MEASURING NONCOGNITIVE
VARIABLES

MEASURING NONCOGNITIVE VARIABLES

Improving Admissions, Success, and Retention for Underrepresented Students

William E. Sedlacek

Foreword by David Kalsbeek

Published in
association with

Sty/us

STERLING, VIRGINIA

COPYRIGHT © 2017 BY
STYLUS PUBLISHING, LLC.

Published by Stylus Publishing, LLC.
22883 Quicksilver Drive
Sterling, Virginia 20166-2102

Library of Congress Cataloging-in-Publication Data
Names: Sedlacek, William E., author.
Title: Measuring noncognitive variables: improving admissions,
success, and retention for underrepresented students/
William Sedlacek.

Description: Sterling, Va. : Stylus Publishing, 2017.
Identifiers: LCCN 2016038176 (print) |
LCCN 2016058096 (ebook) |
  ISBN 9781620362556 (cloth : alk. paper) |
  ISBN 9781620362563 (pbk. : alk. paper) |
  ISBN 9781620362570 (library networkable e-edition) |
  ISBN 9781620362587 (consumer e-edition)
Subjects: LCSH: Minorities--Education (Higher)--United States. |
Women--Education (Higher)--United States. |
Minority college students--Services for--United States. |
Women college students--Services for--United States. |
Universities and colleges--United States--Admisson. |
College student retention--United States. |
Academic achievement--United States.
Classification: LCC LC3727 .S43 2017 (print) |
LCC LC3727 (ebook) | DDC 378.1/9820973--dc23
LC record available at https://lccn.loc.gov/2016038176

13-digit ISBN: 978-1-62036-255-6 (cloth)
13-digit ISBN: 978-1-62036-256-3 (paper)
13-digit ISBN: 978-1-62036-257-0 (library networkable e-edition)
13-digit ISBN: 978-1-62036-258-7 (consumer e-edition)

Printed in the United States of America

All first editions printed on acid-free paper
that meets the American National Standards Institute
Z39-48 Standard.

Bulk Purchases

Quantity discounts are available for use in workshops and for
staff development.
Call 1-800-232-0223

First Edition, 2017

10 9 8 7 6 5 4 3 2

Jacob Bear Sedlacek and Joseph Chance Sedlacek—
May this book help them to know their grandfather.

Este libro se dedica a mi amigo y mentor Darío Orozco Prieto
(1939–2010).
Descansa mi compatriota

CONTENTS

Appendices with further resources are available at sty.presswarehouse
.com/sites/stylus/resrcs/chapters/1620362562_excerpt.pdf

My first exposure to the research and scholarship of William E. Sedlacek was in the late 1980s. As a young policy analyst at Saint Louis University, I was advising some program directors on how to improve the admission and selection of African American students to a special services program. I recall feeling like I had discovered in Sedlacek's work not only a goldmine of empirical validation for new practices but also a whole new way of viewing the precipitating challenge in the first place. His voluminous research on noncognitive factors not only informed our efforts to improve program outcomes by broadening our assessment of attributes that contribute to student success but, more important, also inspired new ways of thinking about our role as educators committed to diversity, access and opportunity for underserved populations of students.

Fast forward to 2004, when tectonic shifts in the policy landscape in higher education admissions created fertile ground for Sedlacek's (2004) book *Beyond the Big Test: Noncognitive Assessment in Higher Education* With intensifying public discourse about the seemingly insurmountable systemic and structural challenges facing colleges and universities pursuing an agenda of social equity, access, and attainment for the public good, there was renewed interest in and receptivity to the solutions Sedlacek's research had surfaced and stimulated over the decades.

Fast forward again to 2017 and we have ample evidence that the challenges remain as plaguing and pervasive as ever; that the gaps in access and attainment are widening; and, unfortunately, that public policy likely will continue to be inadequate to the task. Increasingly it rests with colleges and universities themselves to innovate, experiment, evaluate, and institutionalize programmatic and process responses to the goal of improving access and attainment. And like a beacon from the shore providing guidance to those trying to navigate stormy seas, Sedlacek's new book, this volume, brings timely insight, information, and the confidence instilled by examples and evidence from others who have courageously gone before.

It is no surprise that Sedlacek opens this book discussing the diffusion of innovation. This isn't just a comprehensive summary of Sedlacek's life's work of scholarship; more importantly, it showcases the consequences of that work by sharing examples of institutions that have accepted the challenge and employed these methods to effect change. It therefore brings to us the outcome not only of Sedlacek's analysis but also his advocacy—not only the power of his ideas but their proven impact as ideas in action. This book documents well the diffusion of innovation that characterizes the evolution of the assessment of noncognitive attributes, presented by the person most responsible for these developments.

It is likely and appropriate that leaders in enrollment management in educational institutions, and perhaps particularly in admissions, will be the primary beneficiaries of what Sedlacek has compiled in this valuable resource. Not surprisingly, it is in the professional admissions community where these concepts have taken root, albeit amid difficult dialogue as admissions professionals confront the powerful interests of the standardized testing industry and testing paradigm. Bottom line, it is in the admissions process where we can most directly apply the insights drawn from a deliberate, disciplined assessment of these metacognitive attributes in advancing student success. Every enrollment management and admissions professional should be conversant in this research and literature, this theory and practice or else risk being marginalized in one of the most significant developments of our time in admissions and retention processes.

The enrollment management and admissions leader will find value in this text in several ways. One is that it provides multiple concrete examples of how these noncognitive variables can be integrated into admissions processes and practices. While it might seem that embracing noncognitive approaches to admissions presents daunting logistical obstacles, examples offered here illustrate how straightforward it can be. These new approaches typically and readily graft onto existing processes and admission criteria, and this text offers examples of varying levels of application, from modestly incremental to boldly comprehensive.

A second value is that this text brings a robust empirical and theoretical orientation to using noncognitive factors in admissions, a foundation so solid that even the most entrenched critic would be hard-pressed to argue against at least piloting new approaches. Such a sound theoretical and empirical foundation makes this an intelligent and pragmatic approach to our work. But it's more than that—it's also the right thing to do, and a third value is the compelling moral imperative interwoven throughout this work. In this text, Sedlacek gives the enrollment management professional a powerful response to those asking what can be done to lessen the degree to which the college admissions process in America perpetuates the social and economic divide. The use of noncognitive variables in admissions is a potent response to the pointed criticism of how traditional admissions practices contribute to the systemic, structural barriers to equal educational opportunity in America and how the traditional admissions paradigm in effect exacerbates inequities of opportunity rooted in race and ethnicity, socioeconomic background, parental educational attainment, and so on.

Finally, the reason why today's enrollment leaders should immerse themselves in Sedlacek's work is because of its application beyond the admissions process. While much of the impetus in employing Sedlacek's work in admissions is to assist in better predicting student success, this text outlines how the assessment of these metacognitive attributes can be meaningfully and practically applied in working with students in achieving success over the course of their degree pursuits. One tenet of the overarching evolution of an enrollment management perspective in education is the integration of admissions and retention strategies. Therefore, as educators seek to realize the full potential of the power of these metacognitive assessments in working with students, in effect they are cementing the admissions and the retention efforts and thereby manifesting an integrated enrollment management approach truly oriented to student success. That is another compelling reason why today's admissions professional should take to heart the insights and illustrations of how institutions are adopting and adapting this innovation in educational practice beyond the admissions process.

In contrast to my first engagement as an analyst with Sedlacek's work, I now consider it 30 years later as a senior university officer charged with orchestrating comprehensive institutional enrollment strategy. In that light, I'm prompted to ask, "What characterizes those institutions that have the capacity for embracing, employing, and executing these approaches?" And I'm prompted to wonder what insights come from considering Sedlacek's family of noncognitive attributes introduced in this book, applying them not to individuals but to institutions. Are these attributes predictive of institutional success as much as they are of individual success? Can they be used to assess institutional readiness and capacity for successfully adopting the kinds of change in policy, practice, and perspective that are required for these concepts to be successfully applied? As you review this book, consider with me these factors as predictors of success not only for individuals but for institutions.

A realistic self-appraisal is an essential institutional attribute for systemic change. Organizational change theorist Peter Senge (1990) notes that as important as it is to have a compelling and shared vision for a preferred future, an accurate sense of the current reality is equally critical for change to occur. The successful introduction of innovative uses of noncognitive factors requires a well-informed institutional understanding of its current policies, practices, and processes; their impacts and outcomes; and how those outcomes may be institutional manifestations of deep-seated inequities and injustices. Just as important is an institution's positive self-concept, a broad sense of self-efficacy in managing change and in introducing new practices and processes to shape institutional outcomes. Early adopters are risk-takers, and success requires the courage and institutional self-confidence to entertain new mental models that challenge a status quo grounded in long-standing assumptions.

Using noncognitive factors in shaping enrollment and student outcomes is no quick fix; an institution's preference for long-range plans versus reacting to immediate needs is an essential capacity. Successful innovation is not done well in the urgencies of crisis but rather in a climate that allows sustained experimentation and evolution over the long haul. Moreover, educational outcomes are inherently long-term; altering college admission practices to enhance student educational attainment, for example, can only be fully evaluated years after the introduction of the innovation. And since adopting new policies and practices is always a challenge in educational institutions complicated by processes of shared governance and faculty engagement, for example, understanding how to work within a system is also an essential capacity for long-term change. More broadly, college enrollment practices are systemically entrenched in a professional admissions industry and educational outcomes that are embroiled in a systemic rankings industry; knowing how to navigate change in such intertwined systemic complexities is an institutional competency required for successful innovation.

Leadership experience naturally is an attribute of organizations that successfully bring innovation to life. In the case of noncognitive assessments, leadership experience is necessary in using empirical data to challenge traditional practices and assumptions, establishing long-term goals while introducing short-term changes in policy and practice, and bridging theory with practice. While leadership is critical, it is also insufficient; the successful adoption of innovation requires the availability of a strong support network for the change process. There are many examples of institutions that struggle to close the gap between policy intentions and policy implementation because of inadequate support for change across all of the functions involved; broad-based support is needed for fully integrated, sustainable, and strategic efforts.

Finally, the capacity for change requires a management team extremely competent in their professional roles and responsibilities. Expanding noncognitive factors in college admissions can be a challenging process, and flawed implementation can directly and adversely impact some enrollment outcomes while improving others. If that were not the case, these innovations would be trivial. Because there are inherent and inevitable tradeoffs in such a change effort, it is therefore necessary for the administrative team charged with such innovation to have exemplary knowledge in their field in order to effectively manage this balancing act. Moreover, that team has to be motivated by a commitment to a broader agenda of social change than the impact on the institution's outcomes singularly. Just as a commitment to community service is an attribute indicative of a student's capacity for success, an institution-wide commitment to the social consequences and the public good is likely conducive to the successful adoption of this innovation.

Institutions with these attributes would arguably be more likely to offer fertile ground for introducing and implementing the use of noncognitive variables in promoting student success. At the very least, change advocates wishing to use this text to bring forward a new way of thinking and practice to their institution might be wise to consider if these conditions for success exist.

William Sedlacek's life's work has been to be a preeminent thought leader in a global community of educators seeking to introduce and evolve new thinking and new practice in advancing student success. His scholarship, teaching, research, consulting, and advocacy have together been the dominant catalyst for innovation in noncognitive assessments and its diffusion in educational settings worldwide. Despite his sweeping contributions and the expanding adoption of noncognitive assessments to date, the challenges facing us loom as large as ever. Might this be a Sisyphean effort? Perhaps. But just as Sedlacek has woven pithy and provocative quotes throughout his text, I close with a hopeful one: "The struggle itself toward the heights is enough to fill a man's heart. One must imagine Sisyphus happy" (Camus, n.d.).

David Kalsbeek
Senior Vice President for Enrollment Management and Marketing
DePaul University, Chicago, Illinois

REFERENCES

Camus. (n.d.). *The myth of Sisyphus and other essays.* Retrieved from http://www
.goodreads.com/quotes/296650-the-struggle-itself-towards-the-heights-is-
enough-to-fill
Sedlacek, W. E. (2004). *Beyond the big test: Noncognitive assessment in higher education.*
San Francisco, CA: Jossey-Bass.
Senge, P. M. (1990). *The fifth discipline: the art and practice of the learning organization.* New York, NY: Doubleday/Currency.

PREFACE

The road to success is always under construction.

—Lily Tomlin (n.d.)

As the reader of this book will learn quickly, I love quotations. The book contains many. Why are they there? What do I hope you get from them? The answer is perspective and the beginning of thinking about what is to follow in the book. I view quotations as signposts along a road that I wish the reader to travel. So every time a quotation appears, I ask that you pause and say to yourself, "Why might this be relevant to what I am about to read?" The topics covered are detailed and may provide a different way of thinking, feeling, and ultimately doing something about some complex issues. This book provides answers to the questions raised based on research and practices that have been evaluated in many different situations in academic and student service programs. The road is a metaphor for what can be a way to see an alternative path to problem-solving for student and institutional success.

In chapter 1, "The Innovation Process," I discuss the history of the development of an innovation based on noncognitive variables using models available in the literature. The process of diffusion of an innovation has been studied by a number of researchers and theorists. This chapter is the first of many that will contain references from a variety of fields and publications.

In chapter 2, "Traditional Admissions Measures," I raise the question, "What is wrong with the way we have always evaluated students for admission and then used that information in teaching and student services?" The limitations of previous courses, grades, interviews, portfolio assessments, essays, letters of recommendation, and application reviews are discussed. The history and current problems with the SAT, ACT, GRE, and admission tests in general are discussed in detail. The discussion includes aptitude versus achievement tests and test-optional programs.

In chapter 3, "Noncognitive Measures," I ask if we should hone and fine-tune our tests so that resulting scores are equally valid for everyone in a variety of situations. The answer is that if different groups have different experiences and different ways of presenting their attributes and abilities, it is unlikely that we could develop a single measure, test item, or other construct that yields a score that could be equally valid for everyone in all contexts. If we concentrate on results rather than intentions, we could conclude that it is important to do an equally good job of assessment for each group, not necessarily that we need to use the same instrument for everyone. I then discuss the logic for developing noncognitive assessment tools that are fairer for women; people of color; international students; lesbian, gay, bisexual, transgender, and queer (LGBTQ[1]) students; and students with less traditional backgrounds. The research supporting these measures is discussed in detail. The Noncognitive Questionnaire (NCQ) and other methods of measuring eight dimensions that correlate with success for all students are presented. The eight noncognitive variables that form the core of the book are positive self-concept, realistic self-appraisal, understands and knows how to navigate the system and racism, prefers long-range goals to short-term or immediate needs, availability of strong support person, successful leadership experience, demonstrated community service, and knowledge acquired in or about a field (nontraditional learning).

In chapter 4, "Self-Concept and Realistic Self-Appraisal," I explore in depth the noncognitive variables of self-concept and realistic self-appraisal. Successful students possess a positive self-concept, a strong "self" feeling, strength of character, determination, and independence. Seeing oneself as part of the system and feeling good about it are important components of how self-concept is used here. Feeling a part of the system is generally easier for what I call "traditional" students (White upper-middle-class men), because so much of the system is designed for them. In addition to the usual school pressures, nontraditional students typically must handle racial, cultural, and gender biases and learn to bridge their cultures of origin and the prevailing one.

In chapter 5, "Understands and Knows How to Navigate the System and Racism," I explore the chapter's title with many examples. In this book, *racism* is defined in terms of outcomes or results rather than intentions. If someone does something or says something that affects another person negatively because he or she is a member of another group, we have *individual racism. Institutional racism* is defined as the negative consequences that accrue to a member of a given group because of how a system or subsystem operates in the society (e.g., college admissions), regardless of any other attributes of the individual. Racism can take many forms. The word is used here to cover all types of "isms" (sexism, ageism, "religionism," "disabilityism," etc.). Examples of many types of racism are discussed, including terminology and racism in the news and in the education system. Several practical multistage models of eliminating racism are presented.

In chapter 6, "Long-Term Goals, Strong Support Person, Leadership, Community, and Nontraditional Learning," I present more information on long-term goals, a strong support person, leadership, community, and nontraditional learning. Students of color, women, LGBTQ students, and others for whom the educational system was not designed do better in college if they have long-term goals; develop supportive relationships, and show leadership;

often in race- or gender-related forms. Having a community with which non-traditional students can identify and from which they can receive support is critical to their academic success. In addition, nontraditional students are likely to learn and develop using methods that are less typical and are outside the education system.

As the noncognitive variable system was being developed, I realized that it would take more work in several areas to get institutions and programs to adopt it. Educational systems resist change. In chapter 7, "Additional Measures of Diversity," measurement methods to complement the noncognitive model are discussed. They include measures of information, attitudes, and behavior. Advantages and disadvantages of each method are discussed, and example applications are provided.

Chapter 8, "The Waves of Change Find Many Shores," contains discussions of colleges, universities, groups, and programs that have employed noncognitive variables in some way. Examples from community colleges, public and private baccalaureate programs, and graduate and professional schools are included. In addition, applications from foundations, professional groups, and secondary schools are discussed. Some of the uses of the model are extensive and well evaluated; others are small or implemented with minimum evidence. Some include data and analysis; others are more holistic and part of the philosophy of a program. Some have used the noncognitive model in full with all eight variables; others have used just some of the dimensions, perhaps in a modified form.

In chapter 9, "The Future," I raise the following questions: Will noncognitive variables be discussed, researched, and used in the future? Will future generations recognize the terminology or concepts employed in this book? Will the innovation be sustained, or will it go the way of steam-powered cars, rote memorization, helicopters for every home, and Segways? I answer the questions by suggesting some reasons why noncognitive variables might last and have an effect for a while.

The exhibits and appendices, both in this book and at sty.presswarehouse .com/sites/stylus/resrcs/chapters/1620362562_excerpt.pdf, contain descriptions of noncognitive variables, the behaviors associated with them, and example cases illustrating the variables. The appendices also include examples of instruments and protocols to measure nocognitive variables and dimensions related to diversity.

Note

1. *LGBTQ* is a recently developed and inclusive term. The Texas Tech University Student Counseling Center (2015) provided definitions and a description of its program for LGBTQ students.

ACKNOWLEDGMENTS

I want to acknowledge the contribution of Sarah Burrows to this book. She has guided me through rough waters over multiple drafts. A combination of mother and taskmaster has earned her my admiration and the nickname "Coach." I would also like to thank McKenzie Baker for finding more wording and syntax problems than I thought possible.

I would also like to thank the many students and colleagues who have worked with me on the research and practices that made this book possible.

INTRODUCTION

This book brings together theory, research, and practice related to noncognitive variables in a practical way using assessment methods provided at no cost. Noncognitive variables have been shown to correlate with the academic success of students of all races, genders, cultures, and backgrounds. The eight noncognitive dimensions are independent of one another, and students can be expected to score higher on some and lower on others.

Description of Noncognitive Variables

The noncognitive variables that are the focus of this book are as follows:

1. *Positive self-concept.* The student demonstrates confidence, strength of character, determination, and independence.
2. *Realistic self-appraisal.* The student recognizes and accepts any strengths and deficiencies, especially academic, and works hard at self-development. The student recognizes the need to broaden his or her individuality.
3. *Understands and knows how to navigate the system and racism.* The student exhibits a realistic view of the system based on his or her personal experiences, is committed to improving the existing system, and takes an assertive approach to dealing with existing wrongs but is not hostile to society or a "cop-out." The student is able to handle the system and any "isms" he or she might experience.
4. *Prefers long-range goals to short-term or immediate needs.* The student is able to respond to deferred gratification, plan ahead, and set goals.
5. *Availability of a strong support person.* The student seeks and takes advantage of a strong support network or has someone to turn to in a crisis or for encouragement.
6. *Successful leadership experience.* The student demonstrates strong leadership in any area of his or her background (e.g., church, sports, noneducational groups, gangs).
7. *Demonstrated community service.* The student participates in and is involved with his or her community.

8. *Knowledge acquired in or about a field (nontraditional learning).* The student acquires knowledge in sustained and/or culturally related ways in any field.

A Guide for Academic and Higher Education Professionals

- *Admissions programs.* By incorporating the eight dimensions, admissions programs can improve predictions and reduce error rates in assessing applicants. By going beyond traditional measures such as grades and test scores, admissions policies can more comprehensively assess applicants who may have been overlooked by conventional measures. This will increase the pool of potentially successful students from diverse groups based on race, gender, sexual orientation, disability, and international status. The eight noncognitive dimensions can be coordinated with postmatriculation programs and services on campus.
- *Retention programs.* The eight noncognitive variables are designed to be useful to professionals administering retention programs. By assessing student strengths and weaknesses, professionals can personalize a plan of action for each student. Referrals across campus to different offices and services are encouraged so programs for each student can be developed.
- *Student services.* Counseling, resident life, student union, student development, multicultural, and other student service programs can make direct use of the information from the eight noncognitive dimensions. Student development plans can be assessed, and pre- and postevaluations can be conducted.
- *Teaching and academic advising.* Professors and teaching staff can use the noncognitive variables as an additional tool to learn more about their students and do a better job of advising students and making referrals to services and sources on campus or off.
- *Secondary school applications.* Counselors and teachers in secondary education can make improved recommendations to students who might pursue higher education. By coordinating student assessments at the secondary and higher education levels, professionals can provide students a smoother transition to higher education.
- *Graduate and professional education.* Many examples in this book are from graduate and professional education. Traditional measures such as grades and test scores have been shown to lack the information needed for the success of graduate and professional students. Examples

of how the eight noncognitive dimensions have been employed in a variety of graduate and professional school programs are included in this book.

Examples of admission and postenrollment applications from community colleges, baccalaureate institutions, and graduate and professional schools are included. Additional examples from foundations, professional associations, and K–12 programs are presented. The limitations of traditional assessment methods such as admission tests, grades, and courses taken are discussed.

Possible courses where this book might be adopted include multicultural issues, research in education, student affairs programming, sociology of education, ethics and equity, social change, cross-disciplinary topics, scientific methods, and thesis and dissertation seminars.

This book includes questionnaires, interview protocols, and other assessment techniques that can be implemented at no cost.

I

THE INNOVATION PROCESS

Sextus, you ask how to fight an idea? Well I'll tell you how . . . with another idea!

—Messala, *Ben-Hur* (Zimbalist & Wyler, 1959)

Five-Stage Proactive Innovation Model

There are many models to explain the process of an innovation having an impact in an area. The process of diffusion of an innovation has been studied by a number of researchers and theorists (Dooley, 1999; Rogers, 2003; Sahin, 2006; Sherry, 1997; Stuart, 2000). The Humanitarian Innovation Fund (www.elrha.org/hif/innovation-resource-hub/innovation-explained/humanitarian-innovation-process) developed a five-stage proactive innovation model that I will use to help explain the development and implementation of the noncognitive variable model that is the focus of this book.

Stage 1: Recognition *of a Specific Problem*

In 1970, I was a young assistant professor and director of research at the Counseling Center at the University of Maryland. Student unrest about many issues was rampant. In a study my students and I did, we found that fully half of the student body at the university had participated in a riot or demonstration during the 1971–1972 school year (Collins & Sedlacek, 1973; Kimball & Sedlacek, 1971; Schmidt & Sedlacek, 1971). Among the issues raised was the unfairness of admissions tests for Black students. The university used the ACT test and later switched to the SAT. I was the faculty adviser to a group called the Campus Coalition Against Racism, and on the basis of my training, I went to the literature to find alternatives to the prevailing tests that seemed more fair and that I could present to the campus administration. I was surprised to learn that there were no obvious methods that had been validated for university students (Sedlacek & Brooks, 1976).

We demonstrated the problem of low percentages of Black students and eventually other minority students enrolling in higher education in a series of national surveys initially sponsored by the American College Personnel Association (Brooks & Sedlacek, 1972; Sedlacek, 1987; Sedlacek & Brooks, 1970; Sedlacek, Brooks, & Horowitz, 1972; Sedlacek, Brooks, & Mindus, 1973a; Sedlacek, Lewis, & Brooks, 1974; Sedlacek, Merritt, & Brooks, 1975; Sedlacek & Pelham, 1976; Sedlacek & Webster, 1978). These studies showed that first-year enrollments of minorities in higher education were small and did not change a great deal during that period. Low minority enrollment (about 5% of the student population) was a particular issue at large universities, like the University of Maryland.

Stage 2: Invention *of a Creative Solution or Novel Idea That Helps Address a Problem or Seize an Opportunity*

I decided to develop my own measure based on the best untested ideas from the literature on human abilities, values, and performance. Because the psychology literature tended to label such attributes as *cognitive*, I settled on the term *noncognitive* to describe the measures I was developing. Glenwood Brooks, one of my best students, worked closely with me on the project.

I wanted to use an inductive method. I aimed to develop measures, predict student success using grades and retention, remeasure with changes, analyze results, measure again, and build constructs that would explain the results.

Stage 3: Development *of an Innovation by Creating Practical, Actionable Plans and Guidelines*

In a number of studies over many years, we were able to demonstrate the validity of a series of noncognitive variables useful in predicting the success of students of color; international students; LGBTQ students; and women in higher education at a variety of institutions and programs. We used the term *nontraditional* to describe this diverse group. Current measures did not predict their success in higher education as well as they did for White men (Ancis & Sedlacek, 1997; Bandalos & Sedlacek, 1989; Boyer & Sedlacek, 1988; DiCesare, Sedlacek, & Brooks, 1972; Farver, Sedlacek, & Brooks, 1975; Fuertes & Sedlacek, 1994, 1995; Fuertes, Sedlacek, & Liu, 1994; Pfeifer & Sedlacek, 1971, 1974; Sedlacek, 1972, 1974, 1977a, 1989, 1991, 1996, 1997, 1998a, 1998b, 2003a, 2003b, 2004b, 2004c, 2010, 2011; Sedlacek & Adams-Gaston, 1992; Sedlacek & Prieto, 1990; Sedlacek & Sheu, 2004a, 2004b, 2005, 2008; Tracey & Sedlacek, 1981, 1984a, 1984b, 1985,

1987, 1988, 1989; Webb et al., 1997; T. J. White & Sedlacek, 1986). Much of this research was summarized and discussed in Sedlacek (2004b), and I present it in detail in later chapters of this book.

Edward St. John (2013) stressed the importance of using research and assessment in developing actionable plans to achieve social justice in higher education. He discussed four types of action: *institutionalist action*, when professionals are treated as a group; *closed strategic action*, when initiatives are not open to all groups; *open strategic action*, when actions can be tested openly; and *communicative action*, when partnerships are formed among diverse groups. Sedlacek (2007) discussed an approach to social change using a research base, defining and focusing on audiences that would take action on that research, and becoming a critical source of information for those audiences (also see Sedlacek & Brooks, 1972, 1973).

Stage 4: Implementation *of an Innovation to Produce Real Examples of Changed Practice, Testing the Innovation to See How It Compares to Existing Solutions*

Along with publishing research demonstrating the validity of noncognitive variables in predicting student success at different institutions, workshops on implementing the variables in educational settings were developed (D'Costa et al., 1974, 1975; Prieto et al., 1978; Prieto, Quinones, Elliott, Goldner, & Sedlacek, 1986; Westbrook & Sedlacek, 1988). These workshops focused on an eight-stage model of eliminating racism through the application of noncognitive variables in admissions and postenrollment programs and the development of a variety of measures to support the model (Garcia et al., 2001; McTighe Musil et al., 1999; Sedlacek, 1988, 1993, 1995b, 2003a, 2008, 2013, in press). The basic model is presented and discussed in Sedlacek and Brooks (1976), and I cover it in detail in chapter 3.

Stage 5: Diffusion *of Successful Innovations: Taking Them to Scale and Leading to Wider Adoption Outside the Original Setting*

A key concept in the diffusion of the noncognitive model was to make it available at no cost. Also, the model is not copyrighted, so it can be adjusted, revised, or partially employed. It is not one size fits all. The logic here was to reduce the reasons why people would not try it in a program or research study or for their own benefit in some way. It also allows individuals to take credit for the implementation themselves and receive the reinforcement they need in their system. This reasoning has been employed recently in the development of electric vehicle technology:

Yesterday, there was a wall of Tesla patents in the lobby of our Palo Alto headquarters. That is no longer the case. They have been removed, in the spirit of the open source movement, for the advancement of electric vehicle technology. We believe that Tesla, other companies making electric cars, and the world would all benefit from a common, rapidly evolving technology platform. Tesla Motors was created to accelerate the advent of sustainable transport. If we clear a path to the creation of compelling electric vehicles, but then lay intellectual property landmines behind us to inhibit others, we are acting in a manner contrary to that goal. Tesla will not initiate patent lawsuits against anyone who, in good faith, wants to use our technology. (Musk, 2014)

Here the concept of audience is critical (Sedlacek, 2007). What would motivate someone to use an innovation, in this case the noncognitive model? An admissions director's perspective would likely differ from that of a parent of a student of color, a university teacher, a student affairs programmer, an official of a professional organization, a college president, an administrator at a university outside the United States, a multicultural office administrator, a high school student doing a term paper, a White student applying to college, a women's studies department head, a foundation executive, a faculty researcher, a high school counselor, or a university student doing a thesis. Multiple reinforcements for multiple audiences was the principle employed in diffusing the innovation. I will provide examples for these and other audiences throughout this book.

Adopting the Innovation

Rogers (2003) developed a widely employed model in his book *Diffusion of Innovations*. He discussed five characteristics of an innovation that facilitate adoption of that innovation. The diffusion of the noncognitive variable model will be discussed in terms of Rogers's characteristics.

Characteristic 1: Relative Advantage: *How Is the Innovation Better Than That Currently Employed?*

There were several advantages of the noncognitive variable model. Most important was that the model predicted the success of students of color and other nontraditional applicants better than the typical measures of grades and test scores (Sedlacek, 2004b, 2011, in press). Although the model was available at no cost, there are costs associated with adding a new system, and there are probable scoring costs. However, the noncognitive model would likely cost less for applicants and institutions than traditional measures. Oregon State University (OSU) developed a system of using noncognitive variables in admissions without an increase in the budget (Sandlin, 2008). I will discuss the OSU program further in chapter 8.

Another advantage in employing noncognitive variables is their use in retention, teaching, advising, counseling, and student service programs (Helm, Sedlacek, & Prieto, 1998a; Liang & Sedlacek, 2003a, 2003b; Longerbeam, Sedlacek, & Alatorre, 2004; Noonan, Sedlacek, & Veerasamy, 2005; Roper & Sedlacek, 1988; Schlosser & Sedlacek, 2003; Sedlacek, 1994a; Sedlacek & Brooks, 1981; Sedlacek & Sheu, 2004a, 2004b, 2005; Sheu & Sedlacek, 2004; Warren & Hale, 2016). Grades and test scores are not designed to be helpful in this way. Noncognitive variables are intended to be useful in retaining students and assessing changes in their development and learning.

Characteristic 2: Compatibility: *Does the Innovation Fit With the Procedures and Style Currently Used?*

As noted previously, the noncognitive model can be used with any of the commonly employed methods in admissions or postenrollment programs such as teaching, advising, counseling, or other student services. Also, the noncognitive variable methodology can be modified to fit the situation. For example, some schools use a few of the variables and not others. Other programs combine or alter some of the variables to fit their needs. I will cover throughout the book examples of how the model has been employed in a variety of ways.

Characteristic 3: Simplicity or Complexity: *Is the Innovation Easy or Difficult to Use?*

It is relatively easy to get grades and test scores from applicants or testing organizations. However, the noncognitive model provides more information about students as they enter the institution or participate in a program. This makes it much easier to plan programs and work with students on their needs in a more direct way. A common dilemma at colleges and universities is that it is difficult to get student development information after students enroll. A student may be having difficulties before postenrollment data are collected. At most schools, data collection is decentralized, and one office or department may not coordinate with another. To avoid this problem, OSU provided a profile of student scores on noncognitive variables to all faculty and student service personnel (Sandlin, 2008).

Characteristic 4: Trialability: *Can the Innovation Be Empirically Tested?*

The noncognitive model has been empirically tested in many institutions and programs, using a variety of methodologies including multiple-choice items, short answer questions, essays, interviews, and portfolios (Sedlacek, 1997, 1998b, 2004b, 2004c). I will discuss methods employed by large universities, liberal arts colleges, community colleges, scholarship programs, professional schools, multicultural offices, and others throughout this book.

Characteristic 5: Observability: *Are the Results of the Innovation Visible to All?*

One of the characteristics of many admissions offices is the lack of candor in communicating requirements for admission. Often, admissions materials suggest seeking the well-rounded student, holistic assessment, students seeking a unique experience, and so on, with little detail on what is actually considered. As I watch a college football game on television, I am struck by the lack of differentiation among institutions in their halftime ads. They all have great students and great faculty and promise a fun time. I suggest promoting the institution by discussing how a student will develop on the noncognitive dimensions while enrolled. Throughout this book I will provide examples of schools and programs that have done this.

TRADITIONAL ADMISSIONS MEASURES

Tradition is the prison where change is detained.

—Israelmore Ayivor (n.d.)

Attributes That Determine Students' Success in Higher Education

Should a student come to higher education fully developed, or do we wish to select based on dimensions on which a student will improve through experience at an institution? There has been a recent focus on "college readiness," suggesting information separate from the wide range of attributes a student will need once enrolled (Conley, 2005). Although readiness for college includes taking the appropriate courses, getting good grades, and scoring well on admissions tests, there is evidence that many other attributes determine whether most students will succeed in higher education (Sedlacek, 2011).

Courses

Sedlacek (2011) suggested that although students continue to need courses in math, English, foreign languages, and so on, there has been a tendency among educators and college admissions staff to feel that more is better. The reasoning goes that if we would just require more courses in certain areas (e.g., math), students would be better prepared. However, the law of diminishing marginal utility from economics becomes relevant at some point (Diamond & Rothschild, 1989). The logic behind the law is that beyond a certain level, there is little or no increase in the value of more units in a given area. Thus, at some point, the number of courses in a subject or field may no longer be relevant as a predictor. We may have reached an asymptote, and the variable has become a constant.

For example, Sawyer (2008) studied 245,175 students from 9,507 high schools who took the EXPLORE (8th grade), PLAN (10th grade), and

ACT (12th grade) tests. He concluded that taking additional standard college preparatory courses in high school, taking advanced or honors courses, and earning higher grades would, by themselves, only modestly increase the percentage of students who leave high school adequately prepared to take credit-bearing courses in the first year of college. Sawyer also felt that taking additional courses and earning higher grades mostly benefit students who by grade eight are already well on their way to getting ready for higher education. He concluded that developmental variables also should be considered.

In summary, up to a point, more math and other courses are useful in preparing students for higher education. Beyond that point, other variables, such as those presented in this book, become more important for student success. In fact, one could argue that an overdependence on some courses may detract from time spent on other important aspects of a student's development.

Grades

Recent literature has shown that grades are becoming increasingly less useful as indicators of student achievement or as predictors of future student success (Sedlacek, 2011). This is largely because of the statistical artifact that students at all levels of education are being assigned higher grades. Are current students just smarter and more accomplished than their predecessors? This seems unlikely, but even if true, it does not help us prepare students for higher education, because grades no longer appear as useful in differentiating levels of student academic achievement as they were. Class ranks based on grades have similar problems.

Grades have become more of a constant because of so-called grade inflation. This produces a "ceiling effect" which reduces the size of relationship statistics such as correlation coefficients. For example, Woodruff and Ziomek (2004) found that the mean grade point average (GPA) of high school students taking the ACT assessment had increased a total of 0.20 to 0.26 points on a 4.0-point system from 1991 to 2003, depending on the subject area. Rojstaczer and Healy (2012) showed that the mean GPA in higher education nationally (on a 4.0 system) had risen from 2.94 in 1991–1992 to 3.11 in 2006–2007. Rojstaczer and Healy (2010) concluded that there is a nationwide rise in grades over time of a roughly 0.1 change in GPA per decade. However, they found that relative to other schools, public-commuter and engineering schools tend to grade "harshly," making GPA an even more complex variable of questionable utility when selecting applicants from any group in higher education.

Marquardt (2009) noted that some school districts in Virginia were offering students an increase in their course grades or overall GPA as an incentive to take the Commonwealth's Standards of Learning examination. Marquardt found that between 1995 and 2007 the mean GPA of first-year students in Virginia colleges and universities rose from 3.27 to 3.56 on a 4.0-point system, compared to an increase in GPA in a national sample during that same period of 3.28 to 3.49. In addition, nationally many K–12 schools were not assigning grades to students and were using extramural and portfolio assessments instead (Washor, Arnold, & Mojkowski, 2008).

Rojstaczer and Healy (2010) found that private high schools were grading 0.1 to 0.2 points higher than public schools on a 4.0 scale for a given talent level of student. Because the evidence indicates that private schools may educate students no better than public schools (Pascarella & Terenzini, 1991), private schools seemed to be giving an advantage to their students by awarding higher grades. They graded easier, and there was a tendency for graduate schools, professional schools, and some employers to assume increased competencies for those who attended selective private schools (Bernstein, 2003; Burrelli, Rapoport, & Lehming, 2008). As one Dartmouth faculty member put it, "We began systematically to inflate grades, so that our graduates would have more A's to wave around" (Perrin, 1998, p. A68).

Lahr and colleagues (2014) found that performance-based funding was increasingly popular among both state and federal policymakers in a survey of college administrators in Indiana, Ohio, and Tennessee. These administrators wanted public institutions to graduate more students more efficiently. However, a common way that colleges dealt with those funding formulas was by using grade inflation or admitting fewer "at-risk" students.

There has been an increase in so-called pathway programs for international students matriculating in U.S. colleges and universities (Winkle, 2014). Typically, such programs have an extra year or period of taking courses in a special program at a U.S. institution. The program may be affiliated with a for-profit organization and can be quite expensive for participants. Winkle studied such programs at 12 institutions and concluded that large numbers of pathway students recruited by the corporate partner were not prepared for college-level credit work. Often they were given full academic credit for inflated grades they received in those preparatory courses. The pressure to recruit international students and their related fees has escalated in recent years. The increased income from out-of-state applicants is particularly attractive to state-funded institutions.

I can recall a White female undergraduate student I had in a course on racism. She was uncomfortable with the content and did not participate in class discussions, which she was told were part of her grade. She earned a B in the class and went to the dean to complain that she always got As, and this would ruin her chances to go to law school. I had a long conversation with her on the fairness of her grade and that one grade would be unlikely to decide her future.

Interviews

Interviews are a common method employed by programs in higher education, particularly in professional schools. Muchinsky (1987) noted that interviews can take many forms, from highly structured to open-ended questions that may vary by interviewer. Interviews may be the most difficult method of assessment on which to achieve reliability and validity. Because there are so many variables that need to be addressed and controlled in the interview setting, extensive training of interviewers is necessary. Shaw and Milewski (2004) discussed topics such as having regular calibration sessions and using multiple interviewers in order to achieve reliability and consistency in measurement.

When training interviewers to assess noncognitive variables, I use several key concepts. First, interviewers must be given a rubric to use in scoring. They should feel they have to provide an assessment on certain dimensions before they finish. Second, interviewers should be made aware that their ratings will be evaluated, ideally in open discussion retraining sessions. This makes it easier to get all interviewers using the same methods. Third, interviewers should be told that they are not after their own general assessments of the candidate but part of a team that is scoring specific variables. This reduces the chances that their own styles and ideas will be a variable. These points should be discussed in training and retraining. Fourth, most interviewers will start following the desired structure but will "drift" from that structure over time as they do more interviews, get tired, and so on. Encouraging interviewers to be fresh, take breaks, work at the best time of day for them if possible, and so on is advised. Fifth, interviewers should be made aware of their biases for or against certain candidates. We all have them, regardless of our characteristics or experience. Appendices A1 and A2 provide example scoring systems that can be used in assessing noncognitive variables from interviews.

Whether biases are based on race, gender, religion, sexual orientation, age, country of origin, and so on, some training on this is very important. Various methods of providing such training are available (Sandlin & Sedlacek, 2013; Sedlacek, 2004c; Westbrook & Sedlacek, 1988; M. B. Wilson, Sedlacek, & Lowery, 2014). Prieto and colleagues (1978); Prieto, Quinones, Elliott, Goldner, and Sedlacek (1986); and Sedlacek and Prieto (1990) developed the simulated minority admissions exercise to train admissions committees in medical schools to interview applicants from a variety of backgrounds, races, and cultures.

Longerbeam, Sedlacek, Balón, and Alimo (2005) studied the prejudices of professionals working in diversity and multicultural offices at three universities. These professionals were working in all areas of diversity. They found what they called the *multicultural myth*, in that 70% of participants felt they had no prejudices. The authors also concluded that working in one area of diversity did not free one from prejudice in another. Again, that prejudice could be positive (halo effect) or negative. In my training experience, I have found people with positive or negative predispositions on such variables as physical size, physical attractiveness, accent, field of study, dress, participation in athletics, participation in cheerleading, and interest in hunting, among others. None of these attributes were relevant for the particular purpose of the interview, but variance due to those dimensions came in, often without the awareness of the interviewer.

Letters of Recommendation

Recommendations suffer from a number of measurement problems (Sedlacek, 2004c; Sedlacek & Prieto, 1990). They tend to yield unreliable and invalid results for all groups, often suffering from a positive halo effect. Recommendations tend to give overly positive and undifferentiated comments across candidates; everyone looks great. Dirschl and Adams (2000) found low reliability in multiple ratings of letters of recommendation for a residency at the University of North Carolina School of Medicine. In addition, they found a low correlation with performance in the residency of the selected applicants.

Aamodt and Williams (2005) studied more than 11,000 letters of recommendation from 51 different studies of students and employees and found that they did not add incremental validity to the combination of Graduate Record Examination (GRE) scores and undergraduate GPA. One reason offered was that few references were negative and that two studies indicated fewer than 7% of students or job applicants received average or below average reference ratings. This was especially true when students didn't waive their right to see their references. Aamodt and Williams noted that letters of recommendation might differ in the traits or characteristics used to describe an applicant but will seldom differ in how the evaluator judges the quality of the applicant.

The results of recommendations tend to be more useful if the evaluator knows the recommender or the evaluator requests the recommendation from a particular person. To increase the variability in letters of recommendation and make them more valid and reliable as indicators of student success, writers of letters should be asked to cover specific topics in the letters they write, such as providing examples of behavior or answers to specific questions. If a recommendation is carefully evaluated as one piece of application evidence, then reliability, in the form of corroborative information, might be established. Without being specific, the letters may be of little use to evaluators (Sternberg, 2010). Educational Testing Services (ETS) and those studying law school admissions have used noncognitive skills evaluations that focus entirely on assessments through letters of recommendation. Sternberg felt that ETS did not sufficiently revise their tests. Colleges and universities could get more useful letters by being clear in asking those submitting letters to focus on the issues that the ETS system evaluates, he said. Sternberg felt that a better approach would be to have the applicants themselves submit evidence of their noncognitive skills.

The University of Maryland School of Medicine demonstrated that recommendation letters were an important part of the evaluation of the plaintiff's application to a medical school in their defense of using noncognitive variables in selecting students (*Farmer v. Ramsay et al.*, 1998). Because the letters were written by people known to the medical school, they could be coordinated with other application materials. If there were inconsistencies across different kinds of information presented, candidates could be asked to explain any discrepancies.

In the Gates Millennium Scholars Program, a scholarship program for candidates of color, letters of recommendation were provided to evaluators, along with grades, activities, and personal statements by candidates. Evaluators are trained to consider all the material in assessing applicants. With training and multiple sources of information, evaluators can differentiate among candidates, achieving reliabilities above .90 and validity in predicting success in higher education (Sedlacek & Sheu, 2008). Appendices A1 and A2 provide scoring systems that can be employed with letters of recommendation.

Portfolio Assessments

Portfolios are yet another way to do assessment in higher education (LaMahieu, Gitomer, & Eresch, 1995). In this method, examples of a person's creative work are presented for evaluation. Portfolios have been commonly used in the arts, architecture, and design to demonstrate the work of applicants for admission. Chen and Mazow (2002) discussed the value of electronic learning portfolios for students to present their accomplishments. Smith and Tillema (2003) identified three important issues in portfolio assessment: the clarity and explicitness of the portfolio collection, the feasibility of the collection process itself, and the trust in the outcome of what is being collected.

The school of design at one university has required an additional admissions procedure beyond the general one employed for all undergraduates.

Traditionally, it has required a portfolio containing design-related materials produced by the applicant. Administrators and faculty at the school wished to broaden the content of the portfolio to contain information on noncognitive variables, such as how the applicants had overcome obstacles, how they saw themselves, and what their goals were. The school officials felt this would give them better information with which to judge their applicants, particularly those of color. In another example, to address one potential problem in portfolio assessment—that middle-class students may benefit most—faculty evaluators were trained in identifying examples of high and low scores on noncognitive variables (Koretz, 1993).

The University of California, Irvine, has employed a personal achievement profile, along with SAT or ACT scores, grades, and specific courses completed, as part of its admission profile (Wilbur & Bonous-Hammarth, 1998). The university included, among other things, the noncognitive variables of leadership, community service, and creative achievement. After applicants were screened on their academic credentials, about 60% of the entering class was determined. The additional 40% of the class was selected on the basis of the personal achievement profile. Using a double-blind procedure, admissions staff, who were trained in reviewing the profiles, made the judgments. No interviews or letters of recommendation were employed, and the entering class varied across a number of dimensions.

YES Prep is a program intended to increase higher education attendance and graduation of students from low-income communities. YES Prep has high school students develop a College Assessment Portfolio Project (CAPP) based on the eight noncognitive variables described in Exhibit 1 as one of the pillars in their student success programs (YES Prep Public Schools, 2014). Their progress on improving on the noncognitive variables is documented over the four years of high school and monitored and evaluated by counselors and teachers. I cover more about the YES Prep program in chapter 8.

The Big Picture Learning (BPL) curriculum is mostly experiential without grades in typical courses. To present their potential for admission to colleges and universities, BPL high school students employ portfolios. Students present information about how they are improving on noncognitive variables in their portfolios, as well as about other accomplishments and creative work (Big Picture Learning, 2014). Using different approaches and creating new forms that fit the particular needs of schools or programs are encouraged. This increases the probability that noncognitive variables can be used to benefit students in a variety of contexts. I present a detailed discussion of BPL's uses of noncognitive variables in chapter 8.

Sternberg (2010) noted that the optional portion of the enrollment application at Tufts University, where he was a dean, also included other possible formats that could emphasize applicants' strengths outside of traditional application materials. Students could, for example, submit a YouTube video about themselves, use a sheet of paper to create something, blueprint a future home, create a new product, draw a comic strip, design a costume or a theatrical set, compose a score, or do something entirely different.

Such procedures are useful techniques to generate the material one would need to assess noncognitive variables. The next critical step would be to have a method that could be used to score those materials in a consistent (reliable) way, along dimensions that have been shown to have some validity in correlating with performance criteria for students, such as grades, retention, or other attributes of success in higher education.

Essays

Essays have been shown to be very unreliable indicators of applicant potential, unless raters are trained to score them in specific ways and reliability across raters is established (Sedlacek, 2004c; Sedlacek & Prieto, 1990). With appropriate training, it is possible to have raters score essay material on noncognitive variables. For example, in the Gates Millennium Scholars Program, readers were able to score essays on the applications with high interjudge agreement (Pearson $r = .81$) on the noncognitive variables shown in Exhibit 1. The scores obtained from evaluating the essays were added to an overall score that showed a statistically significant positive relationship with grades and retention in higher education (Sedlacek & Sheu, 2008).

Appendix B1 can be employed to help identify how people may provide information on noncognitive variables in an essay. Appendix A2 contains some sample cases, with names and identification information changed, that could be used in training for evaluation of essays.

Application Reviews

Application review can be seen as similar to essays or portfolios in that an application containing many facets (among them essays and presentations of information on a person) is evaluated. It is important to demonstrate consistency in the ratings of the full application. Shaw and Milewski (2004) called this *composite reliability*. Applications can be reviewed even if there was no a priori intention to evaluate noncognitive variables. For example, in the first year of the Gates Millennium Scholars Program, the applications were designed and applicants completed them before a determination was made on how to evaluate applications. Despite this, the applications contained information that could be evaluated for noncognitive variables. Reviewers were trained to score the applications across all the materials presented, which included grades, personal statements, letters of recommendation, activities, courses taken, and information on the secondary school attended (see Appendices A1 and A2). Interjudge Pearson correlations of between .81 and .85 were achieved using this process in several situations involving admissions and financial aid.

Application review is a good way to start the process of using noncognitive variables in that one can review application materials of current matriculants to do a retrospective study of which noncognitive variables appeared to relate to successes or failures among students. This technique was employed as one of the evaluation methods in the *Farmer v. Ramsay et al.* (1998) medical school case, which I discuss later.

In summary, noncognitive variables present a method of improving assessments for all students and are particularly useful for nontraditional students. Noncognitive variables can be assessed in a number of ways: questionnaires, interviews, essays, portfolios, and reviewing materials not specifically designed to elicit information on noncognitive variables. In chapter 3, I discuss the use of noncognitive variables in admissions and scholarship selection. Chapter 8 includes many examples of how noncognitive variables have been used by schools and programs in higher education.

Tests

Admission tests were created initially to help educators select and advise students (Sedlacek, 2004b). They were intended to be useful to educators making decisions about students. Although they were always considered useful in evaluating candidates, tests were also considered to be more equitable than using prior grades because of the variation in quality among preparatory schools. The College Board has long felt that the SAT was limited in what it measured and should not be relied on as the only measure to judge applicants (Angoff, 1971).

In 1993, the verbal and mathematical reasoning sections of the SAT were lengthened, and the multiple-choice Test of Standard Written English was eliminated. The name was changed from Scholastic Aptitude Test to Scholastic Assessment Tests, while retaining the SAT initials. It is now officially labeled the SAT. In 2003, the College Board announced that an essay would be added and that the analogies questions would be removed in 2005.

The ACT, first administered in 1959, was presented as an alternative to the SAT, emphasizing a wider range of abilities than simply verbal and math. The paradox might be that SAT and ACT scores have always been highly correlated, despite their apparently disparate intentions. The ACT was intended to be more achievement based, whereas the SAT was seen as more of an aptitude test (Sedlacek, 1998b, 2004c; Willingham, Lewis, Morgan, & Ramist,

1990). Both programs' websites provide tables to convert scores from one test to the other, thus assuming equivalence (ACT, 2014; College Board, 2014a). The University of Maryland switched from requiring the ACT to requiring the SAT in the late 1960s. Studies there showed the correlation between the two tests to be .88 for University of Maryland applicants. In other words, the two tests were measuring something operationally very similar.

In 2013, the ACT was administered to 1.8 million people, compared to 1.7 million who took the SAT. Perhaps motivated by this fact, in March 2014, the College Board announced that major changes to the SAT would be coming in 2016 (College Board, 2014b). The SAT redesign is centered on eight key changes. The revised SAT will focus on relevant words, the meanings of which depend on how they are used. When people take the evidence-based reading and writing section of the new SAT, they will be asked to demonstrate their ability to interpret, synthesize, and use evidence found in a wide range of sources.

An attempt will be made to align the revised SAT with the practical work of college and career. In the essay section on the new SAT, students will read a passage and explain how the author builds an argument. The math section will stress problem solving and data analysis, along with algebra and advanced math. In the revised SAT, test takers will be presented an excerpt from one of the Founding Documents or a text from the ongoing Great Global Conversation about freedom, justice, and human dignity. The chief executive officer of ACT has been critical of the new SAT–ACT conversion tables. He feels the new SAT scores are inflated and do not seem to be converted fairly (Roorda, 2016).

Whether these changes result in the measurement of different attributes that are fairer and more relevant to the potential of a diverse applicant pool remains to be seen. Despite various changes and versions over many years, the SAT in essence still measures what it did in 1926: verbal and math ability. It is basically still a general intelligence test that does not assess a wide range of abilities (Sedlacek, 2003a, 2004b).

Most studies on the SAT or ACT focus on student performance in the first year of higher education as the criterion. Why don't standardized tests relate to measures of student success beyond the first year? Aside from not being designed to do so, Sternberg (1996) pointed out that such tests measure only one aspect of intelligence: analytic ability. He defined *analytic ability* as "one's capacity to interpret information in a well-defined and unchanging context." Sternberg felt standardized tests generally do not measure creative ability or practical ability, the two other components of intelligence he identified. Persons with creative ability are able to interpret information in changing contexts. They can easily shift from one perspective to another.

They are likely to be the best researchers or contributors to their fields. Persons with practical intelligence know how to interpret and use the system or environment to their advantage.

If we examine a typical curriculum, many would agree that creative and practical intelligence come into play more in the later years of most programs, because upper-level courses tend to require students to write more, discuss more, and hopefully think more. Analytic skills, as understood by Sternberg, appear less useful by themselves beyond the first year. Sternberg (2010) felt that it has been clear for years that traditional measures account for only some of the difference in academic performance of students and that noncognitive variables also are important, so these changes are long overdue. Noncognitive variables appear to be in Sternberg's (1985, 1986, 1996) creative or practical ability areas, whereas tests tend to reflect analytic ability.

Aptitude Tests Versus Achievement Tests: The Curious Case of the Indestructible Straw Person

The distinction between aptitude and achievement has been a focus of psychometricians for many decades (Jencks & Crouse, 1982). Although psychologists can discuss the differences between the two conceptually, they are difficult to sort out empirically. Kelley (1927) demonstrated that widely used intelligence tests and achievement batteries overlapped by about 90%. Anastasi (1984) discussed the dilemma of constructing a "straw person" that prompts a question that cannot be definitively answered. She felt that all tests assess current status, whether their purpose is terminal assessment or prediction. She added that traditional achievement tests often can serve as effective predictors of future learning, because all tests are measures of a sample of behavior.

Both aptitude and achievement tests can be best characterized as tests of developed ability. It may be most useful to categorize measures by their actual function rather than their labeled or intended function. Anastasi (1984) concluded, in regard to cognitive behavior, that test scores tell us what an individual is able to do at a given time. They do not tell us why individuals perform as they do. To answer that question, we need to know something about each person's experiential background (Anastasi, 1984). Here is where noncognitive measures become relevant.

The GRE

The GRE also has been criticized for not being related to student success in graduate school. Sternberg and Williams (1997) found correlations in the low teens to .20 between grades in graduate school and the GRE. The strongest relationship was found for the analytical portion of the exam, which no longer exists. They noted the methodological issues of studying only students who enrolled in graduate school and the questionable success criterion of grades for graduate students. Kaplan and Saccuzzo (2009) found that GRE scores correlated highest with first-year grades for graduate students, supporting Sternberg and Williams's findings of correlations of .20 or lower. Kaplan and Saccuzzo (2009) concluded, "The GRE predict[s] neither clinical skill nor even the ability to solve real-world problems" (p. 303).

Graduate and professional school students have a smaller GPA range than undergraduates do, making the criterion measure less useful psychometrically. Restriction of range tends to depress relationship statistics such as correlation coefficients. Graduate and professional students also matriculate in much smaller, more relatively independent programs than do undergraduates, making sampling for research purposes much more difficult. Also, we expect different qualities from our graduate students than from undergraduates, further reinforcing the importance of noncognitive variables (Sedlacek, 1972, 2004c; Sedlacek & Prieto, 1990).

Lemann (2000) felt that we had come to a point where the "Big Test" had become the primary object of attention in many schools. It had become the standard by which we judge others and ourselves. Many assume that if an individual has high ACT, SAT, or GRE scores or if a school has high mean scores on such tests, the students must be learning something, and the school must be good. This is ascribing too much power to our tests. Posselt (2016) found that many leading departments, despite saying otherwise, are reluctant to admit anyone who does not have extremely high GRE scores.

ETS began offering the Personal Potential Index (PPI) in 2009 as optional for GRE applicants. It is an online system of evaluation designed to provide additional information on graduate school applicants in six areas:

1. Knowledge and creativity
2. Communication skills
3. Teamwork
4. Resilience
5. Planning and organization
6. Ethics and integrity

ETS studied the validity of this system for evaluating graduate school applicants and its fairness to students of color and other groups. Although ETS felt results were encouraging, too few applicants and graduate programs used the PPI. As a result, when ETS planned large-scale validity studies, it didn't have enough results to be statistically valid and decided to phase out the program (Jaschik, 2016).

ETS will help graduate departments understand why they can admit applicants from a wider distribution of GRE scores than many currently do (Jaschik, 2016). If departments provide data on those who are admitted with slightly lower GRE scores than is the norm for their program, David G. Payne (interview in Jaschik, 2016) said research would show that a broader range of GRE scores can lead to comparable levels of academic success in doctoral programs.

Although it was good to see ETS continuing to pursue alternative variables and approaches as aids to educators in admissions, one of the difficulties in the ETS approach is that there is an attempt to rule out any variance due to diversity on race, gender, culture, religion, and other dimensions. That variance, however, is the key to understanding the potential of many applicants. It is logical that a testing program would want to have a single scoring system that could be applied to everyone in the same way.

There is evidence that noncognitive variables can be viewed as constructs that could be interpreted in the context of the applicant's race, culture, gender, sexual orientation, and other nontraditional dimensions. By doing this for all applicants, including the most traditional, an admissions program can add some unique and useful information that correlates with the success of students beyond their scores on standardized tests or alternative measuring instruments that do not allow for diversity (Sedlacek, 1994b).

C. Miller and Stassun (2014) in their article "A Test That Fails" argued that the GRE should be deemphasized, and measures of other attributes such as drive, diligence, and the willingness to take scientific risks should be added. They felt this would make graduate admissions more predictive of students' ability to do well and would also increase diversity in science, technology, engineering, and math (STEM) fields.

C. Miller and Stassun (2014) stated that in the physical sciences only 26% of women, compared to 73% of men, score above 700 on the GRE quantitative measure. For minorities, it was 5.2%, compared with 82% for Whites and Asians (who are not considered minorities). They felt that the "misuse" of GRE scores to select applicants may be responsible for the underrepresentation of women and minorities in graduate school. Women received 20% of U.S. physical sciences doctoral degrees. Underrepresented minorities, who account for 33% of the U.S. university-age population, earned 6%. They noted that these percentages are similar to the percentage of students who score above 700 on the GRE quantitative measure. They concluded, "In simple terms, the GRE is a better indicator of sex and skin colour than of ability and ultimate success" (p. 303).

A few innovative STEM PhD programs, such as those at the University of South Florida and Fisk–Vanderbilt, have achieved completion rates above 80%, which is well above the national average, and are increasing participation by women and minorities (Powell, 2013). Their admissions process includes an interview that assesses college and research experiences, key relationships, leadership experience, community service, life goals, and perseverance (C. Miller & Stassun, 2014).

The American Astronomical Society (2016) called for limiting the use of the GRE in admissions for graduate admissions in the astronomical sciences.

Why Use Tests at All?

Standardized tests remain controversial, particularly their fairness for people of color (FairTest, 2007; Guinier, 2015; Helms, 2009; Sedlacek, 1976, 1977b; Toldson, 2014). Much of the debate centers on statistical artifacts, measurement problems, and poor research methodology, including biased samples and inappropriate statistical analyses and interpretations (Sackett, Borneman, & Connelly, 2008). Although this discussion and the related controversy are useful and interesting to academics, we may have lost track of why tests were developed to begin with and what their limitations are. Test results should be useful to educators, student service workers, and administrators by providing the basis to help students learn better and to analyze their needs. As currently designed, tests do not accomplish these objectives. The newest SAT, or another test, may change that conclusion, but the results are years away. Many teachers tend to teach to get the highest test scores for their students, student service workers may ignore the tests, and too many administrators are satisfied if the mean test scores rise in their schools. We need something from our tests that currently we are not getting. We need measures that are fair to all and provide a good assessment of the developmental and learning needs of students while being useful in selecting outstanding applicants. Our current tests don't do that.

Test-Optional Programs

Many schools make the ACT or SAT optional for admissions. FairTest (2014) listed more than 800 schools that did not require tests for admission to bachelor's degree programs. Hiss and Franks (2014) studied Bates College graduates for more than 20 years under an admission test-optional program. In addition, they researched optional standardized testing policies in the admissions offices at 33 public and private colleges and universities, using cumulative GPA and graduation rates. The researchers also examined which students were more likely to make use of an optional testing policy and what benefits could derive from such a policy. Four types of institutions were included in the study: 20 private colleges and universities, 6 public universities, 5 minority-serving institutions, and 2 arts-focused institutions, for a total of nearly 123,000 students and alumni. The difference in graduation rates between submitters (those who provided test scores) and nonsubmitters was 0.10%. The mean undergraduate GPA of submitters was 3.11, versus 3.06 for nonsubmitters.

Academic ratings assigned to applicants by Bates admissions staff were equally accurate whether or not test scores were submitted. Under the test-optional policy, application rates increased for students of color and women, as well as those for students from low-income and blue-collar backgrounds. The policy also helped students with learning disabilities and international applicants gain admission. Nonsubmitters were more likely to major in fields that emphasized creativity and originality.

Belasco, Rosinger, and Hearn (2014) studied the relationship between test-optional policy implementation and subsequent growth in the proportion of low-income and minority students enrolling at liberal arts colleges. In addition, they analyzed whether test-optional policies increased numbers of applications. Results showed that test-optional policies tended to increase the perceived selectivity, rather than the diversity, of the participating institutions. Also, after controlling for a number of variables, they concluded that there was no evidence that test-optional policies increased student applications for admission. Schools that implemented test-optional policies reported an increase in mean test scores, which is consistent with past studies (Ehrenberg, 2002; Yablon, 2001). However, adoption of test-optional policies did not increase the proportion of low-income and African American, Latino, or Native American students who enrolled.

Making tests optional for admission does not necessarily guarantee a more diverse student body. It is a start, but experienced admissions staff can make judgments that are less efficient substitutes for the same variance that tests represent. Staff training on how to evaluate a more diverse pool of potential applicants may be required. DePaul University trains its admission staff to do an assessment of noncognitive variables for 5% of its entering class in a test-optional program (D. H. Kalsbeek, personal communication, May 26, 2016). Advice to any institution would be to analyze why a student of color, or students from other groups, would want to attend the institution. Emphasizing variables that relate to campus climate can make a difference to such prospective students. Issues of how racism is handled, courses offered in areas relating to diversity, and student development programs relevant to different student groups may be important.

Although the test-optional movement is interesting and deemphasizes the use of tests for admissions, we are still left with the question, "What will replace tests in our admissions models?" Just because we make tests optional does not mean that we have replaced them with something different. I have done an exercise with a number of admissions committees by presenting applicant materials without test scores and asking them to estimate what their test scores would be. Experienced admissions people can make a quite accurate guess, because they are used to assessing the types of candidates presented at their institution. Experts can make those judgements based on variables related to test scores, such as grades, socioeconomic status, secondary school attended, activities, personal statements, recommendations, and other aspects of the application. The point of the exercise is that if we do not use tests, we need to make sure we are not simply assessing a surrogate for those scores. What we can end up with is a lower quality measure of the same variance represented by a test.

Keeping Up With Change

Change does not roll in on the wheels of inevitability, but comes through continuous struggle.

—Martin Luther King Jr. (n.d.)

The world is much different than it was when the ACT, SAT, GRE, and other tests were developed in the past century. International students, women, people of color, LGBTQ students, and people with disabilities, among others, are participating in higher education in more extensive and varied ways (Kalsbeek, Sandlin, & Sedlacek, 2013; Knapp, Kelly, Whitmore, Wu, & Gallego, 2002; Longerbeam et al., 2005; Meyer, 2003; Sedlacek & Sheu, 2004a, 2004b; Wawrzynski & Sedlacek, 2003). The percentage of U.S. college students who are Hispanic, Asian/Pacific Islander, Black, and American Indian/Alaska Native has been increasing. From 1976 to 2011, the percentage of Hispanic students rose from 4% to 14%; the percentage of Asian/Pacific Islander students rose from 2% to 6%; the percentage of Black students rose from 10% to 15%; and the percentage of American Indian/Alaska Native students rose from 0.7% to 0.9%. During the same period, the percentage of White students fell from 84% to 61% (National Center for Education Statistics, U.S. Department of Education, 2013). Commonly employed tests have not kept up with the implications of these changes (Sedlacek, 2011).

It is not good enough to feel constrained by the limitations of our current methods of assessing abilities or potential. Instead of asking, "How can we make our admissions tests better?" we need to ask, "What kinds of measures will meet our needs now and in the future?" In a presentation I made to the American Astronomical Society (Sedlacek, 2014c), I used the analogy of the multiverse (Greene, 2011). As the name suggests, the assumption of the multiverse is that there are other universes in the cosmos that are outside our own. In statistics, we define a *universe* as the largest group or domain to which we wish to generalize our results. The idea of the multiverse here is that we need to look to another universe of content to measure variables that are unique to that universe. These other variables may not overlap or share variance with the traditional measures but relate to criteria of interest, such as grades and retention. The purpose of chapter 3 is to present the underlying logic and research supporting a method that yields such measures. We do not need to eliminate tests from our admissions systems; we need to add some new measures that expand the range of dimensions we consider. Somewhere in that range is a variable or variables that capture the potential of all comers.

3

NONCOGNITIVE MEASURES

Our work is the presentation of our capabilities.

—Edward Gibbon (n.d.)

One interpretation of how to improve our academic ability assessment measures is to hone and fine-tune them so that resulting scores are equally valid for everyone in a variety of situations. However, if different groups have different experiences and different ways of presenting their attributes and abilities, it is unlikely that we could develop a single measure, test item, and so on from which scores could be equally valid for all in all contexts. If we concentrate on results rather than intentions, we could conclude that it is important to do an equally good job of assessment for each group, not necessarily that we need to use the same instrument for everyone.

The term *noncognitive* has been used to describe many different attributes, including personal and social dimensions, adjustment, motivation, and student perceptions, rather than the traditional verbal and quantitative areas (often called *cognitive*) typically measured by standardized tests (Sedlacek, 1998a, 1998b, 2004c, 2014b). The term *noncognitive* has been criticized by some as being misleading and negative in that it says what it is not rather than what it is (Walton, 2015). In a literature review, Farrington and colleagues (2012) argued that *noncognitive* is an "'unfortunate' word, [reinforcing] a false dichotomy between what comes to be perceived as weightier, more academic 'cognitive' factors and what by comparison becomes perceived as a separate category of fluffier 'noncognitive' or 'soft' skills" (p. 2). Conley (2013) argued that we should instead call these skills, conditions, and mind-sets *metacognition*. Previously, words such as *wireless* and *horseless carriage* were replaced by more positive terms such as *radio* and *automobile*. The evolution of terminology is an issue whenever an innovation enters the lexicon.

Alternative and more positive terms may emerge to supplant *noncognitive*, but as of this date, *noncognitive* reminds us that we are not discussing the usual dimensions. Although noncognitive variables are useful for all students, they also provide viable alternatives in fairly assessing the abilities of people of color, women, international students, older students, students with disabilities, LGBTQ students, or others with experiences that are different from those of young, White, heterosexual, able-bodied, Eurocentric males in the United States (traditional students). Standardized tests and prior grades provide only a limited view of the potential of these diverse groups.

Researchers and theorists alike have studied the use of noncognitive variables in predicting success in higher education. Willingham (1985) concluded that precollege attributes added little to prediction of college success, whereas other researchers have considered student involvement (Astin, 1993), academic and social integration (Milem & Berger, 1997; Tinto, 1993), and study skills (Nisbet, Ruble, & Schurr, 1982) as useful aspects of college success. Ting and Robinson (1998) found socioeconomic background and institutional and environmental variables related to student success in higher education.

Reeve and Hakel (2001) felt that it was important to specify what criteria are being predicted with noncognitive measures and for which groups. They noted seven different areas to consider in evaluating undergraduate or graduate student performance: classroom/examination proficiency, academic effort, personal discipline and self-management, personal administration skills, interpersonal relations, nonacademic effort, and career vision and self-directedness.

DeHaemers and Sandlin (2015) recommended using the noncognitive system discussed in this book in the *Handbook of Strategic Enrollment Management*, as part of the American Association of Collegiate Registrars and Admissions Officers publication series. They stated, "Colleges and universities that have added noncognitive variables to their admissions requirements are finding that these variables are associated with improved outcomes and higher retention, particularly for certain populations. The application of noncognitive variables is allowing for earlier intervention methods. . . . The end result is stronger preparation, better orientation programs, and mentoring and coaching programs that start on day one" (p. 393).

Legal Issues and Noncognitive Variables

The following key legal cases have questioned the legality of using race in admissions where noncognitive variables have been proposed as an alternative to traditional admissions measures (*Farmer v. Ramsey et al.* (1998); *Castañeda et al. v. The Regents of the University of California* (1999); the University of Michigan cases of *Gratz and Hamacher v. Bollinger et al.* (2002) and *Grutter v. Bollinger et al.* (2002); *Fisher and Michalewicz v. University of Texas* (2009); *Fisher v. University of Texas et al.* (2013); and *Schuette v. Coalition to Defend Affirmative Action* (2014).

Farmer v. Ramsey (*Farmer v. Ramsay et al.*, U.S. District Court for the District of Maryland, case no. L-98-1585, 1998) was a case in 1998 that examined the question of using noncognitive variables as an alternative admissions approach. The University of Maryland argued that race was one of many criteria used to evaluate applications for admission to the medical school. The court ruled in favor of the University of Maryland and upheld the university's argument that its limited consideration of race to promote diversity of the student body was narrowly tailored and permissible under *U of California v. Bakke* (1978, 438 U.S. 265, 98 S.Ct. 2733, 57 L.Ed. 2d 750). I discuss this case in more detail in chapter 8.

Castañeda et al. v. The Regents of the University of California in 1999, California's Proposition 209, which passed in 1996 and amended the state constitution, made it illegal to consider race, sex, color, ethnicity, or national origin for preferential treatment within any state organization, including colleges and universities. As in the *Farmer* case, this case raised the question of using noncognitive variables. *Castañeda* challenged Proposition 209, and the parties were able to settle the case by requiring the university to use a comprehensive review process for every applicant.

The University of Michigan cases (*Gratz and Hamacher v. Bollinger et al.*, U.S. Court of Appeals for the Sixth Circuit, No. 02-516, 2002; *Grutter v. Bollinger et al.*, U.S. Court of Appeals for the Sixth Circuit, No. 02-241, 2002) provided more evidence for the use of noncognitive variables to promote diversity within the admissions process. The *Gratz* case challenged the practice of the undergraduate admissions program, where the institution was assigning additional specific weight based on a point system considering race. The U.S. Supreme Court ruled against the undergraduate program. However, in the *Grutter* case, the university's law school was considering race as one of the many factors to admit students in a holistic review, and the U.S. Supreme Court ruled in favor of the law school.

The case at the University of Texas (*Fisher and Michalewicz v. University of Texas*, No. 09-50822, Fifth Circuit Court of Appeals, 2009) before the U.S. Supreme Court has had an impact on the use of noncognitive variables on campuses in the United States. This case centered on the affirmative action admissions policy at the University of Texas, and Fisher's claim that it is inconsistent with the 2003 Supreme Court's ruling in *Grutter v. Bollinger*, which stated that race could play a limited role within an institution's admission policy. This is significant for U.S. public universities in regard to affirmative action. The District Court first heard this case and upheld the university's admissions policy and use of race in its undergraduate admissions process; it was appealed, and the Circuit Court also ruled in favor of the university. Federal judge Sam Sparks declared the state's flagship university "has used and continues to use race-neutral alternatives in addition to its limited consideration of race as part of its admissions process. The undisputed evidence establishes that the University of Texas has done more than merely consider race-neutral alternatives" (p. 22).

In a June 24, 2013, decision on the *Fisher* case, U.S. Supreme Court justice Anthony M. Kennedy wrote in support of a 7–1 decision that was sent down to a lower court for further review:

> A university must make a showing that its plan is narrowly tailored to achieve the only interest that this Court has approved in this context: the benefits of a student body diversity that "encompasses a broad array of qualifications and characteristics of which racial or ethnic origin is but a single though important element." p. 13

On November 12, 2014, the U.S. Court of Appeals for the Fifth Circuit denied a request that it review a decision by a three-judge panel of the court that upheld the legality of race-conscious admissions programs.

On June 23, 2016, the U.S. Supreme Court (No. 14-9801) in a 4–3 decision upheld the decision in the *Fisher* case and ruled that it was constitutional to give racial preferences in admission at the University of Texas. Justice Kennedy wrote, "Considerable deference is owed to a university in defining those intangible characteristics, like student body diversity, that are central to its identity and educational mission. . . . But still, it remains an enduring challenge to our nation's education system to reconcile the pursuit of diversity with the constitutional promise of equal treatment and dignity."

On April 22, 2014, the U.S. Supreme Court, in a 6–2 decision, held that universities and colleges may still employ the limited consideration of race authorized in previous Supreme Court rulings, but voters and legislators also have the right to curtail such plans in public universities and colleges (*Schuette v. Coalition to Defend Affirmative Action*, No. 12-682). The majority ruled state voters have rights, no one class should be protected, and rights could spread to public schools, highways, and so on. Justice Sonia Sotomayor wrote a dissenting opinion in which she argued that the democratic process does not in and of itself provide sufficient protection against the oppression of minority groups, which is why the Equal Protection Clause of the Fourteenth Amendment exists.

For institutions considering the use of noncognitive variables, there is precedence supported by case law for employing noncognitive variables within the admissions process that is narrowly tailored, sophisticated, and research based. This can achieve greater diversity in the student body and aid in the identification of successful students. "Many argue that . . . noncognitive variables are needed to predict adequately which students succeed or fail" (Sedlacek & Sheu, 2005, p. 217). Sedlacek (2004b) and Sternberg and The Rainbow Project Collaborators (2006, in Schmitt et al., 2011) suggested a more holistic view of student potential than the use of traditional measures alone.

Measuring Noncognitive Variables

Measurement is the first step that leads to control and eventually to improvement. If you can't measure something, you can't understand it. If you can't understand it, you can't control it. If you can't control it, you can't improve it.

—H. James Harrington (n.d.)

The Noncognitive Questionnaire

The Noncognitive Questionnaire (NCQ) is designed to assess attributes that are not typically measured by other instruments and that may be common ways for persons with nontraditional experiences to show their abilities (Sedlacek, 2004b). The term *NCQ* will be used here to describe a variety of ways that the eight noncognitive variables that are the focus of this book (see Exhibit 1) can be measured. See Sedlacek (2004b) and williamsedlacek .info/publications.html for examples and norms. Appendices B1, B2, and B3 contain items in various formats that can be used in assessing the noncognitive variables.

The noncognitive variable system appears to measure creative and practical ability (Sternberg, 2010). Thus, the task for education professionals is to tap the student's full range of abilities by doing all the assessments necessary. Members of nontraditional groups tend to need creative and practical abilities to survive more than people with more traditional experience. For instance, realistic self-appraisal appears to be a creative ability, whereas handling racism shows a practical ability. Equality should be equality of outcome not process. If, to do our best job, we need to assess different ways of showing abilities for different people, let's do it.

Scores from the NCQ have been shown to have validity in assessing the academic potential of a variety of nontraditional groups including Blacks (Sedlacek, 2004b, in press; Sedlacek & Sheu, 2004a; Tracey & Sedlacek, 1989), Hispanics (Fuertes & Sedlacek, 1993; Sedlacek & Sheu, 2004a, 2008), Asians (Fuertes, Sedlacek, & Liu, 1994; Sedlacek & Sheu, 2004a, 2004b, 2008, 2013), international students (Boyer & Sedlacek, 1988), women (Ancis & Sedlacek, 1997), and athletes (Sedlacek & Adams-Gaston, 1992). These studies have shown that the NCQ scales predict the grades, retention, and graduation from college and are useful in scholarship selection and retention programs (Sedlacek, 2004b). Several forms of the NCQ have been developed and employed in different contexts. Test–retest and coefficient alpha reliability estimates on NCQ scores for various samples range from .70 to .94 for scores from the eight scales, with a median of .86.

Summary of NCQ Methodology

Different methods of measuring the noncognitive variables shown in Exhibit 1 and Appendices A1, A2, B1, B2, and B3 have been employed by the Gates Millennium Scholars Program (Sedlacek & Sheu, 2004a, 2004b, 2008), the Washington State Achievers Program (Sedlacek & Sheu, 2005), and Oregon State University (oregonstate.edu/admissions/firstYear/requirements.html; Sandlin, 2008), among many others.

Sedlacek (2004b) discussed the history and logic of why noncognitive variables are useful in higher education in admissions and postmatriculation programs. Scholars have long preached the value of personal and social dimensions as important for academic success (Fredericksen, 1954; E. S. Wilson, 1955). Researchers have concluded that student involvement (Astin, 1993), academic and social integration (Milem & Berger, 1997; Tinto, 1993), study skills (Nisbet et al., 1982), and socioeconomic background and institutional and environmental variables (Sedlacek & Sheu, 2008; Ting & Robinson, 1998) are important for student success. However, there have not been comprehensive instruments developed that measure a set of variables designed to compete with the traditional tests employed, such as the ACT, SAT, GRE, and so on. The NCQ was designed to measure noncognitive variables and meet this need.

The noncognitive variables can be used along with any other variables, models, or techniques employed in whatever role or type of mentoring, advising, counseling, administering student services, or teaching is involved. Teachers, advisers, counselors, and student affairs professionals who use the system can expect to obtain better student outcomes in terms of grades, retention, and satisfaction, as well as greater satisfaction themselves as a result of employing something systematic with demonstrated utility in an area that often produces confusion and anxiety. Major benefits of the system are discussed in the following paragraphs.

First, attributes of students can be assessed that correlate well with their eventual success at an institution of higher education. Although a school could select a class that would do well academically solely based on grades and test scores, those predictions could be improved by adding noncognitive variables, which would give a more complete picture of applicants' abilities.

Second, the diversity of an entering class can be increased. Students of color, and those with less traditional backgrounds than what typical students have, can be identified or administering admitted with a high probability of success. This would help discourage future challenges to the lack of diversity at a school.

Third, noncognitive variables can be employed in teaching, advising, counseling, or administering student services on campus (Noonan, Sedlacek, & Veerasamy, 2005; Sedlacek, 1983; Sedlacek, Benjamin, Schlosser, & Sheu, 2007). Sedlacek and colleagues (2007) provided examples and case studies of how noncognitive variables can be used in postmatriculation programs in higher education. This would be beneficial for all students, traditional and nontraditional alike in, for example, designing and implementing retention programs. Aside from their value for nontraditional students, noncognitive variables would be helpful in identifying how to help traditional students, admitted with high grades and test scores, who are having difficulty on some of the noncognitive dimensions.

Fourth, noncognitive variables can provide an important link between K–12 education and higher education. Too often, each system works independently at the expense of student development. If precollege counselors and university admissions officers, student service personnel, faculty, and administrators were to all work within the same system, students could be assisted in their development and transition throughout the educational process. For example, Roper and Sedlacek (1988) discussed and evaluated a course on racism and how to help students develop on noncognitive dimensions. Sedlacek (2007) discussed a model for achieving social justice using noncognitive variables, and Lechuga, Clerc, and Howell (2009) presented an experience-based system of learning activities focused on promoting social justice. I will discuss in chapter 8 examples of secondary school programs using noncognitive variables.

Fifth, noncognitive variables can be successfully employed in graduate and professional education, thus extending the benefits of the system throughout an institution (Prieto et al., 1986; Sedlacek, 2004c, 2014a; Sedlacek & Prieto, 1990).

All programs should be evaluated as to their success. Statistical analyses and models should be employed in program evaluation where possible. However, simpler methods such as noting the increase in students graduating or going on to higher education after initiating the use of noncognitive variables are also helpful.

Criticisms of Noncognitive Variable Assessment Methodology

In a study funded by the College Board, L. L. Thomas, Kuncel, and Credé (2007) provided a critique of the NCQ (Sedlacek, 2004b). On the basis of a meta-analysis of the research available to them, they concluded that it was not a useful instrument. Their work made several assumptions in their analyses that can be questioned. First, there are multiple methods of assessing the noncognitive variables, including multiple NCQ forms, as shown in Sedlacek (2004b) and at williamsedlacek.info/publications.html. Second, studies of the noncognitive variables employing Likert (agree–disagree) items, varieties of short answer questions, interviews, profile analyses, essays, and a review of application materials have all been conducted and are discussed throughout this book. These methods are not versions of the NCQ but procedures that have been used to assess noncognitive variables (see Appendices B1, B2, and B3). This research would not be best summarized using meta-analysis.

Whatever methods researchers employ, there is a chance that the wrong conclusions may be reached. However, we can choose the kind of error we are willing to tolerate. L. L. Thomas and colleagues (2007) employed what can be a conservative technique statistically (meta-analysis), in that the emphasis is on avoiding a Type I error (finding significance where there is none) but risking a Type II error (missing significance when it is present). I believe the best approach to developing new measures is to avoid a Type II error and not miss results that may be useful. There are many studies cited and discussed in this book that have shown some significant results employing a variety of methods.

Also, the noncognitive variable system discussed here is open source and has been modified; shortened; partly employed; and analyzed by many different methods, statistical and otherwise. Many of these studies were not included in the study by L. L. Thomas and colleagues (2007). In addition, the concentration on grades (especially as measured by GPA) as a criterion measure limits the size of any relationship statistics because of increasing grade inflation and a "ceiling effect," as discussed earlier.

Another assumption by L. L. Thomas and colleagues (2007) is that the noncognitive variables were studied only in relation to admissions and not scholarship selection or postmatriculation activity such as teaching, student services, or advising. The noncognitive system I recommend is aimed at student development and goes well beyond admissions. It is an approach to an area of research and student programs, not just a "test."

4

SELF-CONCEPT AND REALISTIC SELF-APPRAISAL

At the center of your being
you have the answer;
you know who you are
and you know what you want.

—Lao Tzu (n.d.)

Self-Concept

Successful students possess confidence, a strong "self" feeling, strength of character, determination, and independence. Marsh, Byrne, and Shavelson (1988) and Wouters, Germeijs, Colpin, and Verschueren (2011) found that a positive self-concept was related to academic success for all students. A strong self-concept seems particularly important for students of color and women at all educational levels where it has been investigated. The student who feels confident of "making it" through school is more likely to survive and graduate. Although many students of color have had to overcome incredible obstacles and setbacks even to reach the point of applying to college, they need even greater determination to continue. Determination is needed precisely because they may come from a different cultural background or have had different gender-related experiences than the students and faculty members they will encounter in college. Some researchers have documented the additional work that must be done by Black and Latino and Latina students to maintain a positive self-identity and negotiate mathematics when images from the media and society portray them as intelligently inferior (Gutierrez & Irving, 2012; McGee, 2009; Stinson, 2008, 2013). Student affairs and multicultural program staff are particularly important in implementing orientation and postenrollment services for students of color. In addition, they can help inform faculty, administrators, and parents of student needs regarding their self-concepts.

Seeing oneself as part of the system and feeling good about it is an important component of how self-concept is used here. Feeling a part of the system is generally easier for traditional students because so much of the system is designed for them. Studies demonstrate that the way students of color feel about themselves is related to their adjustment and success in college (Aries et al., 1998; Neville, Heppner, & Wang, 1997; Patterson, Sedlacek, & Perry, 1984; Trimble, 1988; Trippi & Cheatham, 1989). Patterson, Sedlacek, and Scales (1988) found self-concept to be important for the adjustment of university students with disabilities, and Ju, Zhang, and Katsiyannis (2013) found similar results for elementary and secondary school students with disabilities. Adelstein, Sedlacek, and Martinez (1983) found that a positive self-concept correlated with academic success for older women returning to college.

In addition to the usual school pressures, nontraditional students typically must handle racial, cultural, and gender biases and learn to bridge their cultures of origin and the prevailing one. DiCesare, Sedlacek, and Brooks (1972) found that African Americans who stayed in college and adjusted to these obstacles were usually absolutely certain they would obtain their degree, in contrast to those who left school.

Pfeifer and Sedlacek (1974) noted that good self-concept may take form when successful Black students appear to be considerably different from their White counterparts. They found that Blacks who got high grades tended to have atypical personality profiles compared to Whites who got high grades, according to norms based on White students. Thus, on some measures the opposite use of the same predictor will select the best Black and White students, respectively.

The successful student of color is likely to be experienced in "going against the grain," as well as being atypical. Conversely, African Americans who look like typically successful White students on personality measures may not do well academically. Thus, there is good evidence to suggest that important cultural differences operate between African Americans and Whites in the manner in which self-concept is operationalized. Bennett (2002) found for "underrepresented minorities" who went into teaching, a positive ethnic identity was associated with their graduation from college.

Race and gender identity are important aspects of how one may show ability. Helms (1992) developed identity models for Blacks, Whites, and people of color. Neville and colleagues (1997) found racial identity attitudes of African American college students related to perceived stressors and coping styles. Ossana, Helms, and Leonard (1992) studied "womanist" identity as an important part of self-esteem, and Jones (1997) found that race varied in its importance in the identity development of women in college, depending on their race. Also, Frankenburg (1993) discussed the relevance of exploring the concept of "Whiteness" in the identity development of White women.

Other aspects of self-concept have been explored that might be worth further study. For example, there has been work on religious identity (Duffy & Sedlacek, 2007, 2010; Engstrom & Sedlacek, 1997; Fowler, 1981; Knight & Sedlacek, 1981; Manese & Sedlacek, 1985; Schlosser & Sedlacek, 2003) and lesbian, bisexual, and transgender identities (D'Augelli & Patterson, 1995; Mohr, Israel, & Sedlacek, 2001; Mohr & Sedlacek, 2000; Riddle-Crilly, 2009; Sheets & Mohr, 2009).

Duckworth (2011) identified self-control and determination as important parts of her "grit" scale that measures a preference for long-term goals, a noncognitive variable further discussed in this chapter. Moffitt and colleagues (2011) found self-control to be a predictor of many positive social and educational outcomes in longitudinal studies beginning in childhood. They controlled for intelligence and family background measures in their study. F. G. Lopez, Lent, Brown, and Gore (1997) identified academic self-efficacy in mathematics as an important part of self-concept. Schlosser and Sedlacek (2001b) in a study of 3,271 students entering the University of Maryland found that those with a positive academic self-concept were more likely to pursue postgraduate education and less likely to drop out of school prematurely.

A number of studies have shown that a positive self-concept correlates with college grades, retention, and graduation, particularly the latter two, for regularly admitted African American students (McNairy, 1996; Milem & Berger, 1997; Sedlacek, 2004b; Tracey & Sedlacek, 1984a, 1984b, 1985, 1987, 1988, 1989; Tracey, Sedlacek, & Miars, 1983). O'Callaghan and Bryant (1990) found self-concept to be important for the success of Black American students at the U.S. Air Force Academy. Awad (2007) found that a positive self-concept correlated with student grades but was not related to GRE scores for African American students.

Berger and Milem (2000) and Fries-Britt and Turner (2002) found that successful African American students had their self-concepts bolstered on historically Black campuses, whereas Fries-Britt and Turner (2002) noted that successful Black students had to learn to cope with self-concept issues on traditionally White campuses. Cokley (2000) found that the best predictor of academic self-concept for students attending traditionally White campuses was GPA, whereas the best predictor of academic self-concept for students attending historically Black institutions was quality of student–faculty interactions. Hope, Chavous, Jagers, and Sellers (2013) found that a strong positive racial group identification supported psychologically adaptive connections between self-esteem and achievement among African American students in higher education.

Ting, Sedlacek, Bryant, and Ward (2004) performed a study of 2,138 students attending four universities in North Carolina using the NCQ. They found self-concept to be a statistically significant predictor of retention and grades for all students, including White men and women, as well as men and women of color. The NCQ was a better predictor than the SAT, but the combination of NCQ and SAT scores was the strongest predictor of the criteria studied.

Having a positive self-concept has been shown to be a predictor of success for Asian/Pacific Islander American students (Fuertes, Sedlacek, & Liu, 1994; Sedlacek, 2004b; Sedlacek & Sheu, 2008). Bennett and Okinaka (1990) found that Asian Americans often had feelings of social isolation and dissatisfaction on campus. B. Y. Chung and Sedlacek (1999) also noted that Asian Americans had lower career and social self-appraisal than students of other races. Wawrzynski and Sedlacek (2003) found academic self-concept to be an issue for Asian/Pacific Islander American transfer students; they had trouble deciding what to study and speaking up in class. Among undergraduates from the Gates Millennium Scholars Program, African Americans and Hispanic Americans had more positive self-concepts than did Asian/Pacific Islander Americans. This may be a racial–cultural difference in self-perceptions, but it should be explored further (Sheu & Sedlacek, 2004).

For Latinos, a self-concept problem can be how "Latino" to be: Should I speak Spanish? Should I join a Latino group or a general group? Fuertes and Sedlacek (1995) noted the importance of a Latino self-concept, and Longerbeam, Sedlacek, and Alatorre (2004) found that Latinos were more likely to feel they lacked academic ability than other racial groups. Latinos are also more likely to be uncomfortable on a campus stressing diversity issues (Ancis, Sedlacek, & Mohr, 2000; Helm, Sedlacek, & Prieto, 1998b; Sedlacek, 2004b). However, as entering first-year students, Latinos were more likely to look forward to interacting with other racial groups than were other students (Longerbeam et al., 2004). It may be that Latinos enter college with high expectations around diversity, but the reality causes them difficulties (Sedlacek & Sheu, 2005, 2008).

Boyer and Sedlacek (1988) found self-concept to be predictive of grades and retention for international students, whereas Sedlacek and Adams-Gaston (1992) and Ting (2009) found self-concept related to grades for student athletes using the NCQ as a predictor. Stericker and Johnson (1977), Betz and Fitzgerald (1987), and Ancis and Sedlacek (1997) found women's self-concept related to their academic success. T. J. White and Sedlacek (1986) found self-concept to be predictive of success for students in special programs.

In summary, a positive self-concept is predictive of success in higher education for students of color and other nontraditional students. Although having a good self-concept is important for any student, it becomes even more important for those with nontraditional experiences because of the added complexity of dealing with a system that was not designed for them. Student services, including counseling and student activities programs, can help develop a positive self-concept in students.

Realistic Self-Appraisal

Anyone can plot a course with a map or compass; but without a sense of who you are, you will never know if you are already home.

—Shannon L. Alder (n.d.)

Realistic self-appraisal is a person's ability to assess his or her strengths and weaknesses, allowing for self-development. Realism in self-appraisal by nontraditional persons does not connote cultural, racial, or gender deficiency or inferiority.

Rotter (1966) noted that humans can interpret events as being either a result of their own actions or variables external to their control. He felt that whether people believe a situation or event is under their own control (internal control) will influence their reward expectancy and behavior. Several researchers have found that higher internal control correlates with academic success among U.S. higher education students (Beck, Koons, & Milgrim, 2000; Jansen & Carton, 1999; Nilson-Whitten, Morder, & Kapakla, 2007). Deniz, Tras, and Aydogan (2009) found that external locus of control was related to academic procrastination in Turkish university students.

White students do well pursuing their own interests (internal control) in a society designed to meet their needs, whereas students of color need to also be aware of the external control on their lives that negotiating the racism in the system requires. DiCesare and colleagues (1972) found that African Americans who were better able to assess their strengths and weaknesses were more likely to remain in school than were those who relied on others (teachers, parents) for such assessments. Also, Perrone, Sedlacek, and Alexander (2001) found that White and Asian American students perceived intrinsic interest in a field as the major barrier to achieving their career goals, whereas African Americans, Latinos, and Native Americans cited the lack of personal finances as their major external barrier to success.

White faculty members may give less consistent reinforcement to African American students than they give to White students (Allen, 1992; Sedlacek & Brooks, 1976). For African Americans who are trying to make realistic self-appraisals, overly negative faculty reinforcements cause as many problems as those that are solicitous. Christensen and Sedlacek (1974) demonstrated that faculty stereotypes of African Americans can be overly positive, and S. L. Carter (1996) discussed an example of a colleague who defended his practice of grading his Black students more leniently than his White students.

Harber and colleagues (2012) found that White middle school and high school teachers gave more praise and less criticism to Black and Latino students than to fellow Whites. Teachers lacking in school-based social support (i.e., support from fellow teachers and school administrators) were more likely to display the positive bias. Teachers gave feedback on a poorly written essay supposedly authored by a Black, Latino, or White student. Teachers in the Black student condition showed the positive bias, but only if they lacked school-based social support. Teachers in the Latino student condition showed the positive bias regardless of school-based support. These results demonstrate the importance of developing realistic self-appraisal despite inconsistent reinforcement.

Some researchers have identified poor communication with faculty, particularly White faculty members, as a problem for African American students (Allen, Bobo, & Fleuranges, 1984; Fleming, 1994; Sedlacek, 1995a, 1995b; Sedlacek & Brooks, 1976). Helm, Sedlacek, and Prieto (1998a) and Ancis and colleagues (2000) found communication with faculty to be a problem for African American and Asian American students, which could make it more difficult to assess student ability. Hargrove and Sedlacek (1997) found that African American students were more likely to feel they needed career counseling than did students from other racial groups.

Sedlacek, Benjamin, Schlosser, and Sheu (2007) discussed the importance of employing noncognitive variables in mentoring students of color. Mentoring programs for students of color, based on noncognitive variables, often coordinated through student services, have been shown to correlate with student retention and satisfaction (Castellanos et al., 2016; Sedlacek, 2004b). K. M. Thomas, Willis, and Davis (2007) presented a model for communicating with and mentoring minority graduate students.

Women may experience an academic climate that interferes with their ability to do realistic appraisals of their academic abilities (Ancis & Phillips, 1996; Brush, 1991; Fitzgerald et al., 1988; Sandler, 1987). These difficulties bring about a corresponding decrease in their academic and career aspirations from their first year to their last year in school (El-Khawas, 1980; Ossana et al., 1992). Women who are able to make realistic self-appraisals have been shown to get higher grades in a university than those who have difficulty with such assessments (Ancis & Sedlacek, 1997).

Ting and colleagues (2004) found that Realistic Self Appraisal scores on the NCQ were significantly correlated with grades and retention for White women and women of color, as well as for men in both groups. The NCQ was a better predictor than the SAT, but the combination of NCQ and SAT scores was the strongest predictor of the criteria studied. Kosoko-Lasaki, Sonnino, and Voytko (2006) developed a model for women and "minority" faculty at two medical schools that helped develop their realistic self-appraisal.

Tracey and Sedlacek (1984a, 1984b, 1985, 1987, 1988, 1989) and Tracey and colleagues (1983) found realistic self-appraisal to correlate with college grades, retention, and graduation for students of all races, but the relationships were particularly strong for African Americans. Webb and colleagues (1997) identified realistic assessment of the degree of difficulty of academic work as a correlate of grades for female African American medical students. Boyer and Sedlacek (1988) and Moore (1995) found that international students with higher realistic self-appraisal got higher grades in college. Boyer and Sedlacek (1988) also found that international students with better realistic self-appraisal were more likely to stay in school than were those with lower scores on the variable.

As with any group, Asian/Pacific Islander Americans need to be able to assess their strengths and weaknesses to proceed with their development. Mentors can help students with these assessments, because some issues relating to self-concept can have a negative impact on the ability of Asian/Pacific Islander American students to get a realistic picture of themselves or their interests. For example, the stereotype that Asian/Pacific Islander Americans are interested only in technical fields can interfere with students' ability to adequately appraise their abilities.

The following is an example of the possible problems this could cause: I once had to refer an Asian/Pacific Islander American student for counseling because his peers insisted on seeking computer-related help from him to the point where he had virtually no interpersonal relations on any other basis. His self-concept and realistic self-appraisal suffered, and he began to get depressed. The student wasn't particularly interested in computers, but his peers expected him to be, and they felt they were enhancing his self-concept. Forcing an expectation on people from other races is a form of racism and can damage their self-concept and ability to do self assessments, even if that expectation appears to be positive (Sedlacek & Brooks, 1976).

In summary, women of all races, students of color, and other nontraditional students who are able to make realistic assessments of their abilities, despite obstacles to making those assessments, do better in school than do those less able to make those judgments (Sedlacek, 1977b, 1988, 1995b, 1996, 2004a, 2004b, 2004c, 2011; Sedlacek & Brooks, 1976; Sedlacek & Sheu, 2005, 2008). Realistic self-appraisal is also a predictor of success for students with more traditional experiences. Many student service programs emphasize assisting students in identifying their interests and abilities.

5

UNDERSTANDS AND KNOWS HOW TO NAVIGATE THE SYSTEM AND RACISM

Success is to be measured not so much by the position that one has reached in life as by the obstacles which he has overcome.

—Booker T. Washington (n.d.)

What Is Racism?

Racism is an emotionally charged term, poorly defined and little understood. One set of definitions is as follows:

1. A belief or doctrine that inherent differences among the various human races determine cultural or individual achievement, usually involving the idea that one's own race is superior and has the right to rule others
2. A policy, system of government, and so on, based on or fostering such a doctrine; discrimination
3. Hatred or intolerance of another race or other races (www.dictionary .com/browse/racism)

The preceding definitions are all based on the intention of the purveyor of racism. In this book, *racism* is defined in terms of outcomes or results rather than intentions. If someone does something or says something that affects another person negatively because he or she is a member of another group, we have what we define as *individual racism. Institutional racism* is defined as the negative consequences that accrue to a member of a given group because of how a system or subsystem operates in the society (e.g., college admissions), regardless of any other attributes of the individual (Sedlacek, 1988, 1995b, 2004b; Sedlacek & Brooks, 1976). If we have a policy, procedure, or collective pattern of behavior that adversely affects members of one group over another group, we have *institutional racism*.

Racism can take many forms. The word is used here to cover all types of "isms" (sexism, ageism, religionism, disabilityism, etc.). Sedlacek and colleagues (1976) compared and contrasted the processes of racism and sexism. Although racism can be individual and institutional, the primary concern in this book is one's ability to deal with the policies, procedures, and barriers (intentional or otherwise) that interfere with the development of people. Thus, if we have an admissions evaluation system that yields more useful results for people with traditional experiences than for those with less traditional experiences, we have an example of racism, regardless of the motives involved. In addition, Mullainathan (2015) found racial bias in the presentation of the news regardless of intention.

The following examples are from education and the larger society. It is important to examine how racism, in its many manifestations, can affect our educational system.

Racism and Terminology

It is easy to say, "I didn't intend to say anything to hurt you; you are too sensitive; you should understand and get over it." As noted previously, the premise in this book is that the effect of a policy, procedure, or remark is important, not its intention, honest or otherwise. If we know a word is insulting or hurtful to someone else, why would we continue to use it? Psychologists have defined a *reaction formation* as when a person says the opposite of what he or she really feels or would do (Changing Minds, 2016). Most of us would not like to admit we are wrong, but if we focus on the recipients of our words and deeds, we are the source of change. It is hard to get into another's situation to try to see the world as he or she does. If that person has different cultural experiences, it is all the more difficult.

Throughout this book, words to describe various groups such as *Black* and *White* are considered proper nouns and capitalized because they connote meaning and experience beyond simple description.

Let's Avoid the Topic: The N-Word

We have all seen the *n-word* referred to in our popular media in an attempt to avoid using the word *nigger*, thus evading any serious analysis of the term and the history it represents. *Nigger* has a long and ugly history, particularly in the United States. Derived from the Spanish and Portuguese word *negro* (black) and from the French *nègre* (negro), the term *nigger* had by the 1900s become a pejorative variation (African American Registry, 2015).

There have been recent attempts to eliminate the offensive term from our history, to pretend the word never existed. For example, there has been an effort to remove the word *nigger* from the Mark Twain (1885) classic *Huckleberry Finn* and substitute the word *slave* (Gribben, 2011). Paradoxically, Twain made the point of the evolution of Huck with the following passages, demonstrating that it was possible to change:

> It was fifteen minutes before I could work myself up to go and humble myself to a nigger; but I done it, and I warn't ever sorry for it afterwards, neither. I didn't do him no more mean tricks, and I wouldn't done that one if I'd a knowed it would make him feel that way. (Twain, 1885, p. 121)

As Huck wrote a note that would let the slave owner know where Jim, the runaway slave, could be found, he said, "It was a close place. I took it up, and held it in my hand. I was a-trembling, because I'd got to decide, forever, betwixt two things, and I knowed it. I studied a minute, sort of holding my breath, and then says to myself: 'All right, then, I'll GO to hell'—and tore it up" (p. 272).

Will ignoring the history of a term reduce the racism that exists? Probably not. We should be aware of the language we use, or have used, and the behavior we need to exhibit to confront and eliminate our racism. An excerpt from an editorial in the *New York Times* stated,

> The trouble isn't merely adulterating Twain's text. It's also adulterating social, economic and linguistic history. Substituting the word "slave" makes it sound as though all the offense lies in the "n-word" and has nothing to do with the institution of slavery. Worse, it suggests that understanding the truth of the past corrupts modern readers, when, in fact, this new edition is busy corrupting the past. ("That's Not Twain," 2011, p. A26)

President Obama (2015) used the word *nigger* in a radio interview, when he stated, "Racism: We're not cured of it. It's not just a matter of it not being polite to say *nigger* in public. That's not the measure of whether racism still exists or not. It's not just a matter of overt discrimination." So the context in which the word is used is important. However, we should be aware that some will be offended whenever the word is presented, regardless of the intention.

At the University of Oklahoma, use of the word *nigger* was formalized in a song sung by members of the Sigma Alpha Epsilon fraternity (Moyer, 2015). The university closed the campus chapter of the fraternity and suspended some of its members. Ironically, the university has sponsored the National Conference on Race and Ethnicity (NCORE) since 1988: "The conference focuses on the complex task of creating and sustaining comprehensive institutional change designed to improve racial and ethnic relations on campus and to expand opportunities for educational access and success by culturally diverse, traditionally underrepresented populations" (www.ncore .ou.edu/en/about). I have presented at this conference several times and done some other invited presentations on racism at the university.

Similar incidents have occurred at other universities in recent years (Associated Press, 2015; New, 2015). Oklahoma is one of only four institutions in the Big 12 Conference that did not have a chief diversity officer. The university has taken steps to hire a vice president for diversity in a move criticized by some as overdue.

Additional Examples of Racism in Education

Emory University president James Wagner (2013) angered many by stating in *Emory Magazine* that the "three-fifths compromise" of the U.S. Constitution was a model for how people who disagree can work together for "a common goal." The compromise allowed Whites greater representation in the House of Representatives and is considered by many to be a blatant form of institutional racism: greater power for Whites, and a clear evaluation of the inferiority of Blacks. After much criticism, Wagner apologized: "To those hurt or confused by my clumsiness and insensitivity, please forgive me."

President Martha Nesbitt of Gainesville State College ordered a controversial depiction of the Confederate flag containing images of Klansmen and lynchings removed from the College Art Gallery in 2011 amid much controversy (ncacblog.wordpress.com/2011/02/17/in-censoring-art-gainsevillestate-college-president-violates-academic-freedom). I believe that avoiding controversial racist topics increases the racism we should be confronting in our society. The Confederate flag depiction provided an excellent opportunity to discuss the flag's history and the importance of academic freedom. Where should such issues be addressed and discussed, if not in colleges and universities? President Nesbitt has indeed generated a discussion but not in a way that shows her or her institution in a positive light.

On my own campus, several recent racist incidents have occurred. A member of the Delta Gamma sorority at the University of Maryland reportedly posted a picture of a cake for a 21st birthday on Instagram that included a racist message (Schroeder, 2014). In addition, a student who sent racist and sexist e-mails in January 2014 left the university (Hedgpeth, 2015). The e-mails were condemned by university officials, and a letter was sent to all students, faculty, and staff at the university (Loh, 2015). The university has many courses, offices, programs, and student groups concerned with issues of diversity and racism. I have been actively involved in several of these over many years.

These examples demonstrate how difficult it can be to eliminate racism. Again, we are reminded that results, not intentions, should be the focus. Racism exists in many forms and demands continued attention over time. This book provides a way to approach racism and its effects, as well as models and measures to help reduce or eliminate it.

Westbrook and Sedlacek (1991) studied the labels used to describe nontraditional students in the *Education Index* over 40 years. Terms have varied from a focus on *acculturation* in the 1950s to *disadvantaged* in the 1960s to *cross-cultural* in the 1970s to *multicultural* in the 1980s. *Diversity* was the most common term for the 1990s. Although these terms may suggest different approaches to the groups discussed, operationally we may still be discussing the same people: those with cultural experiences different from those of White middle-class men of European descent, those with less power to control their lives, and those who experience racism in the United States. But does it make sense to include such variables as gender, sexual orientation, or status as an athlete as aspects of cultural experience? I believe it does. By recognizing the complexity of culture, we are more likely to learn about different cultures and increase the probability of reducing racism. Although labels and terminology have important symbolic and conceptual value, they may not help in making decisions in research, programs, or practice about racism.

The successful nontraditional student is a realist based on personal experience with discrimination; is committed to fighting to improve the existing system; is not submissive to existing wrongs, nor hateful of society, nor ready to "cop out"; is able to handle a racist system; and asserts that the school has a role or duty to fight racism.

Young (2011) found conflicting views of racism among educators as either an individual pathology or an institutional problem. She suggested four types of perpetuators of racism: the conscious perpetrators, the unconscious perpetrators, the deceived perpetrators/activists, and the enlightened perpetrators/activists. Young concluded that educators tended to be prevented by their social activism from recognizing their perpetuation of racism through their actions.

Kuh, Kinzie, Schuh, and Whitt (2011), in a study of 20 colleges and universities, found that the most successful programs in increasing student retention and graduation emphasized helping students negotiate the system in four areas. First, an atmosphere of "positive restlessness" was promoted on the campus. In other words, change is positive and possible. Second, data about students and their success were used in evaluating the curriculum and institutional programs. Third, academic and student affairs staff collaborated to achieve student success. Fourth, campus leaders worked to help faculty and staff understand the importance of commitment to student success.

For traditional students, this variable may take the form of handling the system without the addition of racism. How we learn to handle the circumstances with which we are confronted tells us much about our ability and potential. Learning to make the systems of society work for them is important for all students, but the overlay of racism on those systems makes it more difficult to understand and negotiate for students of color, women, and others so affected. Hence, it is critical to their success in school, and it provides a crucial role for student affairs staff in helping students negotiate the racism they encounter. Ting, Sedlacek, Bryant, and Ward (2004) did a study of 2,138 students at four universities in North Carolina, including 523 students of color, using the NCQ. They found the handling racism scale was a significant predictor of grades and retention for male and female students of color but was not significant for their White counterparts.

Models for Handling Racism

Two models of dealing with racism have been developed that may help in understanding this noncognitive variable.

Sedlacek–Brooks Model

Sedlacek and Brooks (1976; Sedlacek, 2004b) proposed a six-stage model for the elimination of racism in educational settings. They felt that individuals or organizations needed to proceed through a linear series of stages before racism can be reduced or ended. The six stages are as follows:

1. Cultural and racial differences
2. Understanding and dealing with racism
3. Understanding racial attitudes
4. Sources of racial attitudes
5. Setting goals
6. Developing strategies

The first stage is an awareness stage in which information is presented about racial and cultural or gender groups and how they perceive issues differently and need different programs and services. Many current student affairs programs emphasizing diversity stress this stage. Institutional data on the number of people in various groups and social science research on the problems, attitudes, and needs of these groups are useful at this developmental level. Research plays an important role in this stage, because it can yield information about diversity within the institution and challenge assumptions and stereotypes. Sedlacek (2004a) discussed a multicultural research program developed in a counseling center that supports this model.

Starbucks, the coffee chain, initiated and then dropped a program titled "Race Together." The program required employees at its more than 20,000 stores to write this on customers' coffee cups as they ordered (Contrera, 2015). It has also placed ads dealing with racial topics in *USA Today*. At one level, this may seem to be a good strategy for bringing people with diverse backgrounds together. However, without a follow-up program as this model suggests, it may do more harm than good. Raising the issue of race by Starbucks's staff is likely difficult as many customers hurriedly move through their day. Increasing awareness is fine, but it must go somewhere beyond that to be successful at improving race relations and/or reducing racism.

The second stage concerns learning to identify manifestations of racism (both individual and institutional) and recognize what might be done to ameliorate them. Research on barriers to achievement of students, administrators, and faculty of color—admissions and retention policies, biased curricula, student affairs programs, and the effects of a negative interracial climate—is useful in this stage.

The third stage involves an analysis of interracial attitudes. Getting the individual or institution to recognize its role in promoting negative interracial attitudes is a critical component of this stage. The Situational Attitude Scale (SAS) discussed in chapter 7 and shown in Exhibit 2 (see website) can be employed at this stage (Sedlacek, 2004b).

The fourth stage focuses on understanding the sources of intergroup attitudes and acceptance of one's role in the process of racism; it leads to later stages. In this stage, research on the history of racial issues at the university or college can be presented and discussed (Sedlacek, Brooks, & Mindus, 1973b). For instance, an analysis of examples of racism from the campus newspaper can be used in this stage (M. D. Hill & Sedlacek, 1994).

The fifth stage involves a synthesis and study of the research material to generate a set of accomplishable goals. In the sixth and final stage, one develops a series of strategies to match each goal.

The purpose of the model overall is to move the person or institution through these stages using a variety of research-related activities. One of the problems for any change agent is recognizing how long it may take an organization to move through these stages (Sedlacek & Brooks, 1976). The change agent must also recognize that the parts of an organization may change at different rates but not necessarily in the same direction. Individual progress in the model can be more monotonic, although individuals can move back and forth through the stages. See Sedlacek (2004a, 2004b, in press) for examples of applications of this model.

Helms Model

Helms (1995) proposed a model of racial identity development for Black and White individuals that can also be applied to organizations. In Helms's White racial identity model, status one (formerly stage) is called "contact." An individual (or organization) is "color-blind" and unaware of racial differences in this stage. The person (organization) assumes that people of other races would want to assimilate into the White culture (the only viable one).

Status two, "disintegration," involves an individual's guilt and confusion at being unable to reconcile being White with the treatment of people of other races. The third status is "reintegration," wherein the White person or organization professes a lack of racism and directs anger and hostility toward people of color. A state of denial exists during this status.

People at Helms's second status still believe that White culture is superior but recognize that racism exists and that a few Whites other than themselves are responsible for it in the "pseudo-independence" status. Whites are seen as having advantages over other racial groups, but this gap can be eliminated by helping other racial groups pull themselves up to the level of White culture.

Though not directly comparable to the Sedlacek–Brooks model at this point, the client (organization) could be seen as processing research or experience on cultural and racial differences (status one), understanding racism (status two), and examining racial attitudes (status three).

The "immersion–emersion" status (status four) entails taking responsibility for the process of racism and feeling angry and embarrassed about it. Again, though not directly comparable to the Sedlacek–Brooks model, it is at this point that an individual (or organization) might begin to set goals (status five).

The sixth and final status, "autonomy," involves the attempt to interact with other races from a positive, nonracist perspective. Here the person or organization truly values diversity. This has been called *universal-diverse orientation* (Fuertes, Miville, Mohr, Sedlacek, & Gretchen, 2000; Miville, Carlozzi, Gushue, Schara, & Ueda, 2006; Miville, Molla, & Sedlacek, 1992; Singley & Sedlacek, 2004, 2009), and several versions of an instrument have been developed to assess this construct (see chapter 7). Singley and Sedlacek (2009) found that White students were less oriented to diversity than were students of color. Helms's last status could be seen as an action phase similar to Sedlacek and Brooks's stage six, where strategies are carried out. Helms believed it was possible to move back and forth from one status to another and to be at some statuses simultaneously.

The second stage in the Sedlacek–Brooks model to eliminate racism concerns learning to identify manifestations of racism (both individual and institutional) and to recognize what might be done to ameliorate them. Research on barriers to achievement by students and faculty of color, such as admissions, retention and student affairs programs, biased curricula, and the effects of a negative interracial climate, is useful in this stage.

Racism and Men of Color: Facing the System

We can all do something about racism, but the focus here is on how men of color can negotiate the racism that they encounter in their lives in their own best interests. There is evidence that handling racism is a skill that is highly correlated with success for men of color (Sedlacek & Brooks, 1976; Sedlacek, 2004b, 2011). Harper (2016), in his summary of research on Black male student persistence, felt that routine encounters with racial stereotypes undermine Black students' persistence rates and sense of belonging on predominantly White campuses.

African American Men

People seem more aware of race than ever. We have scholarship programs (e.g., the Gates Millennium Scholars Program) that fund Blacks in higher education (Sedlacek & Sheu, 2008). Terms like *diversity* and *multicultural* seem common. However, Black men are still the focus of racism in the education system and many other parts of U.S. society, regardless of the intention. We have set up structural barriers that make it difficult for Black men to survive and succeed that have been in place for hundreds of years. Understanding those structural barriers, wherever they may occur, is the key to understanding and eliminating racism. The barriers may be harder to notice; they may be harder to measure, but they are still with us in some form. Harper (2012), in his study of Black men in higher education, concluded that we do not pay enough attention to their own words and stories of success. Black male student athletes were particularly vulnerable to racial stereotypes and institutional racism directed at them by faculty and staff in higher education (Harper, 2016).

Hope, Hoggard, and Thomas (2016) summarized the literature on the effects of racism on young African Americans and concluded that racial discrimination has deleterious effects on their mental and physical health. However, they did not do analyses by gender.

The Trayvon Martin Case

This case (Park, McLean, Roberts, & Tse, 2012) has caused a great deal of discussion, dissent, disagreement, dismissal, and disillusionment. Trayvon Martin was a 17-year-old African American from Miami Gardens, Florida, who was fatally shot by George Zimmerman, a neighborhood watch volunteer, in Sanford, Florida, in 2012. Martin had gone with his father on a visit to the father's fiancée at her townhouse in Sanford. One evening Martin went to a convenience store and purchased candy and juice. As Martin returned from the store, he walked through a neighborhood that had seen several robberies that year. Zimmerman, a member of the community watch, saw Martin and called the Sanford police to report him as suspicious.

Zimmerman was told to stay put and not follow Martin. Zimmerman then followed Martin on foot to prevent Martin from stealing anything from the neighborhood. There was an altercation between the two individuals, and Martin was shot in the chest. Zimmerman, who was injured in the altercation, was not charged at the time of the shooting by the Sanford police, who said that there was no evidence to refute his claim of self-defense. They further stated that Florida's "stand your ground" law prohibited law enforcement officials from arresting or charging him. Zimmerman was eventually charged and tried in Martin's death, a jury acquitted Zimmerman of second-degree murder and of manslaughter in July 2013, and all charges were dismissed in February 2015 (Weiner & Stutzman, 2015).

The term *racism* has been raised often in this heated environment. The lawyers for Martin should have brought up racism at the trial; Zimmerman was motivated by race; Martin was minding his own business and was doing nothing "racial"; Blacks are always profiled; and so on.

The Black Lives Matter movement began as a result of this case. "Black Lives Matter is an ideological and political intervention in a world where Black lives are systematically and intentionally targeted for demise. It is an affirmation of Black folks' contributions to this society, our humanity, and our resilience in the face of deadly oppression" (blacklivesmatter.com/guiding-principles). Swanson (2015) provides a summary of Americans' views of race and policing.

The Michael Brown Case

The Michael Brown case provides another tragic example of how we must look at the results of potentially racist events and not just intentions. Michael Brown, an 18-year-old Black man, was fatally shot by Darren Wilson, 28, a White Ferguson, Missouri, police officer. The disputed circumstances of the shooting and the resultant protests and civil unrest have received considerable attention in the United States and abroad and sparked a vigorous debate about law enforcement's relationship with African Americans and the police use of force doctrine in Missouri and nationwide (Chandler, 2014).

Shortly before the shooting, Brown robbed a nearby convenience store, stole several cigarillos, and shoved the store clerk. Wilson had been notified by police dispatch of the robbery and the suspect's description. He encountered Brown and Dorian Johnson as they were walking down the middle of the street blocking traffic. Although Wilson's initial contact with Brown and Johnson was unrelated to the robbery, Wilson said that he recognized that the two men matched the robbery suspect descriptions. Wilson backed up his cruiser and blocked them. An altercation ensued, with Brown and Wilson struggling through the window of the police vehicle until Wilson's gun was fired. Brown and Johnson then fled, with Wilson in pursuit of Brown. Brown stopped and turned to face the officer. The entire interaction eventually resulted in Wilson firing at Brown several times, all striking him in the front. During the altercation, Wilson fired a total of 12 bullets, probably the last of which was fatal. Brown was unarmed. Witness reports differed as to whether and when Brown had his hands raised and whether he was moving toward Wilson when the final shots were fired. A grand jury declined to indict Wilson on any charges, and a federal investigation later cleared Wilson of civil rights violations in the shooting.

A U.S. Justice Department Civil Rights Division investigation concluded that the Ferguson police department and the Ferguson municipal court engaged in a "pattern and practice" of discrimination against African Americans, targeting them disproportionately for traffic stops, use of force, and jail sentences (U.S. Department of Justice, 2015). The report is the result of an investigation ordered by U.S. Attorney General Eric Holder after the police shooting that killed Brown in 2014.

Among the findings, from 2012 to 2014, 85% of people subject to vehicle stops by Ferguson police were African American, 90% of those who received citations were African American, and 93% of people arrested were African American. However, 67% of the Ferguson population is African American.

In 88% of the cases in which the Ferguson police reported using force, it was against African Americans. From 2012 to 2014, Black drivers were twice as likely as White drivers to be searched during traffic stops but 26% less likely to be found in possession of contraband. Blacks were disproportionately more likely to be cited for minor infractions: 95% of tickets for "manner of walking in roadway," essentially jaywalking, were against African Americans. Also, 94% of all "failure to comply" charges were filed against Black people. African Americans were 68% less likely to have their cases dismissed by a Ferguson municipal judge and were overwhelmingly more likely to be arrested during traffic stops solely for an outstanding warrant by the Ferguson courts (U.S. Department of Justice, 2015).

There was also evidence of racist jokes being circulated by Ferguson police and court officials. One November 2008 e-mail read in part that President Barack Obama wouldn't likely be president for long because "what Black man holds a steady job for four years." Another joke that made the rounds on Ferguson government e-mail in May 2011 said, "An African American woman in New Orleans was admitted into the hospital for a pregnancy termination. Two weeks later she received a check for $3,000. She phoned the hospital to ask who it was from. The hospital said: 'Crimestoppers'" (U.S. Department of Justice, 2015).

As of the date of the writing of this book, the U.S. Department of Justice is negotiating with the city on a court-supervised consent decree that requires the city of Ferguson to make changes in its police and court systems.

President Barack Obama

Let us examine the presidential election of 2012. Barack Obama, the sitting U.S. president, was subjected to a barrage of forms of racism as his opponents tried to get people to vote for someone else. Listen to the words! Do we hear echoes of the long-term experience of Black men? We heard that Obama is a Muslim, he is a terrorist, he was not born here, he is different than we are, he is not very bright, he is lazy, he got his college grades because of affirmative action, all he wants to do is play basketball, and he is "shuckin' and jiving." All these points are based on long-term stereotypes of Black men as dumb, lazy, unaccomplished, scary people who don't deserve the breaks they have been given by White people.

How do we combat these stereotypes? With research and reason. I have been studying racism for many years—not just the process of racism and how to criticize it but what to do about it.

First, we all should recognize and define *racism* such that is possible to do something to eliminate it. The models to eliminate racism discussed earlier in this chapter contain steps to achieve this. It is difficult to do much about racism if a person can say, "Oh, I don't hate Blacks; it is just President Obama's policies." Nearly all who made the statements about Obama said something similar. But it is the effect of the comments that should be our focus. If fewer people voted for Obama because of the comments, we have a racist outcome.

Second, men of color handling racism must decide how to react to the racist structures set up to limit the success of men of color. How should Obama react? What goals in handling the racism can he set for himself and the country? How can he best handle the racism thrust on him? How can he get non-Black voters to choose him? To be elected he needs to do that. Obama chose not to react directly to counter the comments and charges. Although he did present his birth certificate from Hawaii, he showed a positive face regarding the other comments. He demonstrated through his behavior that the charges were not true. He has portrayed himself not as a Black president but as an accomplished, smart president. He has an atypical story as his background; although he did have a Black father, he was raised in Kansas and Hawaii by a White mother and White grandparents, went to top universities, got top grades at Harvard Law School, and was editor of the *Harvard Law Review*, which is a high honor. It is hard to stereotype his background and achievements as a typical "Black" experience.

So, should all Black men downplay their race so they can succeed in our society? The answer is situational and contextual. The answer depends on how society stereotypes them. Let's consider two other Black men who ran for president of the United States recently: Jesse Jackson and Al Sharpton. Each has a different story and would need to work the system differently than did Obama.

Jackson is from North Carolina, with a southern accent and the style of a preacher, both common attributes for Blacks in the United States, which differ from those of Obama. He has darker skin than the president, and it would be difficult for him to ignore his race. Jackson stressed his Black-oriented programs and roots as he ran for office. He did not win, but he used his role as a Black man working positively in White society and got many Whites to vote for him.

Sharpton is a preacher, a broadcaster, and an urban activist from Brooklyn, New York. He has rallied many to the causes of Black people who were being wronged by society. He tried to get enough White people to vote for him based on his activism: Vote for me! I can get things moving and solve societal problems by taking action! Jackson, Sharpton, and Obama could not use the same tactics to handle racism and get elected. Each had to counter the type of racism that was working against him in a different way.

So here is the process: A man of color must analyze how racism may be affecting his development and limiting his success, he must examine the tools he has available to work against the way racism affects him, he should develop a plan to counter the racism that is in his best interests, and then he must evaluate his success and improve his skills at handling racism. He should essentially follow the steps in the Sedlacek–Brooks model.

It won't be easy. Each of the men discussed has faced and overcome many obstacles in negotiating the effects of racism. There is good evidence that working against racism is one of the most important things a man of color can learn to do (Sedlacek, 2004b). Friends, family, teachers, advisers, and counselors can help Black men understand and work through the complex maze that is racism. It is nice to think that racism will end someday, and we will not have to worry about it. Some thought that when Obama was elected that this was the end of racism. It may be an important step along the path to eliminating racism, but we have a long way to go.

Latinos: Other Forms of Racism

I illustrate the racism against Latino males by discussing the experiences of a colleague of mine. We have traveled together and done many joint presentations to professional groups. He has a master's degree and many years of experience in higher education. He is a third-generation Mexican American I will call Carlos. The first of three incidents that I cover involves a time that we were in Chicago for a conference. While I was parking a car at a hotel entrance, someone came up to Carlos, who was waiting for me, gave him a dollar, and said, "My bag is the one on the sidewalk." At first stunned, Carlos said, "I will find you a porter" and returned the dollar. He avoided an awkward situation, but he was hurt, and we spent some time processing the incident. The systematic assumption that Latinos are there for others in service roles is well entrenched in our society (T. J. White & Sedlacek, 1986).

On the second occasion, we were driving together, with Carlos at the wheel, near the Mexican border in Texas. We were pulled over by a police officer. When Carlos asked what the problem was, he was not given a reason but was asked to step out of the car. Despite questions from both of us, Carlos was frisked. I was not asked to step out or be searched. Finally, Carlos was able to produce a passport that satisfied the officer. When I said later that it was lucky that he had the passport with him, Carlos said, "I always carry one with me just in case this happens." When I asked how often this had happened to him, he said, "More times than I can count."

The third incident occurred when Carlos and I were running late to catch a plane, and we were in the security line at a Washington, DC, airport. Carlos was pulled out of line and given a more thorough search, and I was passed through. This was the third time in the past four times we had been in a security line where he was pulled out and I was not. On this occasion, Carlos was mad and challenged the procedure. He was then questioned at length, and we missed our plane. After we discussed the incident, while awaiting another plane, we concluded that Carlos could be seen as a "Middle Easterner" and terrorist suspect. He had a small beard at the time, and we figured that made him look more like he could have been from the Middle East. The next time I saw Carlos, he was clean shaven and said, "The beard wasn't worth the hassle."

Carlos handled the racism well in the first two cases, but the consequence was negative in the third, although he made a change that reduced his chances of confronting racism in that circumstance in the future. In all the incidents, stereotypes of Latinos or "Middle Easterners" set up the situations. Carlos could not choose to avoid them, but he had to be ready to negotiate them for better outcomes for him. Carlos had to be prepared for sudden, unpredictable reactions to him based on how he looked, where he was, and what credentials he had. It was also critical that Carlos had knowledge of the process of racism and that he had someone with whom to process these incidents. The importance of mentoring, advising, and counseling for Latinos in handling racism is well documented (Longerbeam, Sedlacek, & Alatorre, 2004; Santos & Reigadas, 2002; Sedlacek, Benjamin, Scholsser, & Sheu, 2007). Again, we are reminded of the critical role that student services can play in helping people of color handle the system.

When society is experiencing financial difficulties, racism increases. People want to blame someone; men of color are a convenient target. Men of color must be empowered by their ability to identify and handle the racism that confronts them. This is a key role that student affairs programming can provide for men of color. Men of color can make their life better and make it less likely that their children and grandchildren will have to face the same forms of racism that they must work against.

Asian/Pacific Islander American Men

Seeing Asian/Pacific Islander Americans (APIAs) as problem free prevents them from "working the system" and using the student services provided on campus. Interestingly, one of the more destructive forms of racism for APIAs has to do with the so-called model minority myth (Sedlacek & Sheu, 2013). APIAs are not "allowed" to have problems; they are expected to be perfect. The underutilization of help sources has been documented for APIAs (Chin, 1998; Leong, 1986; Sue & Sue, 2015). They are less likely to seek help through advising or counseling than other groups (Liang & Sedlacek, 2003b). Use of student services is correlated with academic success for students of color, and the pressure on APIA students to avoid such services is a form of racism that they need to learn to handle to be successful in higher education (Sedlacek, 2004b). Often, seeking student services is seen as the final option for APIAs, who may try to deal with problems by themselves or ask help from friends or family and community members (Maki & Kitano, 2002).

An additional stressor is that APIAs are expected to pursue the STEM fields. They are limited through cultural traditions, parental pressure, and peer expectations to pursue technical fields, not seek help, and be quiet about it. Whenever we limit the possibilities for a group through institutionalized structures, we have racism.

Adjusting to life on a campus is important to many APIAs. Helm, Sedlacek, and Prieto (1998b) found that APIA university students were more likely to want to know what the rules of conduct were on campus than were other students, whereas Liang and Sedlacek (2003b) reported that they were likely to have fixed value systems. APIAs often see stressing diversity programming and related student services as confusing and sending mixed signals. They tend to relate ambiguous residence hall regulations to their overall satisfaction, so it may be important to have programs on handling racism for them conducted through residence halls (Helm et al., 1998b).

A few instances might help illustrate the problems of handling racism among APIAs. As an example of possible problems this could cause, I refer again to the APIA student, whom I will call Sung, who received counseling at my suggestion. His peers insisted on seeking computer-related help from him to the point where he had virtually no interpersonal relations on any other basis. He didn't know how to handle this, and he began to get depressed. Sung wasn't particularly interested in computers, but his peers expected him to be, and they felt they were acting positively toward him. Eventually, Sung learned that he had to be more assertive and initiate contact with his peers based on topics other than computers and sometimes to decline helping others on computer issues, even though this went against his acculturation that he should be polite. He had to learn to handle the racism that was coming toward him.

On another occasion, I used the information that APIAs were reluctant to seek nonacademic assistance but were more likely to seek help on academic issues (Sedlacek & Sheu, 2008, 2013; Sheu & Sedlacek, 2009). Also, parental expectations for APIAs tend to be that their children should solve their own problems and not seek counseling (Sheu & Sedlacek, 2009). After the tragedy at Virginia Tech, where an APIA student shot and killed other students, many APIA students felt guilty and felt they were viewed differently by their other-race peers. At a forum dealing with the tragedy, I suggested that those wishing to help APIAs might cast their outreach in terms that students who seek help get better grades. By appealing to the academic orientation of APIAs, one can acknowledge their cultural traditions and broaden their options and acceptability of their needs for coping with other problems they may have at the same time. Student affairs professionals can provide an important bridge between academic and student affairs programs that can help APIA students.

In another example, Ronald Takaki, a professor at the University of California, told of the treatment that he received from a cab driver in Virginia, who was surprised that he spoke such good English and that he did not seem to look "American." Takaki explained politely that he was born in the United States and the descendent of Japanese immigrants who had been in the United States for more than 100 years, to the puzzled disbelief of the driver (Takaki, 1993). This had happened to Takaki before, and it was a form of racism that he had to be prepared for. A common form of racism is that those of another race perceive a hard-to-understand foreign accent among APIAs when none is present (Sedlacek, 2004b). This is a way that others can avoid having to deal with APIAs.

Role of Religion Among APIAs

APIAs might employ religion to cope with problems in understanding how to work the system. The development of ethnic identity, including religious identity, has been theorized to be a central aspect of student development among APIAs (Kodama, McEwen, Liang, & Lee, 2002). Min and Kim (2002) suggested that the study of APIAs has generally not included the role of religion in each of APIA ethnic communities.

For example, past research has suggested that Christian churches are a significant source of support for Korean Americans in that they were more likely to cope with problems by engaging in religious practices than were other APIA groups (Yeh & Wang, 2000). However, Sedlacek and Sheu's (2004a) intergroup analysis showed that among undergraduate students in the Gates Millennium Scholars Program, APIAs were less likely to be involved in religious activities than African Americans.

Majors and Sedlacek (2001) found that one university considered some religions to be "cults," and officials were trying to deny the groups access to the campus. However, some APIA students considered some of those so-called cults to be religions (Sedlacek, 2004b). Hence, departments or student services offices that seek to aide in the development of APIA students may wish to include aspects of religion and spirituality.

Native American Men

No group in the United States has struggled more with racism than Native Americans. The long history of mistreatment by the forces of society, public and private, has been well summarized (see, e.g., red-face.us). Many of the stereotypes about Native students come from images that have been portrayed about them in popular media and sports teams. These images are based on assumptions perpetuated by White people and have no basis in fact. Native Americans, like other groups discussed here, are a complex and varied group of many tribes with many different traditions not given to an easy summary in a treatment of this length. I will concentrate on several examples of stereotypes and discuss how Native Americans have handled them.

Violent, fearsome, primitive! These are stereotypes of Native American men from sports teams, movies, and many years of media portrayal. Many groups have approached the National Football League's Washington Redskins to change its name. Team representatives argued that the name and related team symbols are signs of power and ferocity. They do not hear that the name is a stereotype that has limited the potential of Native American men in many ways, including education and employment. Who wants to hire a savage? "Redskins" is insulting and hurtful to many Native Americans. Various tribal leaders have initiated complaints and lawsuits against the team, but the name remains ("Native Americans Unite," n.d.). The term *redskins* is in a class with *nigger*, *spic*, and *chink*, which are names we would likely not attach to a sports team; however, Pekin Community High School in Pekin, Illinois, called its sports teams the "Chinks" for generations until it was changed in 1980. Fans complained that it was not intended to insult anyone and did not want to change it. Again, we see results versus intentions, real or supposed!

The American Counseling Association, the American Psychological Association, the American Sociological Association, the National Association for the Advancement of Colored People, the National Collegiate Athletic Association, most of the U.S. Senate, and President Obama have all called for elimination of team names and mascots insulting to Native Americans and other groups. Many colleges and universities have changed their team names in recent years, including Stanford, Dartmouth, Marquette, and St. John's University. The University of North Dakota was between nicknames, amid great controversy over its "Fighting Sioux" label, until it was voted out in 2012 by North Dakota citizens. A state-mandated "cooling off" period took place, and in November 2015, the school became the "Fighting Hawks."

Another seemingly contradictory stereotype of Native Americans is that they are nonverbal, passive, and spiritual, with little to say of interest to others (Mann, 2005). An example of this is with a Native American student I had whom I will call Martin. He was quiet and did not socialize with other class members. When it came time for students to work in groups, Martin was left out. Everyone assumed he was not very bright or interested in the content of the educational research class. I wanted Martin to have the same experience on a group project that others were having, so I talked to him about how he might get involved with a group. At first he said he was not interested in any of the topics, but I suggested that the methods of research he would learn would be useful in any project that he would study in his future. He joined a group in which he was never very active and finished the course with a C. When I saw him a year later, he told me his fellow students thought his ideas were too abstract and spiritual to be helpful to the group. They knew about his Native American heritage and dismissed it quickly as irrelevant for a quantitative project. Martin said he learned from this experience and now takes a better reading on how people perceive him. He realized he must assert himself into situations in a way he was not taught in his tribal background if he wishes to succeed in the larger White society.

I have tried to discuss a long list of successes and failures in attempts to handle racism among men of color. The virulence of racism lies in its effects, not its intentions, and how men learn to handle those effects is a key to their success in education and in life. Student affairs and multicultural office programs can help men of color develop the skills they will need as students and later in life to handle the racism they are likely to face.

I Am Not a Man of Color; Why Should I Care?

The first thing is to realize that people of every race, ethnicity, nationality, gender, and sexual orientation have a role in some form of "ism" as either a recipient, a purveyor, or an accommodator. We all should make a careful examination of what policies and procedures in our society or on our campuses benefit or harm members of certain groups, actual or perceived. I say "actual or perceived" because if we are grouped incorrectly, such as in the previous example with Carlos, we may still experience racism.

Christian Privilege

Schlosser and Sedlacek (2003) discussed the role of policies on religious holidays in increasing racism on a campus. Christian students routinely are given the opportunity to practice their religion on holidays such as Christmas and Easter through dismissal of classes. Labeled as "Christian privilege," this creates stress among many non-Christian students and fits within the framework of *racist practices* as defined here. Students from other religions typically must miss class or apply to instructors for official leave, which may or may not be granted. Seifert (2007) noted that Ramadan, an important religious observance for many Muslims, often occurs during midterm exams for students.

Many people feel that Santa Claus and a Christmas tree are not religious symbols and do not have religious connotations. For example, Hicks (2003) felt that those symbols were "just part of the culture" (p. 124). As Christian symbols are given central importance in our institutions, non-Christians are marginalized, despite federal law requiring reasonable accommodations for religious expression and observances. C. Clark (2003) noted that the "everyone is Christian" assumption often leads non-Christians to have to verify or document their beliefs. This reinforces the self-concept of many non-Christians as being less worthy than Christians. Seifert (2007) concluded that Christian privilege must be acknowledged and managed before environments truly conducive to spiritual development for all can be created. This is an important role for campus clergy and student affairs professionals.

The Role of Faculty and Staff in Handling Racist Incidents

Fuertes and Sedlacek (1993) developed a five-step program for faculty and student affairs staff to help Hispanic students handle racism. Step one involves teaching Hispanic students during orientation the difference between individual racism and institutional racism. Usually students can identify racism at an interpersonal level but are often unaware of institutional policies (e.g., allocation of funds) that tend to work against the best interests of cultural and racial groups, including Hispanics. Step two involves teaching Hispanic students how to use resources on campus, such as the counseling center, the multicultural student office, or the human relations office. This could be done as part of an orientation program or as a single-credit student development course. Step three involves teaching students to be more flexible by being bicultural or multicultural; that is, to be Hispanic and part of the larger (White or Black) school system at the same time. Fuertes, Sedlacek, and Westbrook (1993) found that Hispanic students who exhibited bicultural attitudes and behaviors were most likely to have support networks in college and to feel a part of the campus community.

Step four involves peer feedback sessions on positive or negative experiences at the institution. These sessions can serve as an emotional outlet and a social event for new students on campus. Such sessions could be organized by the department of resident life or any other student service unit on campus. Finally, step five, where possible, involves matching the student with a Hispanic graduate student, student affairs staff, or faculty member who acts as a mentor and advocate during the student's first year in college. If such mentors are not available, mentors from any group can be trained to provide what a student might need (Sedlacek et al., 2007).

Schlosser and Sedlacek (2001a) proposed a plan for handling racist incidents that occur on a campus. This plan can be employed by individuals, but it is particularly instructive for faculty and student affairs staff. They suggested that although evaluating racist incidents is necessary, it is *not sufficient* to deal effectively with the problems related to those incidents. They proposed a three-stage plan for dealing with those incidents on campus. The procedure includes the following steps: (a) evaluate (i.e., put the incident in context; how does it follow a pattern previously established?), (b) understand (i.e., gather information about the incident and use a variety of sources), and

(c) deal with the incident (i.e., conduct workshops and facilitate ongoing dialogue and involve groups with diverse and competing interests; this may require some processing in both homogeneous and diverse groups). They felt that it is critical that this plan be in place before the incident occurs and that trained facilitators be available.

Women and Sexism

A term that has recently received attention in the research literature is *benevolent sexism*. It is the idea that "women are wonderful, but weak. Benevolent sexism shows up all the time, in this attitude that women are warmer and kinder than men, but at the same time weaker and [needing] to be cared for" (Connelly & Heesacker, 2012, p. 432). Previous research has suggested that benevolent sexism is an ideology that perpetuates gender inequality. But despite its negative consequences, benevolent sexism is a prevalent ideology that some even find attractive. Connelly and Heesacker studied a sample of 274 college women and 111 college men and found that benevolent sexism was indirectly associated with life satisfaction for both women and men. In contrast, hostile sexism was not related to life satisfaction. The results imply that although benevolent sexism perpetuates inequality at the structural level, it might offer some benefits at the personal level for men and women. The authors concluded that benevolent sexism is dangerous and should be confronted to reduce its prevalence.

Women of Color and Sexism

Many times the effects of racism, classism, and sexism are so interrelated that they are impossible to untangle. Women of color have never had the privilege to focus solely on women's issues (Sánchez, 2014). Sánchez suggested four ways women of color experience sexism differently than White women:

1. *Higher wage gap and rates of poverty.* While women in the United States are paid only 77 cents for every dollar a man earns, the wage gap is even larger for women of color. African American women make only 62 cents and Hispanic women make only 54 cents for every dollar earned by White, non-Hispanic men (National Women's Law Center, www.nwlc.org).

2. *Higher health disparities.* Women of color fare much worse when it comes to health. African American women die in pregnancy or childbirth at a rate of three to four times the rate of White women (Center

for Reproductive Rights, reproductiverights.org). These rates have not changed for 50 years. African American women and Latinas combined, for instance, account for 80% of reported female HIV/AIDS diagnoses, even though they represent only 25% of the U.S. female population. Latinas and African American women in the United States also have the highest rates of cervical cancer and are most likely to die from it than any other group (Centers for Disease Control and Prevention, 2016; Sánchez, 2014).

3. *Sexist stereotypes in the workplace.* Women of color are likely to experience discrimination that White women may never confront. The angry, sassy Black woman or the fiery Latina stereotype can affect the ways in which women are treated by employers, educators, and the rest of the world (Sedlacek & Brooks, 1976). Assertiveness can often be misinterpreted as aggression, anger, or "bitchiness." Many women are reluctant to express their feelings for fear of being labeled "too emotional." Although it is against the law to racially discriminate against employees or applicants, White men are three times as likely to get management jobs as similarly qualified Black women (Sánchez, 2014).

4. *Women's bodies are perceived as dangerous.* Women of color are often stereotyped as sexual and promiscuous and the cause of overpopulation (Sedlacek & Brooks, 1976). Latina bodies are often perceived as a threat because of their "uncontrollable fertility" and are blamed for overpopulation (Sánchez, 2014). The derogatory term *anchor baby* (O'Neal, 2010), for instance, refers to U.S-born children of undocumented immigrants used to "anchor" the parents in the country. Because women of color are perceived as undesirables, their bodies have been vulnerable to inhumane practices, such as coerced sterilization (Sánchez, 2014).

Sexist Messages and Behaviors in Higher Education

Women experience individual, interpersonal, and institutional sexism routinely in higher education (Capodilupo et al., 2010). These manifestations are common on college and university campuses. Swim, Mallett, and Stangor (2004) found that women in higher education experience one or two events each week that qualify as "everyday sexism" (p. 117) including gender-role stereotypes and prejudice, degrading comments, and objectification. Nadal (2010) defined *microaggressions* as "brief and commonplace daily verbal, behavioral, or environmental indignities (whether intentional or unintentional) that communicate hostile, derogatory, or negative sexist slights and insults toward women" (p. 158). The following taxonomy of gender microaggressions contains eight themes (Capodilupo et al., 2010; Nadal, 2010).

1. *Sexual objectification.* Objectification encompasses behaviors ranging from using innuendos to catcalling to carrying out sexual violence. When women are referred to as "hotties" or as body parts, they are being objectified.

2. *Second-class citizenship.* Whether they are in the classroom, on the playing field, or in extracurricular settings, women may receive messages that they should not have the same privileges or opportunities as men.

3. *Assumptions of inferiority.* Many people assume that women students are less capable than men in a variety of areas: physical, academic, and emotional.

4. *Assumptions of traditional gender roles.* Women students are expected to show "feminine" behaviors, such as caring for others or displaying "proper" demeanors.

5. *Use of sexist language.* Demeaning terms used to describe women can be commonplace on campus.

6. *Denial of the reality of sexism.* When people minimize the subjugation of women, they perpetuate the cycle of sexism.

7. *Men's denial of individual sexism.* Men contribute to chilly climates when they refuse to acknowledge their own sexist behaviors, such as joking and innuendo.

8. *Environmental microaggressions.* These systemic microaggressions are institutional messages in the social and cultural environment that communicate to women that they are inferior or less deserving.

6

LONG-TERM GOALS, STRONG SUPPORT PERSON, LEADERSHIP, COMMUNITY, AND NONTRADITIONAL LEARNING

Long-Term Goals

If you don't know where you are going, you'll end up someplace else.

—Yogi Berra (n.d.)

Having long-term goals predicts success in college for students. Fauria and Zellner (2014) found that perceptions of accomplishing long-term goals were related to achieving higher student grades and graduation for a sample of mostly White university students. Because role models often are more difficult to find and the reinforcement system has been relatively random for them, many nontraditional students have difficulty understanding the relationship between current efforts and the ultimate practice of their professions. In other words, because students of color tend to face a greater culture shock than do White students in adjusting to a White-student-oriented campus culture, students of color are not as predictable in their academic performance in their first year as are traditional students. By their second year, students of color are about as predictable as others (Sedlacek, 2004b). Therefore, it is important to provide student affairs services that help students learn goal setting in orientation and first-year programs.

Hence, students who show evidence of having long-range goals do better in college than do those without such goals (Sedlacek & Sheu, 2008). Ting (2009) found the long-term goals scale of the Noncognitive Questionnaire

(NCQ) to be a significant predictor of GPA for student athletes at North Carolina State University. In addition, Ting, Sedlacek, Bryant, and Ward (2004) found the long-term goals scale of the NCQ to be a significant predictor of grades and retention for White male students at four universities in North Carolina but not for males of color or females of any race.

Bettinger and Baker (2013) studied 13,555 students in eight institutions, including two- and four-year schools and proprietary schools, in a randomized experiment. Some students received coaching on relating their daily activities to long-term goals, and some did not receive the coaching. Students who were assigned to a coach were more likely to persist during the treatment period and were more likely to be attending their university one year after the coaching had ended.

Duckworth, Peterson, Matthews, and Kelly (2007) found, as part of their development of the grit scale, that perseverance and passion for long-term goals accounted for an average of 4% of the variance in success outcomes, including educational attainment among two samples of adults ($N = 1,545$ and $N = 690$), GPA among Ivy League undergraduates ($N = 138$), retention in two classes of the United States Military Academy cadets ($N = 1,218$ and $N = 1,308$), and ranking in the National Spelling Bee ($N = 175$). Grit did not relate positively to IQ but was highly correlated with conscientiousness from the Big Five personality dimensions. The Big Five traits are extraversion, agreeableness, conscientiousness, emotional stability, and intellect/imagination (Goldberg, 1990). Grit has also been shown to correlate with teacher effectiveness (Duckworth, Quinn, & Seligman, 2009). Duckworth (2011) concluded that self-control is an important part of grit. Self-control is a component of the noncognitive variable self-concept, as discussed earlier.

Many APIAs tend to have fixed value systems (Liang & Sedlacek, 2003a) and be academically focused (Sedlacek & Sheu, 2008; Tracey, Leong, & Glidden, 1986). This may be particularly useful in helping them develop and accomplish long-term goals. More than 90% of undergraduate APIAs who were in the Gates Millennium Scholars Program were interested in pursuing a graduate or professional degree.

Strong Support Person

No person, trying to take responsibility for her or his identity, should have to be so alone. There must be those among whom we can sit down and weep, and still be counted as warriors.

—Adrienne Rich (n.d.)

Be there.

—Matthew Hahn (personal communication, October 5, 2016)

Students who have done well in school tend to have a person who has had a strong influence on them who provides advice, particularly in times of crisis (Sedlacek, 2004b). Curtin, Stewart, and Ostrove (2013) found this for both U.S. and international graduate students. The support person could be in the education system or in the immediate family, but for nontraditional students it is often a relative or a community worker. Fauria and Zellner (2014) found that having support from family, friends, faculty, and student affairs staff was related to success reflected in grades and graduation for a sample composed mostly of White university students. Also, the strong support person scale of the NCQ was significantly correlated with GPA for a sample composed mostly of White students at a western community college (Noonan, Sedlacek, & Veerasamy, 2005).

Many students of color do not have the "props" or support to fall back on that traditional students typically have. Therefore, students of color, women, LGBTQ students, and others for whom the educational system was not initially designed do better in college if they have a history of developing supportive relationships than do those who have not had this experience. Sedlacek (2004b) concluded that the more a student of color was involved academically with course work, other students, and student services, the more likely it was that the student would locate a support person.

Recipients of the Washington State Achievers (WSA) scholarship, who were selected based on noncognitive variables, showed that support and encouragement from faculty, mentors, resident advisers, and other students were positively correlated with time spent in academic activities (Sedlacek & Sheu, 2005). Academic activities included working with other students on schoolwork, discussing ideas from readings and classes with other students, and working harder than they thought to meet instructors' expectations.

Cokley (2000) found that the best predictor of academic success for Black students attending traditionally White campuses was GPA, whereas the best predictor of academic success for Black students attending historically Black institutions was quality of student–faculty interactions. Adviser support was associated with a stronger sense of belonging and academic self-concept for both groups.

Several help-seeking approaches that APIAs tend to use have been identified, including avoiding stress, fitting in on the campus, avoiding student services, and selecting majors within cultural limitations (Liang & Sedlacek, 2003a, 2003b; Sedlacek & Sheu, 2013).

Counseling research has supported the hypothesis that more acculturated APIA college students perceive counseling professionals more favorably as sources of help for personal and emotional issues than do less acculturated ones. It seems reasonable that non-APIA mentors could apply findings from the counseling literature and should take various cultural aspects, such as acculturation levels and Asian cultural values, into consideration when mentoring APIA students (Sedlacek, Benjamin, Schlosser, & Sheu, 2007).

Liang and Sedlacek (2003a) found that student affairs professionals had more positive attitudes toward APIAs when race was not considered in a variety of situations presented to them. This has important implications for how we support APIA students. At first glance, attitudes in the positive direction may be construed as harmless or positive. However, Hune and Chan (1997) suggested that attitudes based on stereotypes that depict Americans of Asian descent as well adjusted, without academic or mental health needs, has hurt many APIAs, particularly those with Southeast Asian ancestry. Sedlacek and Sheu (2008) found that undergraduate APIAs who were students in the Gates Millennium Scholars Program reported more difficulty in finding someone who was interested in their work, could offer support, or could provide academic help than did scholars from other racial groups.

Leadership

Leadership is practiced not so much in words as in attitude and in actions.

—Harold S. Geneen (n.d.)

Nontraditional students who are most successful in higher education have shown an ability to organize and influence others. The key here is nontraditional evidence of leadership among students. Application forms and interviews typically are slanted in directions likely to yield less useful information about the backgrounds of nontraditional students. Many White applicants know how to play the game and will have taken up, and then be sure to list, a wide variety of offices held in traditional school organizations. Many students of color will not have had the time or the inclination for such activities (Allen, 1992).

Educators have consistently been interested in developing future leaders through higher education (Burkhardt & Zimmerman-Oster, 1999; Dugan, 2006). Approaches to understanding leadership have evolved from an industrial model focusing on individual characteristics, use of power, and the accomplishment of tasks to one emphasizing interpersonal variables and collaborative process. Recent research (Dugan, 2006; Komives, Lucas, & McMahon, 1998; Komives, Owen, Mainella, & Osteen, 2006; Rogers, 2003) has focused on transformative leadership (shared partnership among leaders and followers) rather than transactional leadership (exchanges between leaders and followers). This emphasis has led to conclusions that leadership styles may vary in important ways by gender and race (Balón, 2005; Dugan, 2006; Rogers, 2003). Leadership development programs have been a staple part of student affairs programs in higher education (Komives et al., 2006).

Students of color who show evidence of leadership prior to matriculation into college are more likely to be successful students than are those without such leadership experience (Sedlacek, 2004b; Sedlacek & Sheu, 2013). Leadership ability is an important asset to any student but may take different forms in students of color. These forms may vary among different racial groups, and these differences should be explored (Fuertes & Sedlacek, 1993; Garrod & Larimore, 1997; Liu & Sedlacek, 1999).

Because many White students have more support built into the system, leadership ability may not be as critical an attribute for them to demonstrate for admission to college (Sedlacek, 2004b). However, Ting and colleagues (2004) found leadership as measured by the NCQ to be significantly correlated with grades and retention for White men, as well as women of color, in a study of 2,138 students at four universities in North Carolina. The NCQ was a better predictor than the SAT, but the combination of NCQ and SAT scores was the strongest predictor of the criteria studied. Noonan and colleagues (2005) found that the leadership scale of the NCQ was significantly correlated with GPA for a sample of mostly White students at a western community college.

Balón (2005) found that APIAs believed as much as other racial groups in the importance of culture in leadership but tended not to see themselves as leaders and felt less empowered than other racial groups. Dugan (2006) concluded that women had an advantage over men in developing transformative leadership styles, but Liu and Sedlacek (1999) found that Asian American men were more likely to feel they had leadership skills than Asian American women. Bowen and Bok (1998) found that African American students who attended highly selective institutions made important contributions to their communities as leaders after they left school.

The most promising students, however, may show their leadership in less typical ways, such as through their communities, their religious organizations, or even through their leading a street gang (Allen, 1992). It is important to pursue the culture and gender-relevant activities of the applicants rather than to treat them as if they come from a homogenous environment. For example, APIA students may have unique and culturally related ways of expressing their leadership. If an applicant succeeds in his or her culture and is now ready to accept the challenges of college, there is evidence that the student has the potential to succeed (Liu & Sedlacek, 1999; Sedlacek & Sheu, 2013).

Sedlacek and Sheu (2005) studied leadership correlates of 427 students who received the WSA college scholarship compared to a similar sample of 245 students who applied but did not receive a scholarship. WSA recipients were chosen based on the noncognitive variables shown in Exhibit 1. In the sample of WSA recipients, there were 36% men and 64% women and 40% White Americans, 18% APIAs, 18% African Americans, 14% Hispanic or Latino Americans, and 10% other racial backgrounds. The sample of nonachievers was 42% men and 58% women and 45% White Americans, 25% APIAs, 14% Hispanic or Latino Americans, 9% African Americans, and 8% other.

WSA recipients were more likely to hold leadership positions and be engaged in leadership activities in student affairs and academic groups in higher education than a comparison group of similarly achieving students who did not receive the WSA scholarship. A high score on the leadership scale was positively related to academic behaviors, such as working with other students on schoolwork, discussing ideas from readings and classes with students, and discussing ideas from readings and classes with faculty.

Sedlacek and Sheu (2004a) compared a sample of 878 undergraduates in the Gates Millennium Scholars Program to 748 nonscholars who applied but did not receive a scholarship. The 1,626 undergraduate participants were 16% men, 38% women, and 46% unknown and 34% APIAs, 30% Hispanic or Latino Americans, 30% African Americans, and 6% Native Americans. Data from 194 graduate student participants were also analyzed in the study. The graduate students sample included 77% scholars and 23% nonscholars; 32% men and 68% women; and 41% Hispanic or Latino Americans, 32% African Americans, 13% APIAs, and 13% Native Americans.

Analyses indicated racial differences and differences between undergraduates in the Gates Millennium Scholars Program and those who weren't in the Gates program on leadership outcomes and predictors (Sedlacek & Sheu, 2004a). Also, holding a campus leadership position, showing community involvement, and having positive self-concept were predictive of self-leadership perceptions for undergraduate participants. Among graduate students, Gates scholars tended to perceive themselves as leaders, were comfortable being leaders, and expected others to perceive themselves as leaders. About 20% held leadership positions. Graduate student participants tended to have self-confidence and felt that their plans would be successfully completed. Self-leadership perceptions were related to self-confidence, and community involvement was associated with whether graduate participants held a campus leadership position. Among female graduate students, Gates scholars were more likely than nonscholars to believe that they were destined to be a leader.

Assertiveness is likely an important component in leadership as a predictor of success (Sedlacek, 1987, 1996; Sedlacek & Sheu, 2013). A passive operational style for students of color will deny them many opportunities in a system that is not optimally designed for them. Seeking out resources, human and environmental, is correlated with success for students of color.

Tracey and Sedlacek (1984a, 1984b, 1985, 1987, 1988, 1989) and C. J. White and Shelley (1996) showed evidence of the value of leadership in the retention of Latinos and Native Americans. They also found leadership predictive of success in school for African American undergraduate students, as did Webb and colleagues (1997) for female African American medical students. C.J. White and Shelley (1996) also found evidence of the value of leadership in the retention of Latinos and Native Americans. Ancis and Sedlacek (1997), Astin (1977), and Betz and Fitzgerald (1987) all identified leadership as a correlate of success for women in college, and Boyer and Sedlacek (1988) found a similar relationship for female and male international students. Ting (1997) and T.J. White and Sedlacek (1986) found that leadership correlated with academic success for students in special support programs.

In summary, students of color and women who show evidence of leadership, often in race- or gender-related forms, prior to college matriculation are more likely to be successful in college than those who do not have leadership experiences. Leadership ability is important for any student, but it may take different forms for students of color. Further, because traditional students have more supports built into the system, it may not be as critical an attribute for them to demonstrate for admission to college. Student affairs professionals can play a vital role in helping develop leadership skills in students.

Community

> *What we have to do . . . is to find a way to celebrate our diversity and debate our differences without fracturing our communities.*
>
> —Hillary Clinton (n.d.)

For nontraditional students to be successful, it is critical that they have a community with which they can identify and from which they can draw support. Having a community with which nontraditional students can identify and from which they can receive support is critical to their academic success. The community often is based on racial, cultural, gender, or identity issues, but it may not be for all students. Students of color, women, and other persons with nontraditional experiences who are active in a community learn how to handle the system, exhibit leadership, and develop their self-concepts in such groups. Therefore, those who have been involved in a community, often based on race and/or gender, are more successful in college than are those not so involved. Sedlacek (2004b) concluded that the more a student of color is involved academically with course work and other students, the more likely it is that a student will develop a supportive community. Many student affairs programs are designed to help students develop a community on or off campus.

Webster and Sedlacek (1982) documented the importance of college and university student unions in providing a sense of community for African American students. Mallinckrodt and Sedlacek (2009) supported this finding and concluded that African American and international students who used campus athletic facilities were more likely to continue to be enrolled in higher education than were other students. The relationship was not present for White students.

Additional studies found community involvement correlated with academic success for African American university students (Allen, 1992; Hope, Chavous, Jagers, & Sellers, 2013; Sedlacek, 2004b; Tracey & Sedlacek, 1984a, 1984b, 1985, 1987, 1988, 1989; Tracey, Sedlacek, & Miars, 1983; C.J. White & Shelley, 1996).

Ting (2009) found the community scale of the NCQ to be a significant predictor of GPA for student athletes at North Carolina State University. Also, Ting and colleagues (2004) found the community scale on the NCQ to be positively correlated with grades and retention for men of color and White women but not for White men or women of color. Noonan and colleagues (2005) found that the community scale of the NCQ was significantly correlated with GPA for a sample composed mostly of White students at a western community college.

Recipients of the WSA scholarship were selected using the noncognitive variable system discussed in this book. Compared to applicants who were not selected for the scholarship, WSA recipients were more likely to be involved in residence hall activities, events sponsored by groups reflecting their cultural heritage, and community service activities on or off campus (Sedlacek & Sheu, 2005).

Sedlacek and Adams-Gaston (1992) found the community scale of the NCQ to be a predictor of academic success for men and women athletes of all races, whereas C.J. White and Shelley (1996) indicated the importance of community in retaining Latino and Native American students. Having a race-based community correlated with college graduation for "underrepresented minorities" (p. 74) in a teacher training program (Bennett, 2002). Ancis and Sedlacek (1997) found the NCQ community score to be a correlate of success for undergraduate women. Ting (1997) found that the NCQ community score was important for White students in special programs. Boyer and Sedlacek (1988), Moore (1995), and Mallinckrodt and Sedlacek (2009) found community involvement to be important for the academic success of international students.

Understanding the role of community is critical in working with APIA students. Identification with a community has been shown to be important for APIA student success (Fuertes, Sedlacek, & Liu, 1994; Sedlacek & Sheu, 2008, 2013). In general, APIA students operate with cultural values strongly influenced by their families and cultural heritage (Paniagua, 1994). Students are not encouraged to express their problems to people outside their group, especially to strangers. Also, one way to fulfill one's family obligations is not to create problems (D.K. Chung, 1992; Uba, 1994).

Although APIA students may need to find a community within or outside of their ethnic or racial groups, they may feel that to do so would take time away from their studies (Wang, Sedlacek, & Westbrook, 1992). For example, among undergraduates in the Gates Millennium Scholars Program, APIAs were less likely to join fraternities or sororities than were African Americans (Sedlacek & Sheu, 2004a). However, among transfer students, APIAs were more likely than Whites to study in groups and engage in community service on or off campus (Wawrzynski & Sedlacek, 2003).

This presents some real dilemmas for mentors. How does one get APIA students involved with their cultural groups, which will enhance their success in school, while at the same time make them feel that they are not criticizing the school in some way? One answer may be to suggest that all students need a community on campus and that any community based on culture or race is supported by the administration and faculty. Student affairs programs can provide an important role in helping students develop such communities.

Nontraditional Learning

> *We do not learn from experience. . . . We learn from reflecting on experience.*
>
> —John Dewey (n.d.)

There are many ways that knowledge can be acquired, both formal and informal. Terms such as *distance learning, open learning,* and *online learning* have become common (Bureck, Malmstrom, & Peppers, 2003; M. Miller & Lu, 2003; Wedemeyer, 1981). Massive open online courses (MOOCs) have been receiving attention as ways to deliver courses in higher education. Some feel that the delivery system is the answer with no concern for what the system's consequences may be, or how to implement the new system fairly for all students. Evaluations of MOOCs are mixed, in that some students and teachers cite the lack of interaction as a problem in learning the material (Khalil & Ebner, 2013). The focus in this book is on what can be learned from experience. The experience of many nontraditional students may be quite different from that of traditional students and may include aspects of racism and structural barriers to their learning. Whatever the experience, particularly outside the formal education system, the question is as follows: What has the student learned from that experience? Ting (2009) found the nontraditional knowledge acquired scale of the NCQ to be a significant predictor of GPA and retention for student athletes at North Carolina State University.

Kuh (1993) concluded that out-of-class experiences in postsecondary education were positively related to persistence and level of educational attainment. He also found that activities outside of class correlated with the development of (a) cognitive complexity (e.g., critical thinking, intellectual flexibility, reflective judgment), (b) knowledge acquisition and application, (c) humanitarianism (e.g., interest in the welfare of others), (d) interpersonal and intrapersonal competence (e.g., self-confidence, identity, ability to relate to others), and (e) practical competence (e.g., decision-making, vocational preparation). Many out-of-class experiences can be developed as part of a student affairs program.

Nontraditional students are more likely than traditional students to learn and develop using methods that are less typical and outside the education system. The methods may be related to race, culture, identity, or gender, and the field itself may be nontraditional. Assessing what a student learns outside school should be an important part of an evaluation program for any student. Those who have experienced discrimination within the education system may be more likely to show evidence of their ability through nontraditional learning prior to college than are students with a more traditional experience.

Although APIA students are academically focused, they may learn many things outside the education system that school professionals do not consider when evaluating these students' development. They are more likely than other students to learn and develop using methods that may be more culture related (Sedlacek, 2004b; Sedlacek & Sheu, 2013). The learning may have occurred in communicating among family members. APIA students may have experience in helping family members in different generations communicate by knowing English and another language and serving as an interpreter within the family. APIA students may not see this as a valuable or unusual skill. They may also have some experience in a family business, which could include such things as learning about accounting, business practices, or customer relations. Mentors and student affairs professionals can help students explore these and other nonacademic experiences to evaluate their learning (Sedlacek et al., 2007). This process could relate to students' self-concept, realistic self-appraisal, long-term career goals, or efforts to seek other student services.

ADDITIONAL MEASURES
OF DIVERSITY

If a measurement matters at all, it is because it must have some conceivable effect on decisions and behaviour. If we can't identify a decision that could be affected by a proposed measurement and how it could change those decisions, then the measurement simply has no value.

—Douglas W. Hubbard (2014, p. 47)

A s the noncognitive variable system was being developed, there was a realization that it would take more work in several areas to get institutions and programs to adopt it. Educational systems resist change. Additional measures and methods to complement the noncognitive model were needed, as well as a method of dealing with the issue of racism in a proactive way.

Diversity Research

It is important to understand the differences in the areas in which research questions are focused. Sedlacek (2007) proposed that social change research questions can be categorized into one of three areas. Generally, results in one area do not answer questions well in the other area, and confusion on this point often works against the social action researcher.

The first research area is *information*. Anything factual such as demographic information, frequency counts of events, or correct answers to test items would fit here. The change agent often needs information to identify the issues or to know which way to go. At one time, learned people felt that earth, wind, fire, and water were the four elements in nature. Without research we would have no reason to think otherwise.

Sometimes information is compelling and results in immediate change. This is seldom true, however. The people and systems we are trying to change can often ignore or rationalize facts.

Do any of the following statements sound familiar? Blacks prefer to live in certain neighborhoods, women cannot handle management responsibilities, welfare recipients are lazy, and so on. Researchers have often assumed that the facts speak for themselves. Galileo assumed that once he presented his observations about the Earth not being the center of the universe, the Church would accept them. It did, but it was more than 350 years later! Most of us would prefer a quicker response.

The second research area is *attitudes*. Here any affective data concerning feelings, opinions, or perspectives are the focus of research and change. The link between attitudes and information is complex. Presenting information generally does not change feelings, but as part of a larger strategy, the two may be linked. For example, in the stages of eliminating racism discussed in chapter 5, colleagues and I have shown that information on cultural and racial differences and racism, followed by attitude measurement, can lead to the desired reductions in racist or sexist behaviors (Sedlacek, 2004b; Sedlacek & Brooks, 1976). But if you are interested in changes in feelings, do not confuse that with information or behavior. When one is trying to change attitudes among groups, several conditions are required: One of these is that all groups should view the negotiating conditions as favorable. Also, there should be equal power among the groups to affect the outcome, and conditions for continued positive feelings should be developed (Dovidio & Gaertner, 1986). Doing assessments of feelings to determine the status of each of these conditions would be important in any attitude-change process. The Situational Attitude Scale (SAS) is a method of measuring prejudice that can be applied to a variety of situations, using experimental and control forms of a questionnaire, and that can be useful here (Sedlacek, 1996, 2004b, 2004c; Sedlacek, Troy, & Chapman, 1976). I discuss this method in detail in the following section.

The third research area is *behavior*. Often, this area is where we wish to concentrate, but it is an area where it is difficult to get change and where information and feelings may not lead directly to behavioral change. The noncognitive variable research and resulting measures provide a way to change behavior. Some institutions and individuals will be able to focus on behavior and implement the noncognitive model without a reliance on information or attitude measures, but many will not. If institutions or individuals provide multiple measures of relevant variables, it is more likely that behavioral change would occur, and the noncognitive variable model would be used.

Situational Attitude Scale

The SAS methodology is an approach to measuring negative attitudes or prejudiced feelings toward a group. It has been applied to many types of prejudice with some success in providing score reliability and validity in isolating situation-based sources of prejudice. The method can be useful in helping to identify what groups we should include in our conceptions of diversity. Measuring racial attitudes is particularly useful in implementing stage three of the Sedlacek–Brooks model of eliminating racism discussed in chapter 5. The SAS can be helpful to student affairs and multicultural office professionals in their programming efforts. Without such measurement, the calls for reducing prejudice can be too easily dismissed.

When assessing whether a given group is to be considered "nontraditional," it is important to consider whether its members experience prejudice (Sedlacek, in press). *Prejudice* here is defined as some negative attributions or perceived consequences of being a member of a certain group. Measuring the degree of prejudice against a group has been difficult because of the tendency many people have to mask or avoid expressing such feelings because of social acceptability. In response to this measurement problem, Sedlacek and Brooks (1970) developed the SAS. The SAS employs experimental and control forms and provides a situational context to make the psychological withdrawal from the stimulus more difficult.

The SAS methodology has been shown to have evidence of reliability and validity in assessing attitudes toward racial and ethnic groups such as Blacks (Balenger, Hoffman, & Sedlacek, 1992), Hispanics (T.J. White & Sedlacek, 1986), Jews (Gerson & Sedlacek, 1992), American Indians (Ancis, Bennett-Choney, & Sedlacek, 1996), Arabs (Miville & Sedlacek, 1994; Sergent, Woods, & Sedlacek, 1992), and APIAs (Leong & Schneller, 1997; Liang & Sedlacek, 2003a, 2003b).

The SAS has also been employed in measuring attitudes toward persons with disabilities (Linnell, 2001; Marshall, 1983; McQuilkin, Freitag, & Harris, 1990; Stovall & Sedlacek, 1983), older persons (Peabody & Sedlacek, 1982; Schwalb & Sedlacek, 1990), Mormons (Gilman, 1983), women (Herman & Sedlacek, 1973; Minatoya & Sedlacek, 1983), children (Carney & Sedlacek, 1985; Knight, Seefeldt, & Sedlacek, 1984), student protesters (Hopple, 1976), commuting students (Foster, Sedlacek, Hardwick, & Silver, 1977; Lea, Sedlacek, & Stewart, 1980; Wilkshire, 1989), LGBTQ individuals (Engstrom & Sedlacek, 1997; Fox, 1995; J.E. Washington, 1993), athletes (Comeaux, 2011; Engstrom & Sedlacek, 1991; Engstrom, Sedlacek, & McEwen, 1995; Hirt, Hoffman, & Sedlacek, 1983; Spitzer, 2014), African American counseling clients (Stovall, 1989), and groups representing diversity (Longerbeam & Sedlacek, 2006).

The SAS methodology has also been employed in assessing the racial attitudes of Japanese students toward the Edo group (Forrer, Sedlacek, & Agarie, 1977) and Australian student attitudes toward Aboriginal Australians and "New Australians" (Chaples, Sedlacek, & Miyares, 1978). Chaples, Sedlacek, and Brooks (1972) studied attitudes of Danish students toward Blacks (*negre*) and "Mediterranean foreign workers" (p. 235) (*sydlandske fremmedarbejdere*).

This list is intended not to be complete but to illustrate some of the groups to which the SAS has been applied. Also, there is no assumption that there is prejudice against a given group or that it is equally strong or socially relevant for all groups. The SAS methodology can be used to determine the presence or absence of prejudice and the degree to which it is present. The test–retest and coefficient alpha reliability estimates range from .70 to .89.

Bertrand and Mullainathan (2004) used a similar technique to the SAS in studying race in the labor market by sending fictitious résumés to help-wanted ads in newspapers in Boston and Chicago. To manipulate perceived race, the researchers randomly assigned résumés "African-American-sounding" or "White-sounding" names. The fictitious people with the White names received 50% more callbacks for interviews. Callers were also more responsive to résumé quality for the White names than for the African American ones. The racial differential in response was uniform across occupation, industry, and employer size. The authors concluded, "Differential treatment by race still appears to still be prominent in the U.S. labor market" (p. 991).

Creating SAS Situations

To begin, one should develop a set of situations that may generate prejudice toward a given group from another group. These can be obtained from publications (popular or professional) or from focus groups, brainstorming sessions, or pilot studies. For example, research literature and popular press reports have indicated that if we wish to assess attitudes of Whites toward African Americans, living in close proximity may evoke prejudice among some Whites. So several situations such as dealing with college roommates and people living in one's neighborhood were pilot tested prior to inclusion in a final instrument.

A useful technique is a brainstorming session involving representatives of the group to which the scale will be administered where stereotypes and situations that might engender prejudice are discussed. By asking for examples these people might have seen in others, one can reduce the reluctance to discuss one's own feelings. It is important to note that situations should be relevant to the group members being assessed and expressed in their terminology.

For example, in a discussion with able-bodied persons, the word *handicapped* was commonly employed when discussing persons with physical disabilities, so that stimulus term was employed, because the point is to try to elicit a prejudiced response from that group, not to be politically correct or to use terms that might be employed by another group. Exhibit 2 (see website) shows the situations developed in a form of the SAS designed to assess attitudes toward Arabs. The term *Arab* does not have a precise meaning (Patai, 1973) but is used routinely to express negative attitudes by those who do not identify with the group.

Constructing Multiple SAS Forms

After the situations are developed, two or more forms of the SAS version are created. One form (A) is neutral and makes no mention of a particular group in the situation. Another form (B) includes the stimulus term of interest; in online Exhibit 2, the term is *Arab*. The only difference between the forms is a given term, and hence any mean difference noted in responses to the two forms randomly assigned to a group must be due to the stimulus term, using the logic of experimental and control conditions.

The SAS was designed to elicit both overt and less conscious feelings and to control for socially desirable responses. The SAS has typically comprised 10 personal and social situations with some relevance to the particular form of prejudice being studied, followed by 10 bipolar semantic differential scales (Osgood, Suci, & Tannenbaum, 1957) for each situation. Participants are not aware that other forms exist or that comparisons are being made. Consequently, the validity of the SAS is determined by the mean response differences between the two or more forms. Exhibit 2 (see website) shows some situations generated for other forms of the SAS.

Semantic differential items that are evaluative (as opposed to those showing power or movement) usually work best in eliciting reactions to the situations. Situation scores can be calculated, making sure to reflect the polarity of items so they are scored in the same direction. The homogeneity of the situations can be further analyzed using factor analysis or cluster analysis (Sedlacek & Brooks, 1972).

Although it is possible to create more than two forms, it is important that the situations be relevant to expressing prejudice toward the two or more groups in the experimental forms. Situations that might elicit prejudice toward one group might not work with another group. For example, personal situations usually elicit the strongest negative actions toward Blacks from non-Blacks (R.T. Carter, White, & Sedlacek, 1987), but more public situations tend to generate the most negative reactions to LGBTQ people (J.E. Washington, 1993). However, in a study of attitudes toward persons with physical disabilities, three stimulus terms (*neutral, blind,* and *wheelchair*) showed differences with the same series of situations (Stovall & Sedlacek, 1983).

Summary of SAS Methodology

After relevant situations are created and semantic differential evaluative scales are developed, experimental and control forms of the instrument are constructed. Forms are randomly assigned to participants, situation scores are calculated, and differences among forms are determined. A possible way to analyze form differences is with multivariate analysis of variance (MANOVA) with form as an independent variable and situation scores as dependent variables. Exhibit 2 shows (see website) an example of form differences by situation on the SAS (Arab version). Interactions of form by other variables (e.g., gender) are also possible.

Thus, the SAS methodology allows for flexibility of form development in that forms could be uniquely developed for particular circumstances. For example, if a given city were experiencing difficulties in certain situations between members of particular groups, the SAS methodology would allow for a quantification of those circumstances. This could help to determine not only who might be "nontraditional" in certain circumstances but also what situations might be focused on to reduce prejudice and help to solve some of the problems involved.

Cultural Attitudes and Climate Survey

A basic assessment technique useful at the understanding cultural and racial differences stage of eliminating racism (stage 1 in the Sedlacek–Brooks model in chapter 5) is the Cultural Climate Survey. It is essentially a campus audit of programs and perceptions of diversity issues and contains items on information, attitudes, and behavior (Ancis, Sedlacek, & Mohr, 2000; Helm, Sedlacek, & Prieto, 1998b; see also Appendix F at sty.presswarehouse.com/sites/stylus/resrcs/chapters/1620362562_excerpt .pdf). Using factor analysis, the researchers identified 11 independent factors: racial tension, cross-cultural comfort, diversity awareness, racial pressures, residence hall tension, fair treatment, faculty racism, respect for other cultures, lack of support, comfort with own culture, and overall satisfaction. The alpha reliability estimate of the instrument was .81.

Results indicated that significant racial and ethnic group differences existed in regard to perceptions and experiences of the campus cultural climate. African Americans consistently reported more negative experiences compared to Asian American, Latino, and White students. Specifically, African American students experienced greater racial and ethnic hostility; greater pressure to conform to stereotypes; less equitable treatment by faculty, staff, and teaching assistants; and more faculty racism than their Asian American, Latino, and White counterparts. This is consistent with previous research, indicating that African American undergraduates perceive and experience significantly more racism on campus than their non–African American counterparts (Cabrera & Nora, 1994; R. Clark, 2004; Hurtado, 1992; LaSure, 1993; Rucker, Neblett, & Anyiwo, 2014; Sedlacek, 1987).

Asian American and Latino students also reported experiences of stereotyping and prejudice in the form of limited respect and unfair treatment by faculty, teaching assistants, and students; interracial tension in residence halls; and pressure to conform to stereotypes. However, compared to other non-White racial and ethnic groups on campus, Latinos experienced the least racism and experienced a campus climate relatively free of racial and ethnic conflict. Several factors may account for these findings. In the university from which the sample was drawn, Latinos composed approximately 6% of the undergraduate student body, compared to 14% for African American students and 12% for Asian American students.

The limited number of Latino students on this campus may have prevented them from being perceived as a threat or competitors for resources and thus less subject to discriminatory behavior. Different results may be found on campuses with a larger Latino enrollment and with more overt anti-immigrant or antiethnic minority sentiment. Results may also reflect the fact that Latinos are considered an ethnic group rather than a racial group. The lack of ostensible, physical, racial characteristics may render many Latinos less subject to discrimination than other groups, such as Asian American and African American students (see Helms, 1995). Alternatively, given the need to negotiate the rules of conduct of Anglo-American culture in U.S. colleges and universities, including use of the English language, Latinos who attend and persist in college may be more acculturated than their peers who do not attend college (Baron & Constantine, 1997). As such, they may report a greater level of adjustment in college and university settings than their nonacculturated peers. This is consistent with previous meta-analytic research demonstrating that Latino students' familiarity and comfort with Anglo culture is positively related to less stress experienced in predominantly Anglo universities (Quintana, Vogel, & Ybarra, 1991).

Of all groups, Latinos reported the most comfort with their own cultural background, as well as with individuals who are culturally different. These students' acceptance of self and others may serve to buffer the negative effects of discrimination. In fact, positive attitudes toward culturally different others and a secure ethnic identity seem to be associated with lower levels of stress on campus among Latino students (Quintana et al., 1991).

White students consistently reported less racial tension, few expectations to conform to stereotypic behavior, an experience of being treated fairly, a climate characterized by respect for diversity, and the most overall satisfaction. Despite reports of interracial tension and discrimination on campus by students of color who compose approximately one third of the study body, White students seemed relatively immune to such a hostile climate. This reality was most obvious in examining differences on residence hall tension (Quintana et al., 1991). All groups, with the exception of White students, reported interracial tension in residence halls. White students not only experienced limited discrimination but also seemed unaware that interracial tensions and conflict exist for a significant portion of the student body. This last finding is consistent with previous studies that demonstrate significant discrepancies between White and minority students' perceptions of interracial tension and university support for students of color (Cabrera & Nora, 1994; Loo & Rolison, 1986; McClelland & Auster, 1990; Sedlacek, 2004b).

Conducting a Campus Climate Assessment

Campus climate surveys can be extremely useful to student affairs and academic staff as they work to develop effective diversity plans around issues of curriculum, residence life, or student recruitment and retention. Many campus practitioners, however, don't know where to begin to design campus climate surveys. Each institution is different and requires different sorts of evaluations, but a campus climate survey is a good place to start (Sedlacek, 2000).

It is important to know your institution. Rely on your judgment, or someone you trust, about what issues should be surveyed. Check the campus or local newspaper for diversity topics that have come up frequently. Look at what other schools have done, but just because University X used a certain survey does not mean it will be useful for your school. Focus your survey: Don't try to do too much. Perhaps on your campus, issues concerning a particular racial group seem most important. A good survey on a limited topic is better than a wide-ranging survey on many topics. Do several focused surveys over time if necessary.

Another way of focusing is to concentrate on one of three types of content, as discussed previously: information, attitudes, or behavior. The three areas yield potentially much different data.

How Results Will Be Used

Right at the beginning, it is useful to decide on what you want to do with the results of your survey. Are you designing a research study to teach social science students? Will the survey results be used by the school president to help determine and recommend general campus policies? Will the results be used by diversity program or student affairs staff to help plan specific programs? Determine what kinds of data will likely be useful to the intended audience. Consider multiple methods. The use of focus groups, telephone surveys, online surveys, case studies, existing data, historical studies, newspaper files, and interviews has advantages and disadvantages. Use models or theory, where possible, to help organize your thoughts or concepts (Sedlacek, 2004b). This can help you determine the content and methods used in your survey.

Collaborations and Realism: Keys to Success

Collaborate with experienced people wherever possible. Involving faculty who work in multicultural areas, consulting with statisticians and campus assessment offices, and working with student affairs offices and student groups can be beneficial. Keep it practical. Do what you do well. If you don't have the resources for a campus-wide study, do one of just the residence halls or the faculty in engineering, for example. Again, a well-done study that makes good use of resources is preferred. Recognize the limitations in your data. We tend to expect too much of a survey. We want to make cause–effect inferences and solve all our problems with one survey. So don't go beyond what you have. We should use campus climate surveys as background information that is fallible and just a beginning step in our efforts to create change. If it is part of an overall research program with many types of studies, then you can start to make generalizations about your campus.

Watch for sampling problems. It is better to have a small, well-defined sample than a large sample that is poorly drawn. Spend your resources on getting returns and providing incentives that do not interfere with the responses. For example, I have successfully offered credit at the bookstore, a movie pass, and a pen with the school logo. Avoid presuming the nature of the responses. For example, a prodiversity pencil or tickets to a multicultural event may affect responses or make it more likely you would hear from certain segments of your population. Different groups may have different reactions to diversity issues.

Dissemination and Follow-Up

Pay attention to follow-up. Campus climate surveys can be very helpful starting points, but they must be followed up by decisive action that builds on the data that are gathered. To maintain credibility and momentum, members of the campus community need to see any analysis of the survey data that is done and to see any plans of action that emerge from the analyses. Finally, although the primary purpose of any survey should be to improve an individual campus's student affairs and diversity practices and policies, survey results can also be useful to practitioners and policymakers in your state or around the country. If you do a survey, consider publishing the results; they may be useful to others conducting research.

Universal Diverse Orientation

An additional research method that can be useful in the first stage of the Sedlacek–Brooks model to eliminate racism is measuring Universal Diverse Orientation (UDO). The concept of UDO may provide an important direction in multicultural assessment (Fuertes, Miville, Mohr, Sedlacek, & Gretchen, 2000; Fuertes, Sedlacek, Roger, & Mohr, 2000; Longerbeam & Sedlacek, 2006; Miville, Carlozzi, Gushue, Schara, & Ueda, 2006). UDO is the movement toward or away from diversity rather than simply the presence or absence of prejudice and consists of three subscales that measure attitudinal and behavioral aspects of diversity: relativistic appreciation, diversity of contact, and comfort with differences. Together, these three subscales yield a full-scale UDO score that indicates an overall orientation toward diversity. Research has shown the UDO assessment instrument to be correlated with a number of aspects of student functioning, including past academic achievement (Singley & Sedlacek, 2009) and satisfaction (Sheu, Sedlacek, & Singley, 2003). Differences have been found between men and women, as well as among racial and ethnic groups (Asian/Asian American, African American, Latinos and Latinas) on the UDO (Singley & Sedlacek, 2009). White student total scores were significantly lower than those of people of color, Asian Americans had higher scores than White students on the diversity of contact subscale, and men scored significantly lower than women on overall UDO score (Fuertes et al., 2000). See Appendix D for the UDO scale.

Perceptual Mapping

A physical settings approach to environmental assessment called *perceptual mapping* has been developed and researched and can be applied to diversity assessment. The method can yield data on information, attitudes, and behavior and can be useful in all stages of the Sedlacek–Brooks model for eliminating racism. Perceptual mapping is unique in that it uses maps in both the data collection and the data presentation stages of research. Perceptual maps can be developed for any space, inside or outside a building. The perceptual map depicted in Figure 7.1 represents the results of an evaluative study conducted in a student union at a major university (Sergent & Sedlacek, 1989).

Figure 7.1. Perceptual map.

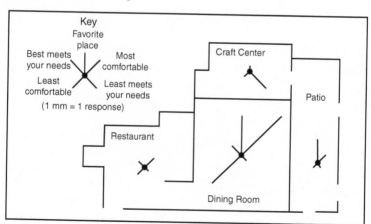

Note. From "Perceptual Mapping: A Methodology in the Assessment of Environmental Perceptions," by M. T. Sergent and W. E. Sedlacek, 1989, *Journal of College Student Development, 30,* 319–322; and "Mapping the University Learning Environment," by A. A. Mitchell, M. T. Sergent, and W.E. Sedlacek, 1997, *National Association of Student Personnel Administrators Journal, 35,* 20–28.

In this study, a map of the student union building was presented to a random sample of undergraduate students. The students were instructed to indicate their responses to each of 10 items by marking their preferences on the map. For example, students were requested to place an "A" on the map in the one place where they felt most comfortable, a "B" on the map in the place that they most often frequented, and a "C" on the map in the place that least met their needs. The measure, which included 10 items to which participants responded, required approximately five minutes to administer. Response frequencies were compiled for each item and were recorded on the map in the format indicated in Figure 7.1.

The perceptual map uses *posies* to depict data quantities. Cartographers use posies to represent geographical characteristics. This posey method was first used in England in the early 1970s to map geochemical properties. Each arm of a posey represents a different item dimension to which participants responded. The relative length of the arm represents the number of participants who chose this area in response to a particular item. In this particular application, posey arms that point down represent negatively valenced items (e.g., the place in which students felt the least comfortable), and arms that point up represent a positively valenced place (e.g., where students felt the most comfortable). Thus, responses to each of five items may be represented by each posey figure. The items used in this application are represented in the key in Figure 7.1.

Methodological Advantages of Perceptual Mapping

One benefit of perceptual mapping is its focus on the *perceptions* of individuals in the environment. It provides participants with an objective representation of the physical environment and assesses perceptions or feelings about the designated space. Perceptual mapping can be useful in several stages of the Sedlacek–Brooks model. The perceptual map may include both behavioral items (e.g., "Designate on the map the place that you most commonly use."), perceptual or attitudinal items (e.g., "Designate on the map your favorite place."), and information items (e.g., "Designate on the map the location of the counseling center."). Items may be designed to measure specific characteristics of the environment. Additional items might instruct participants to designate those areas with which they are familiar, areas in which they most often meet with friends, areas that they would most like to see improved, areas that they tend to avoid, and so on. Flexibility in the choice of items is a unique benefit of perceptual mapping.

Perceptual mapping provides an additional benefit for the evaluation of overall environments related to diversity. Mitchell, Sergent, and Sedlacek (1997) found a number of differences in perceptions of campus space by race. White students had visited the campus prior to enrollment more often than African American students. More African American than White students named a recreational area as a familiar location, whereas more White students than African American students named the student union as familiar. Such information can be used in student affairs and orientation programs and in further exploring why particular feelings or behaviors are associated with certain spaces. Longerbeam and Sedlacek (2006) used the UDO in assessing pre- and post-effects of a living–learning diversity experience. One campus that I worked with used perceptual mapping in identifying the best design for new computer labs being built.

It is a methodology that is easily used by individuals with minimal experience in research and statistical design. Individuals unfamiliar with statistical analyses and tables can interpret the perceptual mapping results because the map format is familiar and makes clear the programmatic and design implications of the results. If statistical analysis of group differences in perceptions of the physical environment is desired, individuals can apply chi-square or other appropriate statistical techniques to test differences in the frequency of responses of two or more groups. It is possible to achieve 90% test–retest reliability of perception locations on a map.

Thurstone Equal-Appearing Intervals

Thurstone equal-appearing intervals (Edwards, 1957; Thurstone, 1959; Trochim, 2002) is a scaling method that could be used in a number of ways in diversity assessment, including measuring attitudes and behavior. It may be particularly useful in the cultural and racial differences stage in the Sedlacek–Brooks model. The technique seems to have been overlooked in recent social science literature (Roberts, 1998), although the original work was published in 1929 (Thurstone & Chave, 1929). The July–August 2002 issue of the *Monitor on Psychology*, published by the American Psychological Association, reported on the top 100 psychologists of the twentieth century. L.L. Thurstone was on the list, but his name was spelled Thurston. Fame has a poor memory and a sense of irony.

To begin the equal-appearing intervals procedure, a group of judges rate the extent to which a large pool of items reflects a certain attribute. Thurstone employed 300 judges in the original work, but many fewer may be necessary. I have had as few as 10 judges be able to make reliable ratings. The number of judges, and initial items required, depends on the simplicity of the content being scaled. The item pool should be much larger than the number of items you wish to use in the final scale.

Judges are instructed to rate the items based on how most people in the target group would rate the items rather than on their own feelings about the items. Thurstone used an 11-point scale on which judges rated the extent to which the items were positive or negative in assessing a certain attitude, although I would recommend any number of scale points from 5 to 11. Judges rated the extent to which the items reflected positive or negative feelings toward "Negroes" in the original work (Thurstone & Chave, 1929).

Another key point about choosing judges is to make sure that they understand the target group and that they are not too ego-involved in the attribute. For example, if you are studying faculty, it is important that judges understand faculty functions. At the same time, judges must be objective enough to make fine distinctions among the items. For example, Thurstone and Chave (1929) found that "Negro" judges could not distinguish among levels of positivity or negativity in attitudes toward "Negroes" in a scale intended to assess attitudes of Whites toward "Negroes."

Items are then selected that judges have agreed on in their value along the 11-point scale (e.g., low variability) and whose medians or means are spread along the 11-point continuum. Therefore, final items may be selected at half-point intervals (e.g., 1, 1.5, 2, 2.5) or approximately equally spaced intervals rather than at exact points. The object is to get a good range of choices in your final scale. The instructions to respondents in your final assessment would be to select the items with which they agree. The respondents' attitudes, behaviors, or score on the scale is the mean or median of the items that they have chosen.

For example, let's say we are developing a measure of interracial behavior and we have 22 items in our final scale. If a given person feels four of those statements seem to be descriptive of what he or she actually does, we would calculate the mean or median of those four items, which would be the score for that person.

In Thurstone's original work, semi-interquartile ranges were used to determine variability, and medians were used for central tendency estimations. However, I have effectively employed standard deviations and means in different projects.

Advantages and Disadvantages of Equal-Appearing Intervals

The primary advantage of the Thurstone equal-appearing intervals method is that the item analysis is done *before* the items are administered to respondents, so the final number of items is smaller. Hence, it can save time and money and be more focused on individual academic or student affairs programs and employee evaluation systems compared to the widely used Likert or summated ratings procedures (Edwards, 1957).

Equal-appearing intervals may be a more ethical approach than summated ratings in that participants are not required to respond to items that may not be used because those items are eliminated in postadministration analyses. Also, because items are preweighted, there is less need for interpretation in decision-making about results.

Another advantage of equal-appearing intervals scaling is that it can be used easily in studies of behavior and attitudes. By scaling behaviors, the problems with a "halo effect" and skewed distributions may be reduced, compared to measuring attitudes. Appendix E shows a scale that was developed in working with a university police force that was having some difficulties with racial issues. Results were used in training, and evaluation systems were developed for the department.

A disadvantage to equal-appearing intervals may be difficulty in finding judges, because it might require eliminating some potential respondents to the final scale, who may be limited in number. A related disadvantage is that the procedure requires two steps of data gathering, rather than one. Also, the assumption is made that the scale values assigned by the judges are independent of their own attitudes. This may not be the case. With judges who may be ego-involved with the dimension being scaled, as discussed previously, scale values tend to not be linear at the extremes (Edwards & Gonzalez, 1993).

The equal-appearing intervals procedure may also be limited to unidimensional scales. If the continuum being judged contains complex variables, it may not be possible to get agreement among judges. In addition, there is some evidence that equal-appearing intervals scaling does not yield truly interval scales (Edwards & Gonzalez, 1993). However, many of the statistical procedures that we might typically employ using equal-appearing intervals scales (e.g., Pearson correlation, analysis of variance) can still be used effectively even if this assumption is violated.

8

THE WAVES OF CHANGE
FIND MANY SHORES

Once social change begins, it cannot be reversed. You cannot un-educate the person who has learned to read. You cannot humiliate the person who feels pride. You cannot oppress the people who are not afraid anymore.

—César Chávez (1984)

In this chapter, I discuss many programs and institutions employing non-cognitive variables for some purpose. They include higher education admissions, student services, scholarship programs, and secondary school applications. Some of the applications of the model are extensive and well evaluated; others are small and/or implemented with minimum evidence. Some include data and analysis; others are more holistic and part of the philosophy of a program. Some have used the noncognitive model in full with all eight variables in Sedlacek (2004b); others have employed some of the variables and modified the model in ways that fit their needs. As stated previously, there is no requirement that users of the system, or any part of it, must notify me of their use. Here I illustrate the final stages of the models of diffusion of an innovation discussed in chapter 1. The hope here is that the reader will be stimulated to think of possible uses of noncognitive variables in whatever work or life purpose comes to mind. *Buena suerte!*

Professional Groups

The following is a list of a number of professional groups that have employed noncognitive variables.

American Association of Collegiate Registrars and Admissions Officers

The American Association of Collegiate Registrars and Admissions Officers (AACRAO) is the primary professional organization of personnel working in the fields of college and university admissions, academic records, and enrollment services. AACRAO was established in 1910; is based in Washington, DC; and has 11,000 members in 40 countries (see www.aacrao .org).

AACRAO publishes books and reports on topics relevant to its membership, including marketing higher education institutions to students, managing enrollment, academic transfer and transfer credit, fraudulent academic credentials, and good practices in management of academic records. AACRAO Consulting offers a variety of services to members in all areas of enrollment management, including assistance in implementing selection and postmatriculation assessment based on the noncognitive variable model presented in this book (AACRAO, 2014). To date more than 20 institutions have taken advantage of this service and initiated programs based on the noncognitive variables (AACRAO, 2013b). By institutionalizing the noncognitive variable model at this level, AACRAO increases the chances of reaching more people and programs, as well as sustaining the innovation. Following is the AACRAO posting on its website announcing the availability of its services concerning noncognitive variables:

> AACRAO Consulting is pleased to announce *FairSelect*, a set of services to assist institutions in adopting the most equitable approaches to comprehensive, holistic admissions and other student selection processes. Delivered by leading researcher William Sedlacek and foremost practitioner Michele Sandlin, *FairSelect* represents a significant step forward from traditional student evaluation and selection practices. Using a unique written interview instrument, backed by 30 years of research and multiple case studies, institutions can augment knowledge gained from test scores and prior academic performance to better assess student potential and institutional fit, improve support services and student success rates, and increase retention.
>
> The *FairSelect* approach has proven successful at a wide range of institutions: large and small, public and private, undergraduate, graduate and professional—including international institutions. The underlying concepts have been shown in research studies to provide for fairer student selections across a wide range of student diversity factors, including socioeconomic status, race, ethnicity, learning style, and national origin. It also has been used to improve scholarship selections, being the basis for selecting students in the Gates Millennium Scholarship Program. This approach has gained wide recognition as an important step forward in admission and scholarship selections.

Our services include campus workshops with faculty and staff, planning assistance, staff training, business process refinement, and technology support. Contact us today to explore *FairSelect* options for your campus. (AACRAO, 2013a)

Luke Schultheis, vice provost at Virginia Commonwealth University (VCU) and AACRAO vice president for admissions and enrollment management, noted that many schools now review students holistically. VCU reviews grades and test scores and uses *FairSelect* as a tool for measuring noncognitive variables.

Schultheis (2014) noted that "Holistic admissions may have included assigning a quantitative value to aspects of student performance or engagement outside of grades," such as athletics, leadership, clubs, and volunteerism "However, students should not discount the importance of standardized tests or grades in school or of anything required in an application for admission. If it is required, it should be considered important in making an admission decision" (Schultheis, 2014).

"What should be most important to the student is identifying a set of institutions where they feel a fit, where they feel encouraged to become engaged both academically as well as socially. Then the student will excel," Schultheis (2014) said. "Conversely, the student who gains access to an institution yet who feels isolated or lost will probably not perform optimally and the chances of graduation could be severely diminished—regardless of high school grades or test scores" (Schultheis, 2014).

Results at VCU show that noncognitive variables were related to retention for students starting in fall 2014 and returning for their second year in fall 2015. Students with the lowest noncognitive score were retained at 77%, whereas students with the highest noncognitive score were retained at 86% (L. Schultheis, personal communication, June 19, 2015).

Association of American Medical Colleges

The Association of American Medical Colleges (AAMC) developed the Simulated Minority Admissions Exercise (SMAE) (Sedlacek & Prieto, 1982, 1990). It is a simulated interview and selection workshop based on actual case studies of applicants to U.S. and Canadian medical schools with the names, schools, and some demographic information changed to protect identities. The cases are African Americans, Native Americans, and Latinos, and 40% are women. The cases were selected to illustrate one or more of the eight noncognitive variables, as either a positive or a negative for each candidate. In a workbook format using a latent image technique, participants can interview candidates and review typical admissions materials. It is typically not possible to uncover the responses to all the interview questions presented in the time allotted, so participants must choose which questions are most important to ask. Cases have consisted of students who were selected by and enrolled in medical schools, some of whom were successful and some who were not. The workshop is scheduled for a full day, during which participants study cases individually. Then, in groups of 6 to 8, they discuss the cases and select 6 of the 10 cases presented. In the final stage of the workshop, participants are told how each student represented fared in school, why, and what he or she is doing now (D'Costa et al., 1974, 1975).

Participants have included admissions committee members, administrators, faculty, and students from most U.S. and Canadian medical schools. Premedical advisers, allied health professionals, and scholarship program professionals have also been included in the sessions. Workshops have been held in medical schools, general campus facilities, and conferences and conventions (Prieto et al., 1978; Prieto, Quinones, Elliott, Goldner, & Sedlacek, 1986). Since 1974, the workshop has been conducted more than 200 times and involved more than 3,000 individuals. More than 90% of participants felt the workshop helped them understand and evaluate minority candidates. In addition, 85% felt they could use the noncognitive variables in admissions and in their advising, teaching, or administrative work.

Many changes have taken place in society and medical education in the past 40 years. The enrollment of female first-year students in U.S. medical schools has more than doubled in that time from 22% to 47% (Association of American Medical Colleges, 2012). Enrollment of minorities as first-year students has remained at about 10%, with the percentage of African Americans enrolled decreasing from 7.5% in 1974–1975 to 6.5% in 2011–2012 and enrollment of Mexican Americans/Chicanos increasing from 1.5% to 2.6%. In addition, the percentage of minority graduates of medical schools has increased. The percentage of African American graduates from U.S. schools increased 30% (5.0% in 1974–1975 to 6.5% in 2010–2011), Mexican American/Chicano graduates increased 189% (0.9% to 2.6%), and American Indian/Alaska Native graduates increased 300% (0.2% to 0.8%) during that same period.

The results at some medical schools have been dramatic. For example, the Louisiana State University (LSU) medical school has seen its percentage of minority students double to 21% after 10 years of sustained effort and repeating the SMAE for admission committee members and staff over that time. In postworkshop evaluations, 80% felt the noncognitive variables were useful in admissions, and 92% indicated that the training helped them assess noncognitive variables in interviews of applicants (Helm, Prieto, & Sedlacek, 1997). Participants reported that self-concept (97%), realistic self-appraisal

(95%), leadership (84%), support person (83%), and handling racism (81%) were the most useful predictors of minority student success. Sixty-one percent indicated grade point average (GPA) and 57% felt medical college admission test scores were useful in assessing minority applicant potential.

Students of color and women have many more career opportunities than they did 40 years ago. Many varied programs and offices designed to deal with recruiting and retention have been developed at virtually all medical schools in the United States and Canada.

Beginning in 1985, a half-day workshop on interviewing to assess noncognitive variables was added to the SMAE offering (Westbrook & Sedlacek, 1988). Principles of interviewing to obtain information on noncognitive variables were presented there and included in Appendix F in this book.

What role the SMAE may have had in the changes that took place in medical education cannot be isolated, but many people were exposed to the perspective of employing noncognitive variables in their work with and for students of color and women.

Colleges and Universities With Religious Affiliations

Many colleges and universities have used noncognitive variables in admissions or student service programs.

Brigham Young University

The Mission of Brigham Young University (BYU)—founded, supported, and guided by the Church of Jesus Christ of Latter-day Saints (LDS)—is to assist individuals in their quest for perfection and eternal life. That assistance should provide a period of intensive learning in a stimulating setting where a commitment to excellence is expected and the full realization of human potential is pursued.

To this end, the University seeks qualified students of various talents and backgrounds, including geographic, educational, cultural, ethnic, and racial, who relate together in such a manner that they are "no more strangers and foreigners, but fellow citizens with the saints, and of the household of God." It is the University's judgment that providing educational opportunities for a mix of students who share values based on the gospel of Jesus Christ and come from a variety of backgrounds and experiences is an important educational asset to BYU. (Findlinson, Strong, & Blackwelder, 2014)

BYU enrolls 35,500 students and 7,000 new freshman each year: 51% are men, 98.5% are LDS, and 14% are "multicultural." BYU employs the noncognitive variables discussed in this book in a "holistic" model. BYU asks the following essay questions on the application designed to elicit information on noncognitive variables, limiting responses to 250 words:

- What is one of the most difficult things you have ever done or experienced? What made it difficult, and what did you learn?
- Explain what will determine which LDS Church Education System (CES) school you will attend.
- Tell us anything else you want us to know about yourself that you haven't had the opportunity to describe elsewhere in the application. Include any special circumstances, experiences, and so on that could influence your admission to the university.
- *Additional transfer essay:* Please share your reasons for seeking admission as a transfer student—specifically, we invite you to address your intended major and your career/life ambitions.

Eighty-three readers from on and off campus were trained online to evaluate the applications using the following policies:

- Every application is thoroughly reviewed.
- Multiple readers review each application.
- Discrepant reader scores are reviewed.
- Readers ask for further reviews on characteristics of interest.
- Readers ask for additional information.
- More frequent committee reviews are offered.

BYU felt the most challenging aspects of a holistic review were the time needed to review files, the difficulty in explaining decisions, and minimizing appeals (Findlinson et al., 2014).

Examples of the "tough cases" that were denied admission for the summer–fall 2014 class include the following (Findlinson et al., 2014):

- 178 students with ACT scores higher than 30
- 76 students with a GPA of 4.0
- 169 students with a GPA of 3.98 or higher
- 54 students ranked number 1 in their class
- 116 students ranked number 5 or higher in their class

Madonna University

Madonna University is an independent, Catholic liberal arts university located in suburban Livonia, Michigan, on the western perimeter of metropolitan Detroit. Conducted by the Felician Sisters of North America, it has six extension campuses. Though strong in its affiliation with the Roman Catholic Church, the school attracts students and faculty of all faiths. Madonna University employs the noncognitive variables in several ways.

Bridging Lost Gaps Program

The focus of the Bridging Lost Gaps (BLG) program is to increase recruitment, enrollment, retention, and graduation rates of African American male students from Detroit, at Madonna University. Students accepted into the BLG program are offered opportunities to develop leadership skills and career goals. With encouragement from mentors and through community service activities, students are challenged to grow intellectually, spiritually, and personally. This mentoring is focused on the noncognitive variable model discussed in this book. The program includes the following:

- a community support network (academic and social)
- access to university student resources
- career development opportunities
- Summer Bridge Program (July–August)
- mentoring (peer and professional)
- financial aid resources
- a sense of belonging

The Need

Too many African American men 15 to 24 years old are unemployed or incarcerated or have been killed. The BLG program was created to save these young men from negative outcomes and provide them a bright future. Each year, Madonna University accepts 20 to 25 students to participate in the BLG program. The program achieved a 97% graduation rate, and multiple students have made the dean's list for their academic success in the classroom. This compares to a 32.6% graduation rate for Black male students across Michigan's four-year colleges and universities (George & Tingson-Gatuz, 2014).

Mentoring and Learning

Students in the BLG program enjoy a safe, learning-centered college community so they can reach their full potential. A support network of faculty, staff, and students provides encouragement and mentoring for students throughout their experience at Madonna University. Through partnerships with local and national companies, organizations, and governmental groups, this unique program offers meaningful opportunities to learn from industry and community leaders. Each student completes an internship and can choose to be employed on campus. Students who are accepted into the BLG program experience the following:

- a weekly meeting
- access to tutoring and academic support
- time for integrated prayer and reflection
- involvement in service-learning and community projects
- attendance at university events

African American men in this program discussed the value of each of the eight noncognitive variables to them (www.youtube.com/watch?v=XmMWwC_8em8). The interviews were produced by the students (see www.youtube.com/watch?v=_3cVSCqRwdY).

Goshen College

Goshen College is a private liberal arts college in Goshen, Indiana. The institution was founded in 1894 as the Elkhart Institute and is affiliated with Mennonite Church USA. It has an enrollment of about 1,000 students. Goshen College is

> dedicated to the development of informed, articulate, sensitive, responsible Christians. As a ministry of the Mennonite Church, we seek to integrate Christian values with educational, social and professional life. As a community of faith and learning, we strive to foster personal, intellectual, spiritual and social growth in every person. We view education as a moral activity that produces servant-leaders for the church and the world. (www.goshen.edu)

Goshen College employs noncognitive variables in admissions, teaching, and student services in order to achieve its mission and goals. By employing the nocognitive variables in admissions, the school hopes to recruit non-Mennonite students with strong self-concepts and the ability to negotiate a system that was not designed for them. In addition, scoring high on the noncognitive variable of community from the NCQ will help students become part of the campus and larger Christian communities.

James E. Brenneman (2010), president of Goshen College, stated,

> Let me be blunt here. It seems I have been too nuanced in the past and have since discovered that sometimes we have talked past one another on the question of Goshen College's future because we have not started with the same basic assessment of the facts as they relate to our future viability

as an institution. So let me be plain. It is more than likely that the make up of the student body of any viable future vision of Goshen College (or probably any Mennonite College) will most likely be about one third local, one third national/international, one third Mennonite (of all stripes). Certainly, we are arriving at the point where the larger majority of our student body will be non-Mennonite. I was surprised when 4 of the 6 seniors who offered senior statements or faith statements at chapel or convocation at the end of last year spoke about how difficult it was to be so different here at GC (presumably, these students were not chosen at random, but were those known to have gained much by being at GC). They used such phrases as "culture shock," "didn't fit in," and "having few things in common." One said she had decided not to come back after her first year, but was persuaded to anyway. They mentioned the "Mennonite Game," "Mennonite cliques" or insensitive questions about their backgrounds. In short, they didn't feel valued for who they were and for the diversity and richness they brought to Goshen College. Fortunately, they all stuck it out and graduated. They all praised the life-changing education they received at Goshen College. They were grateful for the help and support they received from other students and faculty members. . . . I am calling for raising the bar on our minimum GPA entrance expectations and simultaneously adding 8 proven non-cognitive admissions criteria to assist in knowing who will succeed here and how we can help a student do so.

DePaul University

DePaul University is a private university in Chicago, Illinois. Founded by the Vincentians in 1898, the university takes its name from the seventeenth-century French priest Saint Vincent DePaul. In 1998, it became the largest Catholic university by enrollment in the United States. Following in the footsteps of its founders, DePaul places special emphasis on recruiting first-generation students and others from "disadvantaged" backgrounds. The university enrolls about 16,150 undergraduate students and about 7,600 graduate and law students, making DePaul the 13th-largest private university by enrollment in the United States and the largest private university in Illinois. The student body represents a diverse array of religious, ethnic, and geographic backgrounds, including more than 60 foreign countries.

Over the course of several strategic plans dating back to 1997, DePaul set out an ambitious agenda for enrollment growth. As a result, undergraduate enrollment increased by 54% over the next 15 years, including a doubling of the size of the traditional freshman class. The number of freshman applications increased significantly, and admit rates have declined from 80% to below 60%. Measures of academic preparation have improved, and four-year graduation rates have increased from 44% to 56% in the past seven years. This has been achieved while sustaining the university's mission-based goals of access and diversity; Pell recipients compose 27% of the freshman class, 31% are first-generation students, and 34% are students of color. At the same time, net tuition revenue per student has increased dramatically over the same period, an essential element of strategic enrollment management at a university that is among the most tuition dependent of all private, doctoral universities in the United States (Kalsbeek, Sandlin, & Sedlacek, 2013).

It became clear in 2006 that as demand continued to grow for freshman admission and there was less capacity for continued enrollment expansion, DePaul's Enrollment Management and Marketing (EM&M) division faced the inevitable outcome of improved market position, namely, an admission process that would need to be even more selective. This presented a strategic challenge for an institution that affirms the continued relevance and importance of its historical mission to provide college opportunities for students who come from low-income families, who are the first in their families to pursue postsecondary education, and who are from historically underrepresented racial–ethnic groups. These students often face systemic, structural, and societal challenges that are reflected in the academic measures traditionally used in college admissions—namely, ACT and SAT scores, advanced high school curriculum, and high school grades—and are, therefore, more likely to be adversely affected by greater selectivity in a process using only these traditional admission criteria (Kalsbeek, 2013).

The following became strategic questions: How to continue to admit students who may not fare as well as others in these traditional measures of academic preparedness but who have clear potential to succeed at DePaul? How to identify those promising applicants whose background creates disadvantages but who will succeed if given the opportunity to enroll? How to expand the admissions review process to include attributes beyond traditional measures (especially attributes that are known to predict success in college) and ensure that the process is manageable, competitive, equitable, and legal? How to distinguish among applicants who, by traditional measures, may appear equally qualified and admit those with the greatest likelihood for academic success?

The Strategy

DePaul's response was to expand its admission review by collecting more nontraditional data on its freshman applicants and incorporating the insights mined from that data in the admission review process, helping admissions staff decide which students to admit as freshmen. The institutional need was to develop a means for doing this that could be efficiently and effectively brought to scale at a large university receiving thousands of freshman applications annually.

The objective was to directly incorporate in the admissions review process additional information beyond the usual ACT, SAT, and high school GPA—especially information that more directly relates to the likelihood of student success in college—to continue to provide opportunities for students who show promise but who, on the basis of traditional admissions measures, might not be admitted in an increasingly selective process. The overarching enrollment management goal was to improve retention and degree completion outcomes by admitting students who demonstrated qualities and characteristics known to be predictive of student success in college (Kalsbeek et al., 2013).

Turning to the research by Sedlacek (2004b, 2011), the DePaul EM&M team replaced the existing essay on its freshman admissions application with a series of short-answer essay questions designed to offer applicants the opportunity to provide evidence of their qualities and capabilities on noncognitive dimensions of background and college readiness.

The initial intent of the Developing Insights for Admission through the Mining of Non-traditional Data (DIAMOND) program was to complement the admissions review of students graduating from high school with specialized curricula (e.g., the International Baccalaureate), students who had strong academic records but who may have had weaker ACT and SAT test scores, and students graduating from the Chicago Public Schools and Chicago Archdiocesan Schools. In the early stages of the project, however, every applicant was asked to complete these essays.

A senior-level admissions position was created and assigned responsibility for leading and managing the DIAMOND project. A campus-wide volunteer team of readers was selected and trained to rate these short-answer essays using a scoring rubric regarding the extent to which the applicant's responses provided evidence of each of the noncognitive variables; extensive analyses of interrater reliability were used to develop the training regimen and ensure consistency in scoring and minimize rater bias. The readers' ratings were provided to the Office of Admission for inclusion and consideration in the admission review process beginning with the entering freshman class of 2009. A sophisticated online system was developed to efficiently facilitate the entire process of distributing the essays, facilitating the reading and rating process, and managing the overall project; with over 18,300 essays reviewed and rated in the initial two years, this was no small project.

It should be noted that DePaul had no immediate compelling reason to alter its admission program, because by all traditional measures the university was attracting strong candidates who were doing well and were from racially and socioeconomically diverse backgrounds. However, DePaul wished to introduce "new approaches to admission criteria . . . when the institution has the latitude to experiment with innovations and is not doing so under the duress of immediate enrollment challenges" (Kalsbeek et al., 2013).

Analysis: Phase I

From a strategic enrollment management perspective, the initial challenge was to determine if the noncognitive variables added anything new. Test scores, parental education and income, and race were already considered in selection. Analyses showed that the noncognitive ratings were not highly correlated with those dimensions. They were tapping unique variance that would help level the playing field across those characteristics. "The initial analysis offered sufficient confidence that the essays and the ratings provided by trained readers provided a fairly simple yet potentially valuable addition to the admission review process" (Kalsbeek et al., 2013).

In this early phase, the outcome studied was *first-year academic success*, defined as earning a 2.5 GPA or higher and earning 48 credits during the first year. At DePaul, first-year retention is quite high (consistently over 80%), yet a significant share of students who persist into the second year have not made one full year's academic progress in their first year. That progress is what is most predictive of timely graduation, so the focus of the DIAMOND program analysis was less on retention and less on grades alone and more on academic progress as defined previously.

Although high school GPA is the most significant variable in predicting first-year academic success, there is evidence that higher noncognitive scores help predict first-year success for certain populations: students with lower income (in particular, Pell-eligible male students), students of color, and students with lower ACT scores (in particular, students of color with lower standardized test scores). Preliminary results show that noncognitive variables are predictive of first-year retention as well. Specifically for students who perform well in high school but have low ACT scores, noncognitive variables are related to first- and second-year success.

Long-Term Plans

As this innovation at DePaul was executed and evaluated, it evolved significantly in light of changing institutional realities and prevailing evidence. Pressing needs to allocate staff and resources to other university priorities challenged the leadership of enrollment management to sustain the effort required to support the DIAMOND project (D. H. Kalsbeek, personal communication, May 26, 2016). Despite the development of very efficient online systems to manage the collection, review, and rating of the DIAMOND essays and a large pool of willing volunteer readers, managing this element of the recruitment process in the face of the growing complexity of the rest of the recruitment and admissions effort presented difficult decisions about the sustainability of the project.

More important, though, were two considerations. First, although it was clear that the noncognitive measures were additive and independent of income, ACT and SAT scores, race, and first-generation status, the ongoing evaluation of how these measures correlated with and predicted student success at DePaul repeatedly showed very little marginal effect above and beyond the high school academic record. Although differences may have been statistically significant, they weren't sufficiently significant practically to create compelling reasons to sustain the process for the entirety of the freshman class. Although further development of the instruments and rating system would surely improve these assessments of noncognitive attributes, it was judged that this would require more staff time and resources than were available (D. H. Kalsbeek, personal communication, May 26, 2016).

The second consideration was that freshman enrollment outcomes at DePaul demonstrated gains in racial diversity, socioeconomic diversity, first-generation status, and retention and completion rates independent of the impact of DIAMOND, making the continued investment in this process difficult to justify on those grounds (D. H. Kalsbeek, personal communication, May 26, 2016).

DePaul's DIAMOND initiative is instructive in many ways. It is a valuable case study of how to introduce an innovation in the admissions process on a large scale in a way that is grounded in empirical testing and evaluation and that allows the campus community to build an appreciation for the richly diverse experiences our students bring to campus. It is also a case study in using such evaluative data to weigh the merits of sustaining innovation. It has been a potent reminder of the challenges of applying social science research in the real-world setting (D. H. Kalsbeek, personal communication, May 26, 2016).

Most important, it is a reality check about how the pressing demands faced by enrollment management personnel in today's intensely pressured and resource-constrained environment force difficult choices about competing priorities. DePaul remains committed to the core ideas that undergird the importance of noncognitive assessments; however, the noncognitive assessment as implemented was resource intensive both for DePaul and for its prospective students. DePaul moved instead to implement a "test-optional" admission process, in this way removing barriers to admission for the very students DePaul hoped to serve with the noncognitive assessment. The DIAMOND assessment continues to be used as part of this test-optional admissions process at DePaul, through which about 5% of the freshman class is admitted (D. H. Kalsbeek, personal communication, May 26, 2016).

University of St. Thomas

The University of St. Thomas (UST) is a Catholic institution located in Houston, Texas. The school is committed to the Catholic intellectual tradition and the dialogue between faith and reason.

> By pursuing excellence in teaching, scholarship and service, we embody and instill in our students the core values of our founders, the Basilian Fathers: goodness, discipline and knowledge. We foster engagement in a diverse, collaborative community. As a comprehensive university grounded in the liberal arts, we educate students to think critically, communicate effectively, succeed professionally and lead ethically. (www.stthom.edu/About/Mission_and_Vision/Index.aqf)

Sister Marie Faubert is a professor in the School of Education and chair of the Counselor Education Program at UST. Faubert (1992) found that the NCQ correlated with the success of ninth- and tenth-grade rural students in North Carolina. Her results supported the conclusions of Lee (1984, 1985), who found similar results with the same population. In her teaching at UST, Faubert administered the NCQ as part of a course that she regularly taught for those who were the first college-bound students in their family. In addition, Faubert trained graduate students in school counseling in the use of noncognitive variables. "They were invaluable for helping future counselors realize each student has a context to be understood and respected" (M. Faubert, personal communication, January 27, 2015). She had each of her students portray a person who was high or low on a given different noncognitive variable as part of their course work. As an additional aspect of the experience, she had these students use the portrayals as part of their presentations at conferences (Faubert & Sedlacek, 2008).

Johnson C. Smith University

Johnson C. Smith University (JCSU) is a private, coeducational, historically Black four-year research university, affiliated with the Presbyterian Church and located in Charlotte, North Carolina. Its total enrollment was 1,438 in 2015. JCSU offers 24 degree options for undergraduates and one graduate degree in social work (MSW). Students earn their degree through one of three colleges: the College of Arts and Letters, the College of STEM (science, technology, engineering, and mathematics), and the College of Professional Studies.

JCSU has employed several versions of NCQ questions to evaluate the success of its students. Program evaluation data showed that students admitted using the noncognitive measures performed within range of what would be expected of college students and were equally likely to be retained at the university as students who were admitted using traditional cognitive measures (Johnson C. Smith University, 2012). The noncognitive research project employs both quantitative and qualitative methods and focuses on data obtained through short-answer essay questions based on noncognitive variables on the university's admissions application. Essays are scored on a five-point scale by university staff or undergraduate researchers. All essay responses are scored twice by different individuals and checked for interrater reliability. Initial analyses of baseline data using multiple regression suggest "there is a real promise for using noncognitive factors to predict first year performance in Gateway (Math and English) courses" (Henley, Miklaucic, Sandeford-Lyons, Jones-Cameron, & Medlock, 2016, p. 1). Specifically, students who were scored highly on academic self-efficacy by a pair of raters showed statistically significant increases in success in Gateway Math courses, even when controlling for high school GPA and SAT and ACT scores.

In the spring semester of 2015, faculty and staff developed training modules for students with the expressed goal to improve students' understanding of their individual noncognitive strengths.

In the summer of 2016, the university began to develop faculty competencies using noncognitive variable strengths factors in their instruction and to examine the impact of the change in instructional practices and revisions of their course syllabi. Also, faculty will create a two-semester research agenda to explore the impact of their new teaching practices on student learning outcomes.

Secondary School Programs

Some secondary school institutions and program have adopted noncognitive variables to facilitate the transition of students to higher education.

Secondary School Admission Test Board

The Secondary School Admission Test (SSAT) and the Secondary School Admission Test Board (SSATB) began in 1957 as part of the Educational Testing Service (ETS). The first SSAT was administered to just over 5,000 students in 1957. The current SSAT is administered in over 1,085 test locations in more than 100 countries around the world. SSATB uses the admission test to connect to and support the overall independent school admission process. SSATB was built on three principles: to provide a forum for exchange and support among admission professionals, to create a test, and to assist parents and students in their independent school search. In 1993, SSATB became independent from ETS.

Offering a diversity of assessment techniques allows us to enhance our perspective into the breadth of strengths required for success in our schools. For while one important area of aptitude might be less well demonstrated in an applicant, other areas more than compensate. Sedlacek implores us to differentiate our institutions and our learning programs by differentiating our array of assessments—particularly and especially when we consider how we supplement traditional cognitive evaluation with non-cog tools. (Martin, 2013)

SSATB held a "Non-Cognitive Think Tank" on October 8, 2014, to explore noncognitive options for use in admissions and student development. The think tank recommended that "SSATB move forward in developing a non-cognitive assessment tool to be used by schools, in conjunction with the SSAT, which will offer insights into an applicant's character attributes" (SSATB, 2014).

Phillips Exeter Academy

Phillips Exeter Academy (PEA) is a coeducational residential school serving 1,000 students in grades 9 through 12 and postgraduate level. PEA, founded in 1781 by John Phillips, teaches students from "all walks of life" to

- think, discuss, question, and analyze;
- combine knowledge with goodness; and
- acquire the intellectual skills that ensure a love of learning and a lifelong commitment to helping others.

PEA offers over 400 courses in 18 subject areas with a student-to-teacher ratio of 5:1 (www.exeter.edu/about_us/171.aspx).

PEA offers an initiative, "Youth From Every Quarter," in which admitted students from families with annual incomes under $75,000 are provided full tuition assistance. "As you can imagine," admission director (and SSATB trustee) Michael Gary said, "this opened up the floodgates of applications and greatly diversified the applicant pool. The traditional admission assessment process was not in keeping with these changes, nor with the spirit of the new initiative" (Phillips Exeter Academy, SSATB, 2013, p. 19).

As Gary recollects, Exeter's Dean of Faculty heard a presentation by William Sedlacek at a conference about the work he was doing to select students of diverse backgrounds for the Gates Millennium Scholarships, and came back inspired. Before long, they'd engaged Sedlacek as a consultant. The entire faculty and administration read his landmark book, *Beyond the Big Test: Noncognitive Assessment in Higher Education*, and "Sed" spent several days on campus consulting to the team. (Phillips Exeter Academy, SSATB, 2013, p. 19)

According to Gary, "He changed the conversation for us, really opening it up to new dimensions. We were not, of course, doing away with standardized testing, but we came to a much deeper appreciation of another layer of applicant assessment. One of the key things he did for us was to provide us the compelling, authoritative research evidence which corroborated what we already intuitively knew mattered. This helped us immensely" (SSATB, 2013, p. 19).

> Two key changes were implemented. In one, the admission office re-tooled the interview forms and added in small print on the back of every form the "Sedlacek Eight"—the key non-cognitive attributes his research had determined most significant. Interviewers were trained to seek out evidence and examples of these, and to ensure they included this information in their interview write-ups. They also did something very interesting: knowing Sedlacek had advised the admission office of Oregon State in developing short essay questions for their application designed to elicit meaningful information about these same attributes, they asked, and were granted permission to borrow and employ these same questions on the revised application forms for some of their higher-grade level applicants. (SSATB, 2013, p. 19)

Inver Hills Community College

Inver Hills Community College (IHCC) is a community college located in Inver Grove Heights, Minnesota. Founded in 1970, the college is part of the Minnesota State Colleges and Universities System. Enrollment was 5,675 in fall 2013, with 65% part-time students and 31% students of color.

Inver Prep at IHCC is a program that takes a different approach to preparing high school students for higher education (www.inverhills.edu/highschool/InverPrep/noncognitiveassessment.aspx). Inver Prep helps high school students in the "academic middle" prepare for college or university entrance. To qualify, students must place in the 30th to 70th percentile in high school and have adequate reading and math test scores. Potential participants take the NCQ as part of their assessment.

Students who participate in the language arts path of the Inver Prep program are identified and tested during 9th grade and join the program in 10th grade. Students who participate in the math path of the Inver Prep program are identified and tested during 10th grade and join the program in 11th grade.

Students remain in their own high schools to participate in the program and visit IHCC about twice a year for special activities. The Inver Prep program establishes a mentoring system between the college instructor and the high school teacher. The high school teacher may have to put in some additional time initially to learn the new curriculum and to attend professional workshops during the summer, but the program is also designed so the college instructor is there to help and support the high school teacher.

The Inver Prep program is free for participating students, which means substantial savings when compared to a traditional IHCC student. With college preparatory courses completed and an idea of what college is like, Inver Prep students are ready to succeed in higher education. Inver Prep students complete one to three college preparatory courses depending on their path (language arts or math) and learn college success skills that will get them ready for the InCollege program and general college education.

Inver Prep students who successfully complete Inver Prep course work with a C grade or better will be able to apply to the InCollege program and start taking college credits that are part of the Minnesota Transfer Curriculum at IHCC and are guaranteed to be accepted at all of Minnesota's public colleges and universities and most of the state's private colleges and universities.

Inver Prep students benefit from taking college preparatory courses to handle the rigors of college work and get the opportunity to be part of the InCollege program to earn free college credits while they are in high school.

The collaboration between the high school teacher and the college instructor starts in the summer when the teachers participate in two workshops: one about the Inver Prep program itself, and a second one that is discipline specific to prepare the teachers for course instruction. The college instructor provides the teacher with (a) a curriculum that incorporates the accreditation mandates for the college and high school courses, (b) a course outline, (c) learning objectives, and (d) help arranging campus visits and presentations on college basics for the students.

The high school is responsible for providing all course materials beyond the curriculum, and the textbooks can be reused from year to year. The college instructor also visits class regularly and assists in course assessments to ensure the curriculum is the same as an IHCC course. The course assessments include student course evaluations, mandated accreditation exit surveys, and the ACCUPLACER Diagnostic, which is a detailed analysis of a student's strengths and weaknesses. The resulting data enhance his or her college preparedness and academic preference and include an assessment on the noncognitive variables.

YES Prep Public Schools

YES Prep Public Schools is a network of 13 high-performing public charter schools serving 8,000 students in grades 6 through 12 in the Houston, Texas, area and in 2015 expanded to include the students of Memphis, Tennessee.

Founded in 1998 and winner of the inaugural Broad Prize for Charter Management Organizations in 2012, YES Prep "exists to increase the number of students from low-income communities who graduate from a four-year college or university prepared to compete in the global marketplace and committed to improving 'disadvantaged' communities" (YES Prep Public Schools, 2014).

YES Prep graduated over 450 high school seniors, and more than 97% entered colleges and universities across the country (YES Prep Public Schools, 2014). This is an "incredible accomplishment" for their students, the majority of whom reside in some of Houston's highest poverty neighborhoods. More than 90% of the 1,700 alumni are first-generation college students. Over 72% of the alumni either are still persisting in a college or university or have graduated, and since 2001, 44% of the total alumni have earned their higher education degrees. YES Prep's six-year college graduation rate is 41%, which is five times the rate of the students' peers in Houston and more than quadruple the rate of their peers nationally.

Though YES Prep's students have continually outpaced national college graduation statistics for low-income students and students of color, its rates initially began to falter as the size of graduating classes grew. The six-year graduation rate for the class of 2005 was 50%, but for the class of 2006, that rate dropped to 45%, and it dropped to 34% for the class of 2007. The staff concluded that they could not assume college matriculation inevitably leads to college graduation or that a rigorous academic program is all their students needed for success in college. They felt that "nonacademic skills" were the most important determinant of student success (YES Prep Public Schools, 2014).

YES Prep began work with students on the eight noncognitive variables (see Exhibit 1) as one of the pillars in its student success programs. All of YES Prep high school students complete work each year to measure and document their progress toward college readiness with the College Assessment Portfolio Project. The ongoing work for the project focuses on noncognitive skills and allows students to self-identify their own areas of strengths and weaknesses to develop all eight skills, as needed, over the four years of high school. YES Prep developed a rubric and project design that allowed students to gather anecdotal evidence of their progress in developing noncognitive skills, receive regular coaching from their college counselor, and incorporate this work into all of their classes and with all of their teachers.

With the implementation of these new efforts in 2006, the graduating class in 2008 began college "significantly more prepared." The six-year graduation rate rose to 46%. Persistence rates rose for later classes as well. For example, 73% of students in the class of 2010 were still persisting at the end of their fourth year of college. Of YES Prep students in the classes of 2010 to 2012, 87% have persisted to their sophomore year, compared to a national freshman-to-sophomore persistence rate of approximately 72%, regardless of ethnicity or income level.

Douglas County Performance Learning Center

Alternative high schools have begun to employ the noncognitive variables in a variety of creative ways. The Douglas County Performance Learning Center (douglasperformancelearningcenter.ga.dcs.schoolinsites.com/?PageName =%27SchoolPublications%27) in Georgia developed a nontraditional high school program that serves students considered at risk of not graduating on time based on their four-year cohort. The staff at the center implemented the Faces of Change curriculum based on noncognitive variables during a weekly mandatory advisory session (Owens & Beaty, 2016). Faces of Change is a program developed for training parents, teachers, coaches, and mentors in the use of the noncognitive variable system discussed in this book. Their program involves the use of workbook materials and exercises that exemplify a practical use of the noncognitive variables. Student survey results in 2011–2012 showed that the program had helped them set goals for their future (84%); helped them identify their strengths and weaknesses (89%); taught them ways to better interact with their family, friends, teachers, and peers (86%); improved their attendance (98%); improved their grades (95%); and helped develop a better understanding of the importance of earning a high school diploma (83%).

Thomas Jefferson High School for Science and Technology

Established in 1985, Thomas Jefferson High School for Science and Technology (TJHSST) in Fairfax County, Virginia, is the result of a partnership of businesses and schools created to improve education in science, mathematics, and technology (www.tjhsst.edu).

Representatives from business and industry and staff of the Fairfax County Public Schools worked together in curriculum and facilities development for the school. As the Governor's School for Science and Technology in Northern Virginia, the school is also supported by the Virginia Department of Education. Unlike other magnet schools, TJHSST has a four-year, full-day program. TJHSST is interested in selecting a diverse student population that demonstrates "excellence and passion for math, science, and technology."

Noncognitive variables are used as part of the admissions process. The other components include an essay, GPA, test scores, and teacher recommendations. The TJHSST Admissions Office operates independently of the high school under a policy of the Fairfax County school board. Most students enter the school in the 9th grade, with a limited number beginning in the 10th and 11th grades.

Big Picture Learning

The student population of Big Picture Learning (BPL) schools is low income, urban, and non-White, and many students' first language is not English (Arnold et al., 2008; Washor, Arnold, & Mojkowski, 2008). BPL schools employ a number of methods to assess the noncognitive variables, including the basic NCQ (Sedlacek, 2004b; see also williamsedlacek.info/publications .html), behavioral checklists, adviser rating forms, and interview techniques. BPL schools encourage using different approaches and creating new forms that fit the particular needs of schools or programs and that increase the probability that noncognitive variables can be used to benefit students in a variety of contexts. Noncognitive variables are seen as a primary evaluation tool to demonstrate competencies essential to students' success. Appendix G contains a list of resources used in BPL programs. Appendix H contains interview questions used by BPL in evaluating students on noncognitive variables. Appendices I and J show the rubrics used to develop noncognitive competencies in teachers, educators, and students in BPL schools. (Appendices G through J are available at sty.presswarehouse.com/sites/stylus/resrcs/chapters/1620362562_excerpt.pdf)

BPL does not own schools or manage school charters but employs the noncognitive variables in helping set school goals, designing teacher training, and securing funding from public and private sources. It has a primary goal of helping students make the transition to higher education, careers, or community-engagement activities (Washor et al., 2008). Schools affiliated with BPL adopt the philosophy of educating "one student at a time within a community of learners" (Washor et al., 2008).

Schools are built on three basic principles: (a) Learning must be based on the interests and goals of each student, (b) curriculum must be relevant to people and places in the real world, and (c) students' abilities must be measured by the quality of their work. Students tend to come from low-income, urban, and minority backgrounds. Many students' first language is not English, and few of their parents have attended college. In short, BPL school students are members of demographic groups that frequently struggle to complete high school or attain postsecondary degrees. In BPL schools that serve grades 9 through 12, the high school graduation rate is 92%, with 95% of graduates gaining acceptance to college (see www.bigpicture.org for more information on the schools and follow-up data).

More than 100 BPL schools are operating in 18 U.S. states, Australia, Belize, Canada, Israel, New Zealand, and the Netherlands. The creation and transformation of many of these schools was supported in part by the Bill & Melinda Gates Foundation, the Lumina Foundation, the Ford Motor Foundation, the Irvine Foundation, the CVS Health Foundation, and the Nellie Mae Education Foundation, among others.

Faculty at BPL schools define *student success* using measures beyond standardized test scores, grades, or college graduation rates. Success is viewed in terms of whether graduates show evidence of persistence in college, progress in their careers, successful relationships, civic involvement, and happiness. BPL schools track students' trajectories for about 12 years after they graduate (Washor et al., 2008).

BPL schools work to expand the options that disconnected and out-of-school youth have for obtaining both a high school diploma and certificates that demonstrate their skills and understanding with respect to a set of essential competencies. Providing students with opportunities for obtaining high-paid work as they continue with their learning is a program goal. These new forms of certificates require new forms of authentic performance assessments that certify that learners are competent to do the work required and ready to continue learning to do new work requirements (Big Picture Learning, 2012).

The NCQ is administered to alumni enrolled in higher education, and data are related to student retention, college readiness, experiences at college, use of campus resources, and graduation rates, in addition to test scores. BPL schools feel that noncognitive dimensions are more likely to show the learning of students in less traditional programs than are tests and grades. "By using Sedlacek's system we were able to demonstrate student development in many areas that better fit the mission of BPL schools. These noncognitive attributes relate to academic, career and life variables" (Washor et al., 2008). The surveys indicate how graduates are transitioning from high school to work or college, particularly in the calendar year following graduation. Thereafter, alumni enter yearly updates on a spectrum of educational, vocational, and personal measures.

These longitudinal data complement BPL's transition program, which helps students get ready for college and supports them as they proceed through the difficult freshman and sophomore years or assists students who enter the workforce directly after high school. Transition counselors work with students beginning in ninth grade, advising them on the college admissions process and helping them plan a solid college-going strategy or a beginning career move. Counselors keep in touch with their assigned students throughout the summer to make sure they are on track with pursuing the plan they developed and to intervene if necessary. They also follow these alumni once they are in college or on the job and coordinate sending surveys to them through the database (Big Picture Learning, 2012). Once a year, all transition counselors and BPL principals meet to share and discuss alumni responses (Big Picture Learning, 2008).

Findings from the first two years of collecting longitudinal data on students provide evidence that key elements of the BPL model are working well

(Arnold, Soto, Methven, & Brown, 2014). Graduates identified their support system through relationships with their advisers at BPL schools as critical to their success. Community-based experiential internships also helped them develop motivation, resourcefulness, independence, and communication skills.

Research results showed that the long-term goals of many students changed in the summer after graduation. College plans were complicated by financial aid concerns. At least one third of BPL students seriously reconsidered their college plans or changed their intended college during the summer after graduation. At least one in five decided not to begin higher education at all. Although nearly 100% of BPL school seniors were accepted into college, and nearly 90% stated in spring that they intended to start school the next fall, only 70% were actually enrolled in a college or university in September.

College acceptance may not be enough to guarantee college access, particularly for students who may be the first in their family to pursue higher education. NCQ scores on long-term goals, self-concept, handling racism, and community, along with other information, were used by counselors to advise students. One school, for example, employed counselors beyond their usual 10-month contract to do summer follow-up.

Lathram (2015), who is a former teacher and internship coordinator at a BPL school, reported on her experience with noncognitive variables:

> I was hoping students would go on to college, and also was wondering if some would make it to their senior year. . . . When I heard Sedlacek speak, it was as if he was also speaking to my students. . . . I felt more hopeful about my students' successes and their college readiness. The school was non-traditional and my students were doing some great work. Fortunately I had two students with me and (they) became my ambassadors for talking with the rest of the class about the NCCs (noncognitive variables).

In April 2014, BPL held a retreat for coaches and did a survey of their responses on noncognitive variables. Six coaches responded; 100% felt noncognitive variables were important, 50% felt they were very important, 28% shared them with others, and 27% built them into their work.

Los Angeles BPL High School

Los Angeles BPL High School (LABP) was a charter school, founded in 2006, in the Los Angeles Unified School District that ceased to operate in 2016 because of lack of funding. It is discussed here as an example of what can be done with noncognitive variables in inner-city schools. The school served 87 students, mostly Latinos from lower income families, and posted the following mission statement: "The mission of Los Angeles BPL High School is to prepare students for adulthood and beyond, including college/university study and a successful entry into the workforce" (bigpicturela.org). They felt that this was best accomplished through a combination of scholarship, direct experience, and personalized relationships. They sought to "create leaders as opposed to followers; active participants as opposed to spectators; individuals with a transforming vision that transcends doubts from within and limitations from without. They strive to bring positive attention and increased opportunity to our community and its inhabitants" (bigpicturela.org).

An article in the *Los Angeles Times* discussed the uniqueness of having downtown Los Angeles as the LABP classroom (Ceasar, 2014). Jessica Davis, an adviser at LABP, recalled a quick subway ride to Chinatown with some students. "They asked, 'What city are we in?' They'd never heard of Chinatown," she said. "Now, they're constantly talking about how worldly and special they feel" (Ceasar, 2014).

"We can go down to the Metro, go two stops, pop up and go visit City Hall and show them what it looks like instead of only learning about it from a book" (Nicole Nicodemus, LABP principal, cited in Ceasar, 2014).

Vision Statement

LABP created active citizens who served as "change agents," constantly looking to challenge and improve on the accepted status quo. LABP graduates were intended to be confident, disciplined, proactive leaders who will excel in college and beyond. Their focus was on community, and their own function was focused on enhancing opportunities for themselves and their peers.

Implemented in the fall of the 2014–2015 school year, the curriculum had students working in small teams to analyze themselves on a noncognitive competencies (NCC) rubric based on the noncognitive variables shown in Exhibit 1. The goal was to answer survey questions about NCCs and to set goals around NCC acquisition and skill-building, both as individuals and as a group. Students worked on inquiry skills, assessment tools, and research and analysis. Over the course of a few months, groups tracked their NCC-based goal. Following this unit, the school saw an increase in students' math and science grades, as well as a deeper understanding of the NCCs.

Building off the success of the first program, LABP conducted another round of a similar curricular focus. In 2015, students continued to work in teams, conducting various project works around NCCs. One of the goals for the year was for students to develop hypotheses about what NCCs they will see in college students who have demonstrated persistence. Students then created a research approach, came up with interview questions, and interviewed actual college students about their NCCs. Students then completed lab reports on their hypotheses and findings. They compared and synthesized their findings with academic articles about NCCs that they had read (bigppicturela.org).

In May 2015, LABP made a strong case to have its charter renewed by the Los Angeles Unified School District Board (laschoolreport.com/big-picture-makes-big-pitch-to-stay-open-lausd-board-listens). Despite considerable evidence of success, the LABP charter was not renewed in 2015 (boe.lausd.net/sites/default/files/Petition-LABIGPIC-BR%20434-04-14-15.pdf).

LaFayette BPL

Founded in 2008, through the LaFayette Central School District in New York State, LaFayette BPL (LBP) began as a small program of "15 excited over-aged, under-credited and at-risk high school freshmen" (lafayettebigpic.weebly.com/about-us.html). The school has grown to 60 students, nearly half of whom come from the Onondaga Nation. The first class of students from LBP graduated in the 2011–2012 school year; 87% of those who enrolled as freshmen graduated on time. Of this first cohort, 70% went on to attend a college or university.

The LBP "allows students to pursue their passions and provides an environment that supports independent thinking. We will graduate curious learners who have developed a plan for personal growth based on real world experiences" (lafayettebigpic.weebly.com/about-us.html).

LBP is driven by its vision to be a college preparatory school for all students:

> We strive to be viewed and utilized as a resource in our community. We continue to develop positive interactions with surrounding communities as we break educational norms. We are in constant pursuit of improvement and our progress is student driven. Students will always be at the center of learning and we commit to honoring ONE STUDENT AT A TIME. (lafayettebigpic.weebly.com/about-us.html)

Susan Osborn, the LBP principal, attended the BPL principals' retreat in Seattle, Washington, in December 2008. She heard the presentation on noncognitive variables (Faubert & Sedlacek, 2008), brought the information back to LBP, and worked with her colleagues to build a system to help students reflect on their NCCs.

Through a partnership with the Red Group at Syracuse University, the school built a survey of approximately 50 questions, based on the NCCs, which students were asked to take at least once a year at the school. The school keeps a record of student responses.

Along with the survey, there are other ways that the LBP team members have integrated NCCs into their work with students. During the students' 10th-grade exhibitions of learning, called Gateway, students need to identify their support networks, and do that again in their senior year, as part of their autobiography. "Handling systems and navigating racism are constantly a conversation in this building. There are so many factors (to this work)—maturity, awareness. Positive self-concept—it's hard for me to pull them out of what we do. They are central to how we approach students on a daily basis" (S. Osborn, personal communication, February 25, 2015).

Chegg

Chegg (formerly Zinch.com) is an online service that matches students to colleges and universities and scholarship opportunities. As part of its system of matching applicants to schools, the service employs the eight noncognitive variables presented in chapter 3.

"Chegg puts students first. As the leading student-first connected learning platform, the company makes higher education more affordable, more accessible, and more successful for students" (www.chegg.com). Chegg is a publicly held company based in Santa Clara, California, and trades on the NYSE under the symbol CHGG. Chegg announced the results of a poll (January 21, 2015) of high school and college students that asked for opinions and attitudes toward the Department of Education's proposed Federal College Ratings system. A majority of students saw value in a new rating scheme, with 51% of high school students indicating they would use it as a resource. However, the proposal does not include a student satisfaction metric that would give prospective students insight from current students and alumni. When asked what criteria students use or would use in making their enrollment decision, nearly 80% of high school and 70% of college students ranked this metric as being relevant, with nearly 60% of all students ranking the criteria as "very important" to their decision.

Eagle Rock School and Development Center

The school opened in 1993 and is located in Estes Park, Colorado, with an enrollment of 72 students (eaglerockschool.org/about-us/mission-and-philosophy). The school implements practices that foster each student's unique potential using noncognitive variables. Eagle Rock School serves adolescents who are not thriving in their current situations, for whom few positive options exist, and who are interested in taking control of their lives and learning.

Students are admitted between the ages of 15 and 17 years old, are equally represented in terms of male and female, and comprise a purposefully diverse community. Students are from all over the United States and expect to graduate high school.

Fight Your Math Phobia Course

The noncognitive variables discussed throughout this book (see Exhibit 1) are employed in the Fight Your Math Phobia course. According to the instructor, "I felt that the noncognitive variables perfectly addressed what I valued so I decided to implement them in my courses" (K. Ikagami, personal communication, July 30, 2014). "Each week when I meet with students, it is more helping with their noncognitive skills, and less about filling in their math skill gaps. Since using noncognitive variables, I notice a better match with students that I think should earn credit, and the students who do earn credit."

Foundations

Foundations are an important part of funding and support for noncognitive variable programs.

Washington State Achievers

The WSA scholarship program provides funding for students from Washington to attend most colleges or universities in the state to obtain a four-year degree. The noncognitive variables shown in Exhibit 1 are used to select scholarship recipients. The program is funded by the Bill & Melinda Gates Foundation and managed by the College Success Foundation. The scholarship is available to students attending one of 16 WSA high schools in the state of Washington with family incomes less than 35% of the median family income in the state. Most of the WSA recipients are White. The WSA program began selecting scholars in April 2001 and gave 500 awards per year for 13 years (Sedlacek & Sheu, 2005).

WSA recipients reported that receiving the award was a major reason for their attending a college or university. Leadership and community service were positively correlated with time spent on extracurricular activities. Realistic self-appraisal was correlated with higher educational aspirations, and WSA recipients were more likely than nonrecipients to hold leadership positions in their college or university (Sedlacek & Sheu, 2005).

Bill & Melinda Gates Foundation

As funding from federal sources decreases, it is critical that we examine the role of private scholarship programs in attempting to achieve social justice in U.S. colleges and universities (Trent & St. John, 2008). Funded by the Bill & Melinda Gates Foundation, the Gates Millennium Scholars Program was established in 2000 to provide outstanding African American, American Indian/Alaska Native, Asian/Pacific Islander American, and Hispanic American students with an opportunity to complete an undergraduate college education in all disciplines and a graduate education for those students pursuing studies in mathematics, science, engineering, education, library science, and public health. American Indian/Alaska Native applicants must show a certificate of tribal enrollment or proof of descendency to be considered. Additional eligibility requirements include having a secondary school GPA of 3.3 on a 4.0-point scale, having significant financial need (i.e., meeting the Federal Pell Grant eligibility criteria), and demonstrating leadership abilities through participation in community service or extracurricular or other activities. Awards are based on student need and cover the costs of tuition, fees, books, and living expenses at the institution of higher education the student attends. Applicants must submit an application, a nominator form, and a recommender form.

The program chose the scholars for their academic potential using the noncognitive variables shown in Exhibit 1, along with assessments of the academic rigor of their high school curriculum, their high school academic achievement, and their ability to write a good essay explaining their interests in becoming a scholar. A major goal of the Gates Millennium Scholars Program is to develop future leaders of color. The program promotes leadership through its annual Leadership Conferences for Scholars after they begin higher education.

A review of an entire application is scored on the noncognitive variables and makes up about 80% of the weight used in selection. The application includes short-answer questions based on each of the noncognitive variables shown in Exhibit 1; a personal statement by the applicant; letters of recommendation by the nominator and another person; and demographic, background, and activity questions. Raters are trained to identify and consider all this information in scoring each of the eight noncognitive variables. The raters are educators of color, familiar with multicultural issues in education and working with the kinds of students applying. Interjudge reliability was estimated at .83 for a sample of raters in the first year (Sedlacek & Sheu, 2004a, 2008). More than 15,000 Gates scholars have attended more than 1,500 different colleges and universities, with a 97%

first-year retention rate, an 87% 5-year retention rate, and a 78% 5-year graduation rate. More than 60% are majoring in STEM fields. In a study comparing scholars and nonscholars, Sedlacek and Sheu (2004a, 2008) found the following:

- The measure of noncognitive variables employed in selecting scholars showed very high internal consistency reliability (.92).
- Scholars were more involved than nonscholars in academic activities, such as working with students outside of class, discussing ideas with students and faculty outside of class, and working on creative projects.
- Scholars were more likely than nonscholars to perceive their school as helpful in navigating the system.
- American Indian/Alaskan Native scholars tended to perceive climates as less discriminatory than nonscholars. However, Hispanic American scholars tended to perceive climates as more discriminatory than nonscholars.
- Nearly all scholars (95%) indicated that they were very unlikely to drop out of school and were strongly committed to earn a degree at their current institution.
- The great majority (about 90%) of scholars expected to complete an advanced degree (master's degree or higher). African American scholars had higher educational aspirations than African American nonscholars. Among women, African Americans had higher educational aspirations than American Indians and Asian/Pacific Islander Americans.
- Among scholars, APIAs and Hispanic Americans experienced more difficulties with school work than did African Americans.
- Among APIAs, scholars spent more time (27.58 hours) than nonscholars (23.22 hours) studying per week.
- American Indian/Alaskan Native scholars were significantly less engaged in academic activities than African Americans or Hispanic Americans.
- Among scholars, APIAs tended to spend more time studying per week (27.58 hours) than American Indian/Alaskan Natives (17.89 hours).
- Scholars and nonscholars who had more realistic self-appraisal and strong support persons tended to spend more time studying.
- Graduate student scholars tended to seek out help for academic problems from faculty and were less likely to seek assistance from clergy.
- Leadership and working the system scores correlated with a positive academic experience for graduate student scholars.

- For graduate student scholars, realistic self-appraisal was a significant predictor of GPA.

The Bill & Melinda Gates Foundation initiated an additional program focusing on college readiness. This program's major goal is ensuring that 80% of students graduating from high school are prepared for college, with a focus on low-income and minority students reaching this target. The foundation recognizes that preparing for higher education involves more than course work. Having elementary and secondary teachers work with students on behaviors beyond the typical classroom activities is critical to the success of this initiative (Bill & Melinda Gates Foundation, 2015).

The noncognitive variables shown in Exhibit 1 provide a method for achieving those program goals in college readiness (Sedlacek, 2011). Appendices A1 and A2 and Sedlacek (2004b) provide information on the behaviors that students might demonstrate that would positively or negatively affect each noncognitive variable. Teachers can work with students to encourage the positive behaviors and reduce the negative ones. Administrators and student affairs professionals also can evaluate students' school environments to determine how the school supports or hinders student development on each of the variables.

Jack Kent Cooke Foundation

The Jack Kent Cooke Foundation (JKCF) is a private, independent foundation dedicated to advancing the education of exceptionally promising students who have financial need. The foundation supports students from elementary school to graduate school through scholarships, grants, direct service, and knowledge creation and dissemination. The foundation also offers grants and supports research to further advance high-performing students with financial need. Founded in 2000 by the estate of Jack Kent Cooke, the foundation has awarded $125 million in scholarships and $79 million in grants to organizations that support its mission (www.jkcf.org/scholarship-programs).

JKCF was selected as the first-ever recipient of the College Advising Corps Investor Impact Award. This award is intended to recognize donors whose significant and sustained support has enabled the College Advising Corps (CAC) to provide college counseling to thousands of high-need students throughout the United States. Since it began, the JKCF has awarded more than $13 million to CAC and its university-based programs (www.jkcf.org/scholarship-programs).

JKCF staff were trained in using the noncognitive variable system in evaluating applications for each of the scholarship programs. Specific evaluation models that included the eight noncognitive variables shown in Exhibit 1 were developed for each scholarship program. These include the following:

- The Young Scholars Program provides students with comprehensive educational advising and financial support from the eighth grade through high school. Up to 65 students are selected for this program each year.
- The College Scholarship Program is an undergraduate scholarship program available to high-achieving high school seniors with financial need who seek to attend four-year colleges and universities. Scholars receive up to $40,000 per year, college planning support, ongoing advising, and the opportunity to network with the larger JKCF scholar community. Up to 40 scholars are selected for this program each year.
- The Undergraduate Transfer Scholarship is for community college students seeking to complete their bachelor's degrees at four-year colleges or universities. The foundation provides up to $40,000 per year for up to three years, making it the largest private scholarship for community college transfer students in the country. Up to 85 scholars are selected each year.
- JKCF awarded funds through the Graduate Arts Award and the Dissertation Fellowships through 2014.

Colleges and Universities

Institutions of higher education have been sources of direct assistance to students in selection and program development.

Southern Illinois University

Southern Illinois University (SIU) uses the noncognitive variables discussed in chapter 3 in a class for first-year students. Students are administered the NCQ at entrance, and the results are used in advising and counseling in referring students to academic and student services offered at SIU. The Center for Learning Support and Testing Services provides a printout based on noncognitive variable scores and other information for each student, which is made available to faculty and staff. The printout suggests resources associated with a scoring rubric developed by SIU. The printout was considered a useful tool in helping students adjust to SIU in a proactive manner (L. Blair, personal communication, January 30, 2015).

University of Texas Rio Grande Valley

The University of Texas Rio Grande Valley (UTRGV) is a new university, begun in 2015, that was formed from the consolidation of the University of Texas at Brownsville and the University of Texas–Pan American. The university will include a new medical school.

UTRGV is employing the eight noncognitive variables presented in chapter 3 as an addition to the Apply Texas Common Application used in the state. Faculty and staff will be trained to assess the noncognitive variables where they appear in the Apply Texas application or the additional questions added to the UTRGV application.

Washington State University Vancouver

Washington State University Vancouver (WSU Vancouver) began 25 years ago as a branch campus of the university and was authorized by the legislature to expand to lower division students beginning fall 2006. As of the 2014–2015 school year, WSU Vancouver enrolled 3,264 students; 54% were women, and 21% were students of color. In preparation for admitting freshman, WSU Vancouver evaluated the current admission requirements. Although WSU Vancouver could not modify the actual admission requirements (e.g., GPA, test scores), there was an opportunity to alter the essay question.

"At the time, we were aware of Oregon State University's work with Dr. Sedlacek and were intrigued by the noncognitive variables—it was a good fit with WSU Vancouver's mission of access and serving a diverse student population" (N.T. Youlden, personal communication, April 17, 2015). After a site visit to Oregon State University in 2005 followed by on-campus training by Sedlacek, WSU Vancouver adopted the noncognitive variable questions in what was called the "personal statement."

These questions became part of the admission process for all new undergraduates who entered fall 2006 and were included as part of the online application. WSU Vancouver developed an interface so readers could read the personal statement responses remotely. Although students could complete a paper admission application with their personal statement questions, the majority of students completed their admission application, including their personal statement, electronically. In fall 2007, the main WSU campus in Pullman implemented the same noncognitive questions for its undergraduate students.

At WSU Vancouver, the personal statement questions were used primarily to help rather than hinder an admissions decision, particularly for borderline applicants: those with negative grade trends or a weak college prep curriculum or those in an alternative admission category (e.g., home-school).

At WSU Vancouver, the personal statement questions also were used for the annual scholarship process. Students completed the personal statement online, and the scholarship committee (e.g., faculty, staff, administrators) reviewed and scored scholarship applications electronically as well. "The information provided by the personal statements has been extremely help-ful with scholarship decisions for our student population" (N. T. Youlden, personal communication, April 17, 2015).

The rubric used was designed for assessing the noncognitive variables for both admissions and scholarship scoring (see Appendices A1 and A2). In addition, training was required for any faculty or staff who helped read personal statement responses.

> There are a number of benefits of the personal statement information for both the admission and scholarship process at WSU Vancouver and a few key examples are outlined below:
>
> - Better understanding of what applicants faced in their personal lives to help explain grade trends. For example, in some cases applicants clearly articulated challenges they faced in their personal lives and the steps they were taking to cope and get themselves back on track.
> - Leadership potential of our applicants and how they could poten-tially contribute to the campus community.
> - More information about applicants to help further our mission of access (applicants would sometimes disclose additional information about being first generation, underrepresented, undocumented, etc.).
> - More information about academic/career goals and steps taken to prepare for college.
>
> The personal statement questions were also very telling by what stu-dents *didn't* share; for example, the applicant with negative grade trends who chooses to make no mention of this in the personal statement. (N.T. Youlden, personal communication, April 17, 2015)

After several years, it was found the majority of new students at WSU Vancouver were admissible without the personal statement, and for some it was actually an obstacle. Consequently, the personal statement questions were made optional for admission applicants but continued to be used as necessary with borderline applicants. WSU Pullman also discontinued man-datory use of the personal statement questions several years ago. "However, the personal statement questions continue to be a valuable piece of our scholarship selection process at WSU Vancouver" (N.T. Youlden, personal communication, April 17, 2015).

Oregon State University

Founded in 1868, Oregon State University (OSU) is the state's land-grant university, with an enrollment of more than 30,000 students; about 20% are U.S. minorities. OSU has developed a student evaluation system based on the noncognitive variables shown in Exhibit 1 (see oregonstate.edu/admissions/firstYear/requirements.html; Sandlin, 2008). The OSU admissions application contained six short-answer questions that cover the eight noncognitive variables. Responses are limited to 100 words and were scored independently from other application materials. Raters from many parts of the campus were trained to score the six questions. Interrater agreement was estimated at .85. OSU used its Insight Résumé system in selection, academic advising, student services, on- and off-campus referrals, financial aid, and teaching.

Insight Résumé score profiles were provided to faculty, student affairs staff, and administrators for their use in teaching, advising, and counseling students. The university's students were made aware that the scores are employed widely on the campus for their benefit. In addition, Insight Résumé scores were employed successfully in an "early warning" program to identify students who might be in danger of academic probation. OSU noncognitive scores correlated with retention, and since OSU began employing noncognitive variables, its retention rate increased, and there was more diversity in the applicant pool and first-year class. Campus offices were working better together, applicant GPA was up, and referrals were better based on the noncognitive information.

A particularly creative technique was developed for use at OSU. OSU staff developed profile sheets for each noncognitive variable depicting a student who was high on each dimension. The caption on each profile was "A Great Student Is More Than a Number," and a discussion of the noncognitive variables and the Insight Résumé was included. The university's marketing office received a national award from its professional organization for the program.

Texas A&M University

Texas A&M University (TAMU) is a coeducational public research university located in College Station, Texas. It is the flagship institution of the TAMU system, the fourth-largest university in the United States, and the largest university in Texas. The school enrolled 62,185 total students in 2014, including 47,567 undergraduates.

TAMU implemented the use of the noncognitive variables discussed in chapter 3. It developed its own questionnaire and called it the "Aggie Vision Questionnaire." The university found it "very helpful" in managing about 400 applicants that TAMU had for the cycle in which it was used initially. From there, the university collected the responses online, scored them, and then made decisions based on the final results. "I found it to be very useful, and it really gave us some insight into the students and their level of maturation. Overall, I was very pleased with the results and it did well to dramatically reduce our long-term expenses" (R. Jenson, personal communication, February 10, 2015).

> We utilized the non-cognitive variable review for two years. This helped us to phase out of utilizing interviews to select applicants. After the two years our number of scholarships available for the Century Scholars program grew by such a large amount that to continue to review the non-cognitive variables was not feasible with the amount of staff we had. We adjusted our holistic review model to make awards based off of data review. We appreciate all you shared with us. When our program was smaller and we had to cut the expenses that went into interview, this helped us out immensely. (L. Uptain, personal communication, February 16, 2015)

University of North Carolina Conference

The University of North Carolina General Administration held a conference on January 21 and 22, 2015, titled "Redefining Student Success: The Role of Non-Cognitive Skill Development Strategies" hosted by the University of North Carolina at Chapel Hill. More than 100 representatives of the 16 institutions that are part of the university system attended. This conference was part of exploratory work associated with the State Systems Transformation Grant funded by the Bill & Melinda Gates Foundation. The purpose of this grant was to explore the ways in which state systems of higher education have the ability to influence transformative change in student success and degree completion. The University of North Carolina chose to focus on the role and development of noncognitive or "dispositional skills" with respect to these goals. "Although research in this area is strong, higher education scholars and professionals are in many ways still in the early stages of dialogue about the role, effect, and development of dispositional skills in educational programs" (K.E. Stewart, personal communication, October 8, 2014). The goal of this conference was to bring together "thought leaders" to inspire conversations and thinking among professionals from across the university and its campuses.

As part of the conference, each institution attending formed a team that was to select several noncognitive variables in the system shown in Exhibit

1, which could be implemented on their campus. Attendees heard several presentations on noncognitive variables and were given a copy of *Beyond the Big Test: Noncognitive Assessment in Higher Education* (Sedlacek, 2004b).

North Carolina State University

The North Carolina General Assembly founded the North Carolina College of Agriculture and Mechanic Arts, now North Carolina State University (NCSU), on March 7, 1887, as a land-grant college. Today, NCSU has an enrollment of more than 34,000 students; 56% are men, and 16% are minority.

On the basis of several studies, researchers found the NCQ to be predictive of success for undergraduate students at NCSU (W. Hill, 1995; Hoey, 1997; Ting, 1997, 2009; Ting & Gales, 2014; Ting & Robinson, 1998; Ting & Sedlacek, 2000; Ting, Sedlacek, Bryant, & Ward, 2004). The studies showed predictive and construct validity for NCQ scores of White applicants and applicants of color. For White applicants, self-concept and long-term goals were the best predictors of college GPA, while self-concept and negotiating multicultural experiences were the best predictors of retention. For applicants of color, self-concept, strong support person, and handling racism were the best predictors of college grades and retention.

Hoey (1997) found that a combination of first-year fall GPA and NCQ scores could correctly predict 92% of the retention of African American students from first to second year at NCSU. For other students of color (Asian American, Latino, Native American, and other), a combination of fall first-year credit hours enrolled and NCQ scores also correctly predicted 92% of the retention from first to second year at that institution. Multiple regression and multiple discriminant analyses were employed in these analyses.

Construct validity evidence through a factor analysis showed that seven of the eight noncognitive variables described students at NCSU. The community dimension took the form of extracurricular activities, but all of the other NCQ dimensions emerged in the factor analysis.

The Park Scholarship Program at NCSU has also made use of noncognitive variables:

> While we have not conducted any assessments that focus directly on noncognitive variables, this is an ongoing topic of conversation among our staff and the faculty who guide and mentor our Park Scholars. We take noncognitive variables into account throughout our scholar selection processes, as well as in shaping and re-tooling the leadership and development programming in which the Park Scholars participate over the course of their four years with us. (V. Schwartz, personal communication, January 6, 2015)

University of Puget Sound

The University of Puget Sound (UPS) is an independent, liberal arts institution located in Tacoma, Washington. The undergraduate enrollment of roughly 2,600 students is primarily residential. Though established in 1888 by what is now the United Methodist Church, UPS today is governed by an independent board of trustees.

Many UPS students take on multiple minors, major in interdisciplinary fields, and travel abroad. The 2,600 students are 57% women and 43% men from 44 states and 16 countries. UPS students come from most of the 50 states, and approximately 75% of the student body is from outside Washington State. The university's "ethnic minority" student enrollment is about 27%. Students who identify as Asian American or Pacific Islander compose the largest ethnic minority group on campus, with a strong Hawaiian community. About 85% of UPS students are receiving some form of financial aid (www.pugetsound.edu/about).

UPS participates in the Common Application (www.commonapp.org/Login), which is a nonprofit membership organization that promotes equity, access, and integrity in the higher education admissions process. Applications can be submitted to over 500 member institutions by students and school officials. Common Application membership is open to institutions that promote access by using a holistic selection process in evaluating students (Rickard, 2015).

Those applying to UPS for the 2016–2017 school year can choose to respond in writing two short essay questions in lieu of submitting standardized test scores. Those questions will be scored based on the noncognitive variable system presented in this book (see Appendix K in the online resources).

Student applicants for fall 2016 who choose to take this alternative route will provide 100-word essays in response to two questions: one about a personal goal, and another about a community with which they identify. The essays will be assessed by UPS employees trained in noncognitive assessment. The assessors will have no information about the individual candidates.

These essays, in conjunction with the Common Application and essay, teacher and counselor recommendations, and high school transcripts, will provide more information to fully evaluate the potential of a student's success at UPS.

The following are statements from Jenny Rickard, vice president for enrollment at UPS:

- "We believe that this new policy will help level the playing field for students, not only in decisions on admission, but in allocating merit scholarships."

- "We are working locally, nationally, and internationally to expand the diversity of our campus to create a rich learning environment for talented young people from all backgrounds."
- "Educators have long known that personal characteristics such as leadership ability, determination, and resourcefulness are essential qualities for college success, as well as academic preparation and performance in high school" (www.pugetsound.edu/about).

The following are selected quotes from new admission materials provided to prospective students interested in attending UPS:

- "We aspire to increase the diversity of all parts of our University community through commitment to diversity in our recruitment and retention efforts."
- "Our students are proudly unclassifiable and universally kind."
- "We're ambitious and modest. We're collaborative and independent-minded. We're rooted in the pioneering Pacific Northwest and in love with the world."
- "We live in the real world, and we try to make it better."
- "Be interesting in a way that isn't necessarily flashy or obvious; just be the kind of person you'd like to know. Also, be smart—in ways that aren't necessarily flashy or quantifiable."
- "The general ethic is: Be brave. Be kind. Work together."
- "Conventional wisdom tells you that college is all about the mountaintop, all about the frenzied pursuit of some high golden peak. We're not interested in conventional wisdom. We're interested in every kind of landscape, every kind of life, every destiny. We make our own wisdom."
- "Puget Sound is a place of continual movement and action. These traits guide the voice and imagery used to portray the Puget Sound experience."
- "*Pioneering.* Sense of adventure, groundbreaking, willing to take risks.
  Confident. Voice of a leader, honoring true self while respecting others.
  Independent. Driven by an internal compass with a strong point of view.
  Creative. Interdisciplinary, original thinking, collaborative, curious.
  Open. Welcoming, inviting, supportive, genuine concern for others, friendly, eager to share" (www.pugetsound.edu/about).

Montgomery College

Montgomery College is a public, open access community college located in Montgomery County, Maryland, just outside Washington, DC. The college has three campuses, the largest of which is in Rockville, Maryland. Approximately 38,000 students are enrolled in the three campuses, including the distance education program. Enrollments by race are African American 32%, White 29%, Asian 14%, Hispanic 11%, and multirace or other 14% Sixty-five percent are part-time. Those who graduate or transfer by group are Asian 54%, White 53%, African American 37%, and Hispanic 36% (Montgomery College, 2013).

> The Montgomery College mission clearly states, "We empower our students to change their lives, and we enrich the life of our community. We are accountable for results." This mission statement holds true for not just a portion of the community, but applies to all of the county's residents. Still, the evidence indicates that the lives of our African-American and Latino students are enriched at a rate far lower than that of their peers. Clear evidence of an achievement gap exists when the placement, retention, success in gateway courses and graduation rates of these students compared with the rest of the student population are examined. (Montgomery College, 2013)

The college has begun an initiative to close the gap in achievement using the NCQ administered to students and basing counseling, teaching, and mentoring programs on those scores. "Identifying the cognitive and noncognitive barriers to success will give these students greater opportunity to take advantage of the benefits of higher education, and improve the academic performance of the underserved" (Montgomery College, 2013).

Central New Mexico Community College

Central New Mexico Community College (CNMCC) is located in Albuquerque, New Mexico, and has an enrollment of about 35,000 students

Six CNMCC programs have chosen to use noncognitive essays for admission criteria (biotechnology, respiratory therapy, paramedic, alternative teacher licensure, radiologic technology, and medical laboratory technician). The variables thought to be most relevant to their programs were as follows:

- Realistic self-appraisal
- Long-term goal setting

- Involvement
- Leadership
- Handling the system and racism
- Support

About 30 campus faculty and staff have completed grader training on scoring noncognitive variables. Graders' feedback was generally positive; they felt the noncognitive variables resonated with their experience. "We had some difficult conversations around the 'handling the system/racism' variable—I think that was the most difficult to explain, and for them to grade" (K. Gross, personal communication, February 15, 2012).

Questions were developed from Sedlacek (2004b) and the experience of other schools and then tailored to the college's population. The education department at CNMCC helped develop a scoring rubric. A student focus group was conducted, followed by two pilot studies. These groups were small, so we don't have enough data to draw any conclusions yet. Student participants felt it was a positive addition to the application process (i.e., considering them as a person rather than considering just their GPA).

> I did not run any statistics, but in my estimation, inter-grader reliability was actually fairly good for the pilots. We plan to track students' retention and performance in the programs, which will take one to two years (depending on program length). If it goes well, other programs may decide to adopt this as admissions criteria as well. . . .
>
> In sum, we are excited to include this to balance the "academic preparation" piece that historically has been weighed most heavily. As a community college, we have had a lot of conversations about the open-access mission and how we can value the diversity of our students' experiences in the admission process for these programs. We're hoping this will help us meet that mission. (K. Gross, personal communication, February 15, 2012)

Professional Schools

Professional schools are often highly selective in their admissions policies and provide evidence of the use of noncognitive variables at all levels of the educational system.

University of Maryland School of Medicine

Established in 1807, the University of Maryland School of Medicine (UMSM) is the first public university and the fifth-oldest medical school in the United States and the first to institute a residency training program. UMSM includes Davidge Hall, which was built in 1812 and is the oldest building in the Northern Hemisphere in continuous use for medical education.

UMSM has employed interviews to assess applicants on the noncognitive variables shown in Exhibit 1. It has defended their use in a lawsuit challenging their fairness (*Farmer v. Ramsay*, 1998).

The plaintiff, Rob Farmer, a White man, alleged that he was denied admission to UMSM on the basis of race. Farmer applied for admission to UMSM twice and was rejected each time. Farmer admitted that his first application did not qualify him for admission. After this initial application and rejection, however, Farmer applied for and participated in UMSM's Advanced Premedical Development Program. The program was designed to increase the number of medical students from "minority and/or disadvantaged" backgrounds.

Program participants received a free Medical College Admission Test (MCAT) preparation course and special counseling on the medical school admissions process. Farmer retook the MCAT following his participation in the program and significantly improved his scores. Farmer's second application to UMSM, however, was also rejected.

The essence of Farmer's complaint was that his second application to UMSM would have qualified him for admission had he been considered as a minority applicant. Farmer alleged, "The average MCAT scores for Blacks who were accepted to UMSM was lower than the average MCAT scores for Whites who were rejected without even being interviewed." The complaint further alleged this disparity results from a UMSM "policy of preferring Blacks and members of other minority groups for admission" (*Farmer v. Ramsay*, 1998).

As we discussed in chapter 2, the court in *Farmer* ruled that it will permit UMSM to employ noncognitive variables in admitting students.

University of Sri Jayewardenepura, Sri Lanka

Medical students at the University of Sri Jayewardenepura, Sri Lanka, were administered a modified version of the NCQ (Ranasinghe, Ellawela, & Gunatilake, 2012). Students were stratified into two equal groups: Group A (high achievers) included students who had obtained an honors degree at their final examination, and Group B (low achievers) included students who have referred in one or more subjects at the same examination. Group A demonstrated significantly higher mean scores on positive self-concept and confidence, realistic self-appraisal, leadership, and preference for long-range goals. The authors concluded that noncognitive characteristics were important predictors of academic success, and a combined system incorporating both past academic performance and noncognitive characteristics might help improve the selection process and early recognition of those who may be struggling.

Fiji School of Medicine

The Fiji School of Medicine is a regional health professional educational institution with a mission to provide medical training and research facilities to the Pacific Islands region (Ezeala, Ezeala, & Swami, 2012). This geographic region is characterized by ethnic, religious, generational, cultural, and socioeconomic diversity. The authors felt that limiting selection criteria to purely quantitative academic performance data was effectively a policy of restriction because it disproportionately disadvantaged candidates from underprivileged backgrounds. They noted that those candidates may possess desirable characteristics required for a successful career in health care but who face many barriers to accessing higher education. Results from a study of key stakeholders from the College of Medicine, Nursing, and Health Sciences (CMNHS) and Fiji Ministries of Education and Health showed that nearly two thirds of respondents supported the introduction of supplementary assessments for student selection, including the NCQ.

North Carolina State University–Tuskegee University

The Veterinary Medicine Pipeline (VMP) collaboration with Tuskegee University's School of Veterinary Medicine (TUSVM) is built on the noncognitive variables discussed in chapter 3. The goal of the VMP program is to better prepare North Carolina State University (NCSU) underrepresented preveterinary students and make them more competitive for veterinary school admissions. Ethnic minorities are vastly underrepresented in the veterinary sciences. NCSU preveterinary "minority" students will be exposed to interactive seminars and webinars with faculty and students from TUSVM, and some will even participate in the Annual Veterinary Medicine Symposium at Tuskegee.

Another aim of the collaboration is to provide access to minority practicing veterinarians who serve as role models, supporters, and motivators to underrepresented preveterinary students at NCSU. The VMP program also includes a VMP student club that operates under the auspices of the preveterinary track of the Minority Association of Pre-Health Students (MAPS) at NCSU.

East Carolina University School of Dental Medicine

The East Carolina University School of Dental Medicine (ECUSDM) was established specifically by the North Carolina legislature in 2007 to address the significant need for dentists within the state of North Carolina. North Carolina ranked 47th nationally in the number of dentists per capita (M.B. Wilson, Sedlacek, & Lowery, 2014). The state faced a number of additional issues further affecting access to dental services: a concentration of practicing dentists in urban areas, an aging dental workforce, rapid population growth, and a shift in racial composition. It was therefore essential that graduates possess the attributes and skills necessary to meet the needs of vulnerable populations in the state (M.B. Wilson et al., 2014).

The ECUSDM inaugural class of 52 students, all North Carolina residents, matriculated in August 2011; a second cohort of 52 students matriculated in August 2012. The school will continue to admit approximately 50 students, all North Carolinians, per year. The school specifically sought to educate dentists from "rural, disadvantaged and under-represented minority backgrounds, with a commitment to providing primary care dentistry services in communities of need across the state of North Carolina" (M.B. Wilson et al., 2014). Health professionals who come from disadvantaged backgrounds or are members of underrepresented minorities are more likely to provide care in communities of need (Butters & Winter, 2002).

The American Dental Education Association (ADEA, 2012) reported that for the 2010 entering classes, of the 4,947 students enrolled as first-time enrollees in U.S. dental schools, Hispanics and Latinos composed 7.2%, African Americans composed 5.4%, and Native Americans composed less than 1% of first-year enrollees. Underrepresented minority students collectively accounted for less than 13% of the total first-year enrollment. Total U.S. dental school enrollment followed a similar pattern (ADEA, 2012).

Traditionally, U.S. and Canadian dental admissions committees have relied on academic and cognitive data such as completion of prerequisite courses, Dental Admission Test (DAT) scores, and GPAs to inform admissions decisions (Ranney, Wilson, & Bennett, 2005), although Curtis, Lind, Plesh, and Finzen (2007) demonstrated that such variables are not predictive of academic performance in dental school.

The recognition of the limitations of traditional cognitive measures in predicting dental school outcomes, combined with the compelling need for increased diversity within the dental workforce, has led many admissions committees to move toward a more holistic approach to admissions. Within such a framework, variables such as leadership, community service, and shadowing experiences are often included in the admissions deliberation process. N. Lopez, Self, and Karnitz (2009) described a systematic process for including nonacademic variables in a quantifiable format.

Admissions Committee Training

ECUSDM began use of the Sedlacek (2004b) noncognitive variable system in its inaugural admissions cycle in 2010–2011, which included a workshop for admissions committee members on assessing noncognitive variables conducted by Sedlacek. Prior to the start of the 2012–2013 admissions cycle, Sedlacek made a presentation to all faculty regarding the use of noncognitive variables in admissions and student development and did additional training with the admissions committee. For the 2013 admissions cycle, noncognitive variables were given more weight and the DAT was given less weight in making decisions regarding which applicants to invite for interviews.

Initial Application Review Process

Students seeking admission to ECUSDM submitted applications through the Associated American Dental Schools Application Service (AADSAS). Once AADSAS applications were received, applicants were invited to complete the supplemental application.

The completed AADSAS and supplemental applications underwent a holistic review, including a personal statement and a description of community, leadership, and extracurricular activities. Given the limitations of time available for interviews, the school determined that reviewing students' written responses to questions could effectively assess some of the noncognitive variables, whereas other noncognitive variables could be assessed in personal interviews with specifically designed questions on its supplemental application to address four of the noncognitive variables: availability of a strong support person, successful leadership experience, demonstrated community service, and knowledge acquired in or about a field (M.B. Wilson et al., 2014).

- *Availability of a strong support person:* Other than your parents, describe someone who has been a strong support person for you. In what specific ways was that person supportive?
- *Successful leadership experience:* Describe a situation where your attempts at leadership were not successful? Why do you think that was?
- *Demonstrated community service:* Describe the role you played in a group that worked together toward a common goal. What did you learn from that experience?
- *Knowledge acquired in or about a field:* Describe a crisis in your life and what you learned from dealing with the crisis.

On the basis of a preliminary application review, applicants whose noncognitive variable responses indicated that their potential for fitting the mission of ECUSDM and whose academic record and DAT scores met the minimum criteria for admission were invited to interview with members of the admissions committee (M.B. Wilson et al., 2014). Interview questions were as follows:

- *Positive self-concept and realistic self-appraisal:* Do you think that you are good at most things? Why or why not? In what areas do you anticipate that you will excel in dental school? What kinds of things are you *not* good at? Why? What challenges do you anticipate facing in dental school?
- *Understands and knows how to navigate the system:* Describe a situation where you believe you were not treated fairly. Why do you think that happened? Do you believe that there are inequities in our dental health care system? Why or why not?
- *Long-range goals:* If it turns out that for some reason you do not receive an offer of admission to dental school for this application cycle, what are your plans? Aside from dentistry, what other goals do you have in your life?

Each of three interviewers independently assessed and scored each applicant on scale of 1 to 4 (where 4 was the highest) for each of the eight noncognitive variables. Each interviewer also provided an overall desirability score for each applicant, where 1 was extremely desirable and 4 was a rejection.

Admissions Committee Review and Action
At regularly scheduled meetings, the committee considered the recommendations of the interviewers, including noncognitive variable scores, and all available information in making admissions decisions. Although the admissions committee did not use a decision algorithm or rubric to make admissions decisions, noncognitive variable scores played a key role in the decision to admit.

Applicants who were not interviewed and scored by three members of the admissions committee were eliminated, resulting in an $N = 204$ for the 2010–2011 cycle and $N = 195$ for the 2011–2012 cycle. Interviewer mean scores of the eight noncognitive variables ranged from 2.33 for leadership to 2.70 for positive self-concept for the 2011 cohort and from 3.07 for nontraditional learning to 3.51 for strong support person for the 2012 cohort. Applicant total scores were 20.10 for the 2011 entering class and 26.15 for the 2012 entering class. Mean scores for the 2012 cycle were higher overall than scores for the 2011 cycle.

Pearson correlation coefficients were calculated for the noncognitive variable scores and total scores for each applicant with "desirability" and "final admissions action." Total score showed the highest significant correlations with desirability (.05 level). Positive self-concept, realistic self-appraisal, long-range goals, and leadership showed higher correlations with desirability than the other noncognitive variables, although all noncognitive variables showed correlations with desirability, which were significant at the .05 level.

Total score showed the highest correlation with final admissions action. Among the individual noncognitive variable scores, positive self-concept, realistic self-appraisal, long-range goals, and leadership showed higher correlations with final admissions action than the other noncognitive variables. All were significant at the .05 level except for strong support person. Generally, the correlations with final admissions action were lower than with desirability.

For both admissions cycle samples, the correlations were highest for total score and were significant (.05) for desirability and final admissions action. Four of the noncognitive variable scores—positive self-concept, realistic self-appraisal, long-range goals, and leadership—showed the highest correlations with both desirability and final admissions action.

Applicants with higher noncognitive variable scores received higher desirability scores from their individual interviewers and were more likely to receive offers of admission. Applicants with lower noncognitive variable scores received lower desirability scores from their individual interviewers and were more likely to be denied admission.

The finding that the same four noncognitive variable scores showed higher correlations for both desirability and final admissions action indicated that the individual interviewers and the admissions committee were more likely to emphasize those variables in selection.

The correlations for final admissions action may indicate that those students who were the best match for ECUSDM were more likely to accept offers of admission. This will continue to be monitored closely over the years, as well as evaluated as part of assessing student development on the noncognitive variables for the matriculating students.

The increase in mean scores from the 2011 cycle to the 2012 cycle is worth further study. It may indicate that the applicants to the 2012 cycle were stronger on noncognitive variables than their predecessors. Word may be out that ECUSDM is emphasizing those dimensions in admissions. An important part of the ECUSDM program is to communicate its unique mission to advisers and prospective applicants.

The increase in mean scores could also be a result of the halo effect, in that evaluators were assigning higher scores in the second year, independent of applicant attributes. This is a problem that can occur in ratings as a program develops and raters feel positive about its mission and their role as evaluators. This underscores the need for continual calibration and training of interviewers to ensure that the noncognitive variable scoring can be used to effectively differentiate among applicants, which is the desired outcome regardless of the characteristics of the applicant pool.

This preliminary data analysis demonstrated that noncognitive variables were related to admissions decisions in ways that are compatible with the Sedlacek (2004b) model as implemented at ECUSDM. The next stage of data analysis will be to relate the noncognitive scale scores to outcome measures such as grades; retention; graduation; and, ultimately, variables such as career choices.

Performing more comprehensive assessments were seen as moving toward a determination of which persons might be considered nontraditional in work with individuals or groups. In addition, postenrollment counseling, advising, and mentoring programs based on noncognitive variables were developed (Sedlacek, Benjamin, Schlosser, & Sheu, 2007; Warren & Hale, 2016). The noncognitive variables were designed to be predictors of both student success in educational programs and developmental dimensions. Although the noncognitive variables are particularly helpful in working with students from nontraditional backgrounds, they can be employed to increase the likelihood of success of all students. Noncognitive profiles of all students were provided to faculty advisers, and faculty and staff have received training in helping students improve on the noncognitive variables in what will be a continuing program.

Additional Organizations and Programs Using Noncognitive Variables

U.S. Dream Academy

The U.S. Dream Academy was founded by Grammy-nominated gospel singer Wintley Phipps through his work with Prison Fellowship Ministries (www.usdreamacademy.org/about/program). His work with incarcerated parents identified a struggling and overlooked population, namely, children of incarcerated parents. The vision for the U.S. Dream Academy emerged out of a desire to break the cycle of incarceration many families experience, particularly when living in high-risk communities.

The U.S. Dream Academy sponsors an after-school mentoring program, which served over 1,000 students in grades three through eight during the 2008–2009 school year. The program starts with this principle: "Beyond school, every young person served must spend 11 to 15 hours each week in a stimulating learning environment" (www.usdreamacademy.org/about/

program). One-on-one sessions with carefully matched mentors complement after-school activities that combine academic fundamentals. The focus builds on three pillars: skill building, character building, and dream building. The overall goal is to nurture the whole child while altering attitudes, enhancing self-esteem, supporting emotional and intellectual growth, and stimulating academic interests.

According to the program, academic failure has been shown to be the most important predictor of future incarceration. The core components for this pillar are assistance with homework and online learning. Students use SuccessMaker, a computer-based educational program that focuses on literacy and math instruction. Students use the Education in Human Values curriculum, a universal, values-based program that lays the foundation for students to understand and apply the five fundamental values of peace, love, truth, right action, and nonviolence in their lives. The program helps students broaden their understanding of what their options and opportunities are while eliminating the possibility of incarceration from their framework of reference. Mentoring plays a part here because mentors act as role models, showing students positive options for their life.

The U.S. Dream Academy concentrates on 101 attributes that form the basis of the program. A system of noncognitive variables was developed for the program based on the research of Sedlacek discussed in chapter 3 and augmented by work in assessing values based on spirituality (Duffy & Sedlacek, 2007, 2010). The noncognitive variable system is used in implementing the program and in evaluating outcomes.

The following section is from "Free Higher Education for All!" (Sedlacek, 2014a), which appeared on the Insidetrack Blog on February 13, 2014.

Sounds Great! MOOCS, courses on your smart phone, a world-wide classroom of millions, and the promise of free online higher education for all. Innovation; Change; The latest innovation is seen by many as the answer to all our problems. They feel the delivery system is the answer; not what its implications are for learning or implementing the system fairly to all.

The system that we have learned to work to fit our needs evolves, and students, parents, and educators must adjust. If we examine the models that have been developed that describe the stages that people go through to deal with change, they usually involve denial, skepticism, insider coping, wider understanding, and eventually more change to begin the process anew. While descriptive, these models of change do not consider the attributes that one must possess to move through those stages. I have been studying and designing measures of noncognitive variables that may help us understand and develop such attributes in people.

The attribute I would like to discuss is "Negotiating the System." Some people are very good at analyzing the ways that the institutions of society treat them and may facilitate or interfere with their best interests. This is an important attribute for all, but it is a particularly critical ability for anyone experiencing discrimination. The discrimination can be on the basis of race, gender, age, disability, religion or many other categories. The students most vulnerable to discrimination are the least likely to possess the insider knowledge and skill to successfully navigate this increasingly complex system. Those who already enjoy certain advantages in the system are more likely to possess the skills to interpret the many routes to a degree now available. My research suggests that people need to anticipate how change will affect them, and then do what needs to be done to maximize its benefit or minimize its damage to them.

This is a skill that can be developed in individuals at all levels by helping them examine the implications of changing systems. A number of universities, colleges, and scholarship programs admit and provide services for their students on handling the system.

The Gates Millennium Scholars scholarship program includes evidence of overcoming obstacles and negotiating the system, among other noncognitive variables, in its selection of Scholars. Over 15,000 scholarships have been awarded to students of color attending over 1,500 different institutions, including the most selective in the country. More than 90% have graduated with a mean GPA of 3.25. They are more likely to interact with faculty and use student services than other students, and hence are working the system for their benefit.

The East Carolina University School of Dental Medicine selects students, in part, on the basis of their ability to negotiate the demands of rural North Carolina. Helping students work that system is a major faculty and staff goal.

We can all learn to analyze how a series of policies and procedures works for or against us, and do what is necessary to handle that system. We can stay ahead of the demands of change, and not leave some behind struggling with the implications of the latest innovation.

9

THE FUTURE

There are grounds for cautious optimism that we may now be near the end of the search for the ultimate laws of nature.

—Stephen Hawking (n.d.)

Will noncognitive variables be discussed, researched, and used in the future? Will future generations recognize the terminology or concepts employed in this book? Will the innovation be sustained, or will it go the way of steam-powered cars, rote memorization, helicopters for every home, and Segways? Let's look at some reasons why noncognitive variables might last or at least have an effect for a while.

In the discussion in chapter 1 of the models of diffusion of an innovation, once an innovation becomes useful and observable to many, it might survive. I see the final stage of innovation as a series of plateaus, much like we see in learning (www.intropsych.com/ch07_cognition/learning_curve.html). We reach a certain point in the development of an innovation, and understanding and behavior (individual and institutional) consolidate around it. Whether we move to the next plateau depends on many variables, including whether, in an inductive model, we can organize and document where we are and then move up to the next plateau of integrating our knowledge. In any area of science or scholarship, this is an important step.

Weick (1984) argued that social problems are solved when innovative action allows for a strategy of small wins where a series of concrete, complete outcomes of moderate importance build a pattern that attracts allies and deters opponents.

I feel we may be at a plateau where a series of small-scale examples can be consolidated to move to the next level or plateau. There are many research studies and applications of noncognitive variables available to consider. In addition, issues around diversity, communication, and interest in reaching and teaching a wider range of students worldwide are upon us.

The hope is that this book can aid in the process of documenting where we are on a plateau and where we might go next. The energy and interest seem available at present. Whether the noncognitive concept evolves and becomes a natural and common concept or becomes an oddity of our times remains to be seen.

EXHIBIT 1

Description of Noncognitive Variables With Reliability Estimates of Scale Scores

Variable Number	Variable Name
1	*Positive Self-Concept* (α = .79) Demonstrates confidence, strength of character, determination, and independence
2	*Realistic Self-Appraisal* (α = .78) Recognizes and accepts any strengths and deficiencies, especially academic, and works hard at self-development; recognizes the need to broaden his or her individuality
3	*Understands and Knows How to Navigate the System and Racism* (α = .80) Exhibits a realistic view of the system based on personal experience of racism and overcoming obstacles; committed to improving the existing system; takes an assertive approach to dealing with existing wrongs but is not hostile to society and is not a "cop-out"; able to handle the system
4	*Prefers Long-Range Goals to Short-Term or Immediate Needs* (α = .80) Able to respond to deferred gratification; plans ahead and sets goals
5	*Availability of Strong Support Person* (α = .79) Seeks and takes advantage of a strong support network or has someone to turn to in a crisis or for encouragement
6	*Successful Leadership Experience* (α = .78) Demonstrates strong leadership in any area of his or her background (e.g., church, sports, noneducational groups, gang leader, etc.)
7	*Demonstrated Community Service* (α = .80) Participates and is involved in his or her community
8	*Knowledge Acquired in or About a Field (Nontraditional Learning)* (α = .80) Acquires knowledge in sustained and/or culturally related ways in any field

Note. Composite score α = .83. From "Early Academic Behaviors of Washington State Achievers," by W. E. Sedlacek and H. B. Sheu, 2005, *Readings on Equal Education, 21*, pp. 207–222.

Scoring System for Noncognitive Variables on Interviews and Essays

In the following section, you will find the definition of each of the noncognitive variables and a list of questions to guide you in the assessment of each variable.

Variable 1: Positive Self-Concept	
This variable assesses the applicant's confidence, self-esteem, independence, and determination, all vital components of future achievement and success.	
Positive Evidence	**Negative Evidence**
Does the applicant feel confident of making it through graduation?	Does the applicant express any reason he or she might not complete school or succeed and attain his or her goals?
Does the applicant make positive statements about himself or herself?	Does the applicant express concerns that other students are better than he or she is?
Does the applicant expect to achieve his or her goals and perform well in academic and nonacademic areas?	Does the applicant expect to have marginal grades?
Does the applicant provide evidence how he or she will attain his or her goals?	Does the applicant have trouble balancing his or her personal and academic life?
Does the applicant link his or her interests and experiences with his or her goals?	Does the applicant appear to be avoiding new challenges or situations?
Does the applicant assume he or she can handle new situations or challenges?	

(Continues)

(Continued)

Variable 2: Realistic Self-Appraisal	
This variable assesses the applicant's ability to recognize and accept his or her strengths and deficiencies, especially in academics, and to work hard at self-development to broaden his or her individuality.	
Positive Evidence	**Negative Evidence**
Is the applicant aware of his or her strengths and weaknesses?	Is the applicant unaware of how evaluations are done in school?
Does the applicant know what it takes to pursue a given career?	Is the applicant not sure about his or her own abilities?
Is the applicant realistic about his or her abilities?	Is the applicant uncertain about how his or her peers or superiors rate his or her performances?
Does the applicant show an awareness of how his or her service, leadership, extracurricular activities, or schoolwork has caused him or her to change over time?	Does the applicant overreact to positive or negative reinforcement rather than see it in a larger context?
Has the applicant learned something from these structured or unstructured activities?	Is the applicant unaware of how he or she is doing in classes until grades are out?
Does the applicant appreciate and understand both positive and negative feedback?	Is the applicant unaware of positive and negative consequences of his or her grades, actions, or skills?
Does the applicant provide evidence of overcoming anger, shyness, and lack of discipline?	
Does the applicant face a problem, like a bad grade, with determination to do better?	

Variable 3: Understands and Knows How to Navigate the System and Racism	
This variable assesses the applicant's ability to understand the role of the "system" in life and to develop a method of assessing the cultural and racial demands of the system and respond accordingly and assertively.	
Positive Evidence	**Negative Evidence**
Is the applicant able to overcome challenges or obstacles he or she is confronted with as a result of racism in a positive and effective way?	Is the applicant unaware of how the "system" works?

Does the applicant understand the role of the "system" in his or her life and how it treats nontraditional persons?	Is the applicant preoccupied with racism or does not feel racism exists?
Does the applicant reveal ways that he or she has learned to "deal" with the "system" accordingly?	Does the applicant blame others for his or her problems?
	Does the applicant react with the same intensity to large or small issues concerned with race?
	Is the applicant's method for successfully handling racism that does not interfere with personal and academic development nonexistent?

Variable 4: Prefers Long-Range Goals to Short-Term or Immediate Needs

This variable assesses the applicant's persistence, patience, long-term planning, and willingness to defer gratification and success in college.

Positive Evidence	Negative Evidence
Does the applicant reveal experience setting both academic and personal long-term goals?	Does the applicant lack evidence of setting and accomplishing goals?
Does the applicant provide evidence that he or she is planning for the future?	Is the applicant likely to proceed without clear direction?
Has the applicant determined a course of study and does the applicant anticipate the type of career or path he or she might or could pursue?	Does the applicant rely on others to determine outcomes?
Is the applicant aware of realistic and intermediate steps necessary to achieve goals?	Does the applicant focus too much attention on the present?
Has the applicant participated in activities (volunteer work, employment, extra courses, community work) related to his or her anticipated career goal?	Is the applicant's plan for approaching a course, school in general, an activity, and so on nonexistent?
	If the applicant states his or her goals, are the goals vague or unrealistic?

(Continues)

(Continued)

Variable 5: Availability of Strong Support Person

This variable assesses the applicant's availability of a strong support network, help, and encouragement and the degree to which he or she relies solely on his or her own resources.

Positive Evidence	Negative Evidence
Does the applicant have a strong support system? This can be a personal, professional, or academic support as long as it is someone to whom the applicant can turn for advice, consultation, assistance, encouragement, and so on.	Does the applicant avoid turning to a support person, a mentor, or close adviser for help?
Is the applicant willing to admit that he or she needs help and able to pull on resources, other than himself or herself, to solve problems?	Does the applicant keep his or her problems to himself or herself?
	Does the applicant state that he or she can handle things on his or her own?
	Does the applicant state that access to a previous support person may have been reduced or eliminated?
	Is the applicant unaware of the importance of a support person?

Variable 6: Successful Leadership Experience

This variable assesses the applicant's skills developed or influence exercised from his or her formal and informal leadership roles.

Positive Evidence	Negative Evidence
Has the applicant taken leadership initiative, for example, by founding clubs or organizations? What evidence is there?	Is the applicant unable to turn to others for advice or direction?
Does the applicant describe the skills he or she has developed as a leader, skills such as assertiveness, effectiveness, organizing, and time management?	Does the applicant lack confidence or leadership skills?

Has the applicant shown evidence of influencing others and being a good role model?	Is the applicant passive, or does he or she lack initiative?
Is the applicant comfortable providing advice and direction to others?	Is the applicant overly cautious?
Does the applicant describe a commitment to being a role model for siblings, community members, or schoolmates?	Does the applicant avoid controversy?
Does the applicant show sustained commitment to one or two types of organizations with increasing involvement, skill development, and responsibility?	
Does the applicant take action and initiative?	

Variable 7: Demonstrated Community Service

This variable assesses the applicant's identification with a cultural, geographic, or racial group and his or her demonstrated activity within that community grouping.

Positive Evidence	Negative Evidence
Does the applicant show sustained commitment to a service site or issue area?	Does the applicant lack involvement in a cultural, geographic, or racial group or community?
Does the applicant demonstrate a specific or long-term commitment or relationships with a community?	Is the applicant involved in his or her community in name only?
Has the applicant accomplished specific goals in a community setting?	Does the applicant engage more in solitary activities rather than group activities (academic or nonacademic)?
Does the applicant's community service relate to career or personal goals?	

(Continues)

(Continued)

Variable 8: Knowledge Acquired in or About a Field (Nontraditional Learning)	
This variable assesses the applicant's experiences gained in a field through study and experiences beyond the classroom. This variable pays particular attention to the ways the applicant gains nontraditional, perhaps culturally or racially based, views of the field.	
Positive Evidence	**Negative Evidence**
Does the applicant use his or her knowledge to teach others about the topic?	Does the applicant lack evidence of learning from the community or nonacademic activities?
Is the applicant working independently in his or her field? (Be sensitive to variations between academic fields and the experiences that can be gained; for example, if in the sciences, by doing independent research, or if in the arts, by participating in competitions or compositions.)	Is the applicant traditional in his or her approach to learning?
Did the applicant learn from internships or employment?	Is the applicant unaware of his or her possibilities in a field of interest?

Note: From Sedlacek, W. E. (2004b). *Beyond the big test: Noncognitive assessment in higher education.* San Francisco, CA: Jossey-Bass.

Example Cases for Training Raters in Evaluating Admissions or Financial Aid Applications

Noncognitive Variable Scoring System

When scoring each of the noncognitive variables for each applicant, be sure to consider the complete application. The following is a description of a five-point system that can be used to assign scores.

Score	Description
1 Low score	There is evidence that the applicant *does not do well* on the variable. Examples: • Not sure of ability • Plans to leave school before finishing • Avoids seeking help from others • Is a loner
2 Minimal evidence	There is some *slight positive evidence* on the variable. Examples: • Minimal involvement in a community • Shows low-level leadership in a group • Handles small examples of racism • Has medium-range goals
3 Neutral or inconsistent evidence	There is *contradictory or no information* on the demonstration of success on the variable. This is the *default option* if the evidence is unclear. Examples: • Shows some good examples and some bad examples of external learning • Fails to provide information on goal setting • Is ambivalent on the value of a support person

(Continues)

(Continued)

Score	Description
4 Solid evidence	*Clear evidence* of success on the variable is presented. Examples: • Has experience with a cultural or racial group • Has knowledge of a field that the applicant has not formally studied in school • Has a mentor • Evaluates good and bad experiences
5 Outstanding evidence	There is evidence that is *unusually well done or consistent* over time on the variable. *Ten percent of applicants or less will score this highly.* Examples: • Possesses goals that are interconnected in stages over time • Demonstrates leadership at many levels and situations over time • Articulates strengths and weaknesses and what can or has been done on them • Shows that noncognitive variables are well integrated (e.g., long-term goals are tied to leadership, feelings about self, and extramural learning)

APPLICATION 1: ADSILA WILLIAMS IS AN 18-YEAR-OLD NATIVE AMERICAN FROM THE SOUTHWEST

1. Positive Self-Concept	Score
Evidence from the personal statement: • Although Adsila's classes are difficult, she is doing well in most subjects. • Adsila keeps at a topic until she gets it. • Adsila is good at reaching out to others outside her tribe. • She wants to work with people in her future. Evidence from the recommendation letter: • Adsila has a positive style of interaction. • She never gives up. • Adsila chose to take some advanced placement courses and did well. • Adsila is quiet but confident.	5

Evidence from the application: • She has taken difficult courses. • Adsila has taken more than the required courses. Summary of the scoring: • Adsila seems confident of her strengths and abilities and gets a 5. She has taken on more work and courses than necessary.	
2. Realistic Self-Appraisal	**Score**
Evidence from the personal statement: • Sometimes she takes on too much. • Adsila challenged herself by selecting difficult courses. • She is confident but does not know about some areas of life. Evidence from the recommendation letter: • She may be too trusting of others. • Eventually she figures things out. • She is not always sure of what she can do. Evidence from the application: • She has done many things that suggest she has a good sense of herself. • She could be more experienced in activities outside school. Summary of the scoring: • Adsila shows some evidence of realistic self-appraisal but has some areas that need work. She gets a 4.	4
3. Understands and Knows How to Navigate the System and Racism	**Score**
Evidence from the personal statement: • Adsila has some experience with nonnative groups but shows little understanding of how those groups may view her. Evidence from the recommendation letter: • There is the suggestion that she should learn more about how the world works outside her tribe.	2

(Continues)

(Continued)

Evidence from the application: • No evidence is present. Summary of the scoring: • Adsila has little experience in understanding how others outside her tribe may treat her, so she gets a 2.	
4. Prefers Long-Range Goals to Short-Term or Immediate Needs	**Score**
Evidence from the personal statement: • Adsila wants to go to college but is not sure where or what she will study. • Someday she would like to work with people but is not sure how. Evidence from the recommendation letter: • Adsila has potential, but it is unfocused. Evidence from the application: • She has some focus on the future by going to college but is unclear after that. Summary of the scoring: • Adsila looks to the future but is not sure what it will be, so she gets a 3.	3
5. Availability of Strong Support Person	**Score**
Evidence from the personal statement: • Her mother and father encouraged her to do her best, but they have not had a strong influence on her. • Adsila developed a close relationship to a teacher to whom she feels she can turn. Evidence from the recommendation letter: • One teacher sounds supportive. Evidence from the application: • No evidence is present. Summary of the scoring: • Adsila seems to have some support, but it is not clear how available it is. She gets a 4.	4

6. Successful Leadership Experience	Score
Evidence from the personal statement: • Adsila has trouble being assertive within her tribe. • Adsila is seen as a leader among her friends. • Adsila works with young people in her tribe. Evidence from the recommendation letter: • Adsila is active with her friends. • Adsila serves as a mentor for her peers and younger people. • Adsila is not active on tribal issues. Evidence from the application: • Adsila shows some signs of being a role model for others. Summary of the scoring: • Adsila scores a 3 because she shows leadership in some areas but not others.	3

7. Demonstrated Community Service	Score
Evidence from the personal statement: • Adsila has done some work with young people in the tribe. • Adsila helps her friends get involved in tribal activities. Evidence from the recommendation letter: • Adsila is well liked and always busy in some activity. • Adsila volunteers to help others within the tribe. Evidence from the application: • Adsila is a volunteer in several tribal groups. Summary of the scoring: • Adsila gets a score of 4. She is involved in the community, but that activity is not necessarily related to any of her goals.	4

8. Knowledge Acquired in or About a Field (Nontraditional Learning)	Score
Evidence from the personal statement: • Adsila has not expressed any information she has acquired from her activities.	3

(Continues)

(Continued)

Evidence from the recommendation letter: • She is always busy, but it is unclear what she is learning from the activity since it seems unfocused. Evidence from the application: • Adsila is active, but there is little evidence of any learning. Summary of the scoring: • Adsila gets a 3, because there is no evidence of learning from her activities.	
Total Score	28

APPLICATION 2: CARLOS LOPEZ IS A 19-YEAR-OLD LATINO FROM THE MIDWEST

1. Positive Self-Concept	Score
Evidence from the personal statement: • Carlos likes figuring things out. Evidence from the recommendation letter: • Carlos always does what he says he will do. • He approaches everything he does with a positive attitude. Evidence from the application: • No evidence is present. Summary of the scoring: • Carlos is positive in his approach to life, so he gets a 4.	4
2. Realistic Self-Appraisal	**Score**
Evidence from the personal statement: • Carlos does everything pretty well. Evidence from the recommendation letter: • No evidence is present. Evidence from the application: • No evidence is present. Summary of the scoring: • There seems to be little evidence of any self-reflection, so Carlos gets a 2.	2

3. Understands and Knows How to Navigate the System and Racism	Score
Evidence from the personal statement: • No evidence is present. Evidence from the recommendation letter: • No evidence is present. Evidence from the application: • No evidence is present. Summary of the scoring: • Because no evidence is provided, Carlos gets a 3 as the default option.	3

4. Prefers Long-Range Goals to Short-Term or Immediate Needs	Score
Evidence from the personal statement: • Carlos wants to do some work with his hands, but he is not sure what; maybe a carpenter. He likes making models. Evidence from the recommendation letter: • Carlos is unclear about his future. Evidence from the application: • No evidence is present. Summary of the scoring: • Carlos scored a 2 because he has some general but unfocused idea of his future.	2

5. Availability of Strong Support Person	Score
Evidence from the personal statement: • No evidence is present. Evidence from the recommendation letter: • No evidence is present. Evidence from the application: • No evidence is present. Summary of the scoring: • Because there is no evidence, Carlos scored a default option, 3.	3

(Continues)

(Continued)

6. Successful Leadership Experience	Score
Evidence from the personal statement: • Carlos is active on several sports teams and is captain of his soccer team. • He was selected to represent his class in a school assembly. Evidence from the recommendation letter: • Carlos is a good role model for some of the younger students. • He does his work and still has time for sports. Evidence from the application: • Carlos lists sports and homeroom leadership activities. Summary of the scoring: • Leadership is shown in several ways in his application materials. It does not relate directly to other aspects of his life, so Carlos gets a 4.	4
7. Demonstrated Community Service	**Score**
Evidence from the personal statement: • He is involved with his soccer team but does not mention anything else. Evidence from the recommendation letter: • He is involved in his sports team and as a school representative. Evidence from the application: • No evidence is present. Summary of the scoring: • Carlos described some activity with his school and sports team but nothing else, so he gets a 2.	2
8. Knowledge Acquired in or About a Field (Nontraditional Learning)	**Score**
Evidence from the personal statement: • Carlos learned something about people from sports. Evidence from the recommendation letter: • He learned some leadership skills as a class leader.	2

Evidence from the application: • No evidence is present. Summary of the scoring: • There is some, albeit minimal, evidence, so Carlos gets a 2.	
Total Score	22

APPLICATION 3: J'WAUN BROWN IS A 19-YEAR-OLD AFRICAN AMERICAN STUDENT FROM THE EAST

1. Positive Self-Concept	Score
Evidence from the personal statement: • J'waun has done well in history and tended to excel in these courses by paying attention and preparing for exams. • J'waun has become really proficient at library research. • He has a strong motivation to learn and do well in everything. • J'waun realizes his weakest subject is math and that he must work extra hard on it. • He is well liked by his classmates. Evidence from the recommendation letter: • J'waun is working on many school projects. • J'waun feels sure of himself. • He does most things well. Evidence from the application: • No evidence is present. Summary of the scoring: • J'waun scores a 5 because he is confident and does most things well.	5
2. Realistic Self-Appraisal	**Score**
Evidence from the personal statement: • J'waun has done well in history courses. • J'waun realizes his weakest subject is math and that he must work extra hard on it. • He feels that he does not do well in math because he has not concentrated on it.	5

(Continues)

(Continued)

Evidence from the recommendation letter: • J'waun's strength is figuring out what he needs to do to succeed. • J'waun likes learning, which has helped him do well in school. Evidence from the application: • J'waun has participated in numerous scout and community activities. Summary of the scoring: • J'waun gets a 5 because he has some understanding of his weak area and works at it.	
3. Understands and Knows How to Navigate the System and Racism	**Score**
Evidence from the personal statement: • No evidence is present. Evidence from the recommendation letter: • No evidence is present. Evidence from the application: • No evidence is present. Summary of the scoring: • No evidence is provided on whether J'waun is aware of working the system to his advantage or any aspect of racism, so he scores the default option of 3.	3
4. Prefers Long-Range Goals to Short-Term or Immediate Needs	**Score**
Evidence from the personal statement: • Once completing college, J'waun plans to go to graduate school and eventually become a college professor in history. • He wants to study history in college. He also wants some other courses, including education, to be more well rounded. Evidence from the recommendation letter: • J'waun has a good idea of what he wants to do in life. Evidence from the application: • J'waun gets high grades, which will help him achieve his goals.	5

Summary of the scoring:	
• J'waun has clear long-term goals, with some shorter term ones. He is also specific about stating his goals, so he scores a 5.	
5. Availability of Strong Support Person	**Score**
Evidence from the personal statement:	1
• J'waun likes to do things by himself.	
• He studies best on his own and is distracted by others.	
Evidence from the recommendation letter:	
• J'waun is accomplished but seems to be alone too much.	
• J'waun does not have regular contact with his family.	
• He does not have a close relationship to any teachers.	
Evidence from the application:	
• No evidence is present.	
Summary of the scoring:	
• J'waun is a loner who does not have a support system, so he gets a 1.	
6. Successful Leadership Experience	**Score**
Evidence from the personal statement:	1
• J'waun is usually studying and does not make time for group activities.	
Evidence from the recommendation letter:	
• J'waun is not seen with other students.	
• He keeps to himself.	
Evidence from the application:	
• No evidence is present.	
Summary of the scoring:	
• J'waun is not involved in any groups and keeps to himself, so he gets a 1.	
7. Demonstrated Community Service	**Score**
Evidence from the personal statement:	2
• He does not spend time in any community activities outside school.	
• He is a member of the History Club at school and helped coordinate an event last year.	

(Continues)

(Continued)

Evidence from the recommendation letter: • No evidence is present. Evidence from the application: • No evidence is present. Summary of the scoring: • J'waun has shown minimum interest in any community activities, with some minor activities, so he gets a 2.	
8. Knowledge Acquired in or About a Field (Nontraditional Learning)	**Score**
Evidence from the personal statement: • J'waun has learned a great deal about history from reading, visiting museums, and watching the History Channel on television. He has a special interest in nineteenth-century U.S. history. Evidence from the recommendation letter: • J'waun has written some college-level papers on historical topics. Evidence from the application: • He has taken lots of history-related courses and activities. Summary of the scoring: • J'waun learned from cases and on his own about history, so he gets a 5.	5
Total Score	27

APPLICATION 4: MOHAMED BASARA IS A 20-YEAR-OLD FROM THE MIDDLE EAST

1. Positive Self-Concept	**Score**
Evidence from the personal statement: • No evidence is present. Evidence from the recommendation letter: • No evidence is present. Evidence from the application: • No evidence is present.	3

Summary of the scoring:

- Because there is no evidence provided, Mohamed scored a 3.

2. Realistic Self-Appraisal	Score
Evidence from the personal statement: • Mohamed is from a wealthy family and does not feel he has to say much about himself. Evidence from the recommendation letter: • Mohamed has great possibilities and will do well when he returns to his home country. Evidence from the application: • Mohamed was well educated in Europe before coming to the United States. Summary of the scoring: • Mohamed provides limited information on this dimension so he scores a default option 3.	3

3. Understands and Knows How to Navigate the System and Racism	Score
Evidence from the personal statement: • He feels others in the United States are racist and do not understand him. • He feels there is no racism in his home country. Evidence from the recommendation letter: • No evidence is present. Evidence from the application: • No evidence is present. Summary of the scoring: • Because there is negative evidence and denial, the score is a 1.	1

4. Prefers Long-Range Goals to Short-Term or Immediate Needs	Score
Evidence from the personal statement: • He is going to major in engineering and expects to graduate with a bachelor's degree and then get a master's degree. • Mohamed expects to work for a big engineering company in his home country.	4

(Continues)

(Continued)

Evidence from the recommendation letter:

- He was sent by his government to earn an engineering degree and expects to oversee large projects at home.
- He has focused his course work on civil engineering and large-scale applications.

Evidence from the application:

- Mohamed's course work over a long period has focused on math and engineering.

Summary of the scoring:

- Mohamed has plans and experience related to his long-term goal, so he gets a 4.

5. Availability of Strong Support Person	Score
Evidence from the personal statement: • Mohamed's father is a government official in his home country and has directed his education. Evidence from the recommendation letter: • His father is a dominant figure in his life. Evidence from the application: • No evidence is present. Summary of the scoring: • Mohamed's father is a support person but is not always available where he is. Mohamed has no others to turn to, so he gets a 3.	3
6. Successful Leadership Experience	**Score**
Evidence from the personal statement: • Mohamed is turned to for advice by some students from his country. Evidence from the recommendation letter: • Mohamed is sought out by other students for his advice. • He takes the initiative on group projects. • Mohamed keeps to himself. Evidence from the application: • No evidence is present. Summary of the scoring: • Although Mohamed shows some leadership, it is inconsistent, so he gets a 3.	3

7. Demonstrated Community Service	Score
Evidence from the personal statement: • No evidence is present. Evidence from the recommendation letter: • No evidence is present. Evidence from the application: • Mohamed has worked on some engineering projects in the communities where he has been in school. Summary of the scoring: • Mohamed has some experience in the community, but it is inconsistent, so he gets the default score of 3.	3

8. Knowledge Acquired in or About a Field (Nontraditional Learning)	Score
Evidence from the personal statement: • Mohamed has learned some applications of his course work on local projects. Evidence from the recommendation letter: • His letters stress his family and government ties rather than what he knows. Evidence from the application: • No evidence is present. Summary of the scoring: • Mohamed has acquired some knowledge, but it is unclear and not consistent, so he gets a 3.	3
Total Score	23

APPLICATION 5: ANN SWIFT IS A 23-YEAR-OLD WHITE STUDENT FROM THE SOUTHEAST WITH A LEARNING DISABILITY

1. Positive Self-Concept	Score
Evidence from the personal statement: • Ann refers to her own abilities often. • She knows she is smart.	4

(Continues)

(Continued)

Evidence from the recommendation letter:

- She has had to demonstrate many times that she can do the work.
- Ann approaches challenging tasks with resolve to complete assignments and have in-depth understanding.

Evidence from the application:

- Ann has accomplished many things despite her disability.

Summary of the scoring:

- Ann shows self-confidence despite obstacles, so she gets a 4.

2. Realistic Self-Appraisal	Score
Evidence from the personal statement: • Ann states some things she can do well, as well as others she would like to improve on. Evidence from the recommendation letter: • Sometimes Ann overestimates what she can do, because she must take much longer to do her homework than other students. Evidence from the application: • Ann lists many accomplishments and activities. Summary of the scoring: • There is some inconsistency in whether Ann understands what she can and can't do, so she gets a 3.	3
3. Understands and Knows How to Navigate the System and Racism	Score
Evidence from the personal statement: • She has had to exceed the expectations of friends, family, and teachers over many years. • She cites examples of showing great patience in helping others to understand her situation. Evidence from the recommendation letter: • She does not let others make her feel inferior. Evidence from the application: • She has undertaken all the activities that anyone of her age might pursue.	5

Summary of the scoring:	
• Ann has worked the system well in her behalf, so she gets a 5.	
4. Prefers Long-Range Goals to Short-Term or Immediate Needs	**Score**
Evidence from the personal statement: • Ann wants to be a teacher. • She says she is going to attend College X and major in education, with a minor in English. • She plans to travel after graduation before going to graduate school. Evidence from the recommendation letter: • Ann has it all worked out, better than most students with or without a disability. • She knows what she will be doing for the next 10 years. • Her commitment to helping others is indicative of her desire to become a teacher. Evidence from the application: • Ann was president of the English Club in her school. Summary of the scoring: • Ann has a clear path to achieving her long-term goals, so she gets a 5.	5
5. Availability of Strong Support Person	**Score**
Evidence from the personal statement: • Ann believes God will show her the way. Evidence from the recommendation letter: • Ann seems to do well without anyone to turn to for a discussion of her goals. Evidence from the application: • No evidence is present. Summary of the scoring: • Ann has only a vague support system. She says she will seek help if needed but currently lacks a clear support person and may have trouble if she encounters some barriers to her success, so she gets a 2.	2

(Continues)

(Continued)

6. Successful Leadership Experience	Score
Evidence from the personal statement: • She is president of the Future Teachers Club. • She works in an elementary school with children with learning disabilities. Evidence from the recommendation letter: • She is looked to by others. • Ann is president of the Future Teachers Club. • Others seek her advice. Evidence from the application: • Ann is president of the Future Teachers Club. Summary of the scoring: • Ann has shown leadership in many ways, consistent with her long-term goals, so she gets a 5.	5
7. Demonstrated Community Service	**Score**
Evidence from the personal statement: • Ann works in an elementary school with children with learning disabilities. Evidence from the recommendation letter: • She has always been active in her campus community. • Ann takes active roles in several high school clubs and church groups. Evidence from the application: • Ann works with students with learning disabilities. Summary of the scoring: • Ann gets a 4 because of her activities in several areas. She does not get a 5, because it is not clear how all her activities are coordinated.	4
8. Knowledge Acquired in or About a Field (Nontraditional Learning)	**Score**
Evidence from the personal statement: • She is president of the Future Teachers Club, which has gone on field trips to schools and invited local teachers to meetings for presentations and discussions.	4

Evidence from the recommendation letter: • Ann has picked up lots of practical information about teaching and any difficulties she may have with a learning disability. Evidence from the application: • Ann is president of the Future Teachers Club. Summary of the scoring: • Ann has learned a lot about teaching, including possible problems she may have with a learning disability, so she gets a 4.	
Total Score	32

APPLICATION 6: LIN CHUN IS A 17-YEAR-OLD ASIAN AMERICAN FROM THE WEST

1. Positive Self-Concept	**Score**
Evidence from the personal statement: • Lin does not like to talk about herself, believing that is for others to do. Evidence from the recommendation letter: • She is very hardworking and expects a lot from herself. • Lin can be successful in whatever she chooses to do. Evidence from the application: • No evidence is present. Summary of the scoring: • Although there is some information provided, it is minimal and lacks detail, so Lin gets a 2.	2
2. Realistic Self-Appraisal	**Score**
Evidence from the personal statement: • Lin really likes to solve problems, and nothing gives her more satisfaction than to get the right answer. Evidence from the recommendation letter: • Lin excels in her schoolwork and in a student club for students of her race. • Lin has demonstrated the ability to succeed in all areas of high school life.	4

(Continues)

(Continued)

• In each of these areas, Lin has demonstrated her ability to handle problems effectively. Evidence from the application: • No evidence is present. Summary of the scoring: • Lin's interest in solving problems and her awareness of her ability is evidence of realistic self-appraisal. This is supported in her recommendation letter, so she gets a 4.	
3. Understands and Knows How to Navigate the System and Racism	**Score**
Evidence from the personal statement: • No evidence is present. Evidence from the recommendation letter: • No evidence is present. Evidence from the application: • No evidence is present. Summary of the scoring: • Because there is no evidence, Lin gets a 3.	3
4. Prefers Long-Range Goals to Short-Term or Immediate Needs	**Score**
Evidence from the personal statement: • In the fall, Lin will be attending University X with a major in engineering and a minor in mathematics. Evidence from the recommendation letter: • Lin intends to study engineering in college, and I believe she will be successful in reaching her goals. Evidence from the application: • Lin is in the math club and spends time as a volunteer math tutor. Summary of the scoring: • There is some relationship between Lin's intended major and other parts of the application, so Lin gets a 4.	4

5. Availability of Strong Support Person	Score
Evidence from the personal statement: • No evidence is present. Evidence from the recommendation letter: • No evidence is present. Evidence from the application: • No evidence is present. Summary of the scoring: • Because there is no evidence, Lin gets a 3.	3

6. Successful Leadership Experience	Score
Evidence from the personal statement: • Lin has developed her own computer program that she employs with her work in tutoring. Evidence from the recommendation letter: • Lin works well with others, and many look to her for advice. Evidence from the application: • She lists work with her brothers and sisters in helping them with schoolwork. Summary of the scoring: • Lin shows leadership in several areas, so she gets a 4.	4

7. Demonstrated Community Service	Score
Evidence from the personal statement: • Lin was in leadership positions and helped a student group set up a tutoring program. Evidence from the recommendation letter: • Lin is very involved in a local club that does some charity work. • Lin has been very active in several extracurricular activities of the school. Evidence from the application: • She set up a tutoring program for fellow students. Summary of the scoring: • Lin is engaged in some activities, though not extensive, so she gets a 3.	3

(Continues)

(Continued)

8. Knowledge Acquired in or About a Field (Nontraditional Learning)	Score
Evidence from the personal statement: • Lin learned a great deal about math and tutoring on her own. Evidence from the recommendation letter: • Lin is a quick learner and read a lot to set up her tutoring program. Evidence from the application: • Lin set up a tutoring program. Summary of the scoring: • Lin showed learning and experience about math and tutoring, so she is scored a 4.	4
Total Score	27

APPLICATION 7: CENISA HOWARD IS AN 18-YEAR-OLD AFRICAN AMERICAN FROM THE MIDWEST

1. Positive Self-Concept	Score
Evidence from the personal statement: • She is the older sister who has taken care of her four younger siblings. • Cenisa has worked part-time jobs babysitting and as a clerk and salesperson. • Cenisa feels she can do great things with her life. Evidence from the recommendation letter: • She has the potential to accomplish anything she wishes. Cenisa is the most talented student one teacher had over 20 years. • Cenisa is very quick to pick up on a concept. • She is particularly interested in science and math. Evidence from the application: • Cenisa joined a self-exploration student group. Summary of the scoring: • There is information on her confidence, determination, and ability to achieve her goals, so she gets a 5.	5

2. Realistic Self-Appraisal	Score
Evidence from the personal statement: • Cenisa is confident in her potential and assumes she can choose from a number of careers. • Although she played violin in the school orchestra, she feels her future is in medicine. Evidence from the recommendation letter: • Cenisa is good with people. • She is interested in science and has done some extra reading on medical careers. Evidence from the application: • Cenisa realizes the high school does not have all the courses she might need in college, so she has taken some science and math courses in a special program at the community college. Summary of the scoring: • Cenisa has a strong sense of what she needs to succeed and gets a 5.	5
3. Understands and Knows How to Navigate the System and Racism	Score
Evidence from the personal statement: • Cenisa has some sense that an African American woman may encounter some prejudice, but she feels she can handle it. Evidence from the recommendation letter: • Cenisa knows how to get what she wants. • She had one experience where she was singled out in a class as a Black woman and was confused by it. Evidence from the application: • No evidence is presented. Summary of the scoring: • Cenisa has some sense of what it is to be Black and a woman but has not had much experience in dealing with any negative treatment, so she gets a 4.	4

(Continues)

(Continued)

4. Prefers Long-Range Goals to Short-Term or Immediate Needs	Score
Evidence from the personal statement: • Cenisa is clear that she wants to attend a certain undergraduate school, work in the summers in a clinic, and then go to medical school. Evidence from the recommendation letter: • Cenisa has a great deal of potential to accomplish anything she wishes. She has a plan laid out for her success and will be successful in her future life and career. • Cenisa has the combination of hard work, ability, and motivation that should make her successful. Evidence from the application: • Cenisa has specified her goals by year of accomplishment. Summary of the scoring: • Cenisa has clear long-term goals linked to shorter term ones, so she gets a 5.	5
5. Availability of Strong Support Person	**Score**
Evidence from the personal statement: • Cenisa has not sought support from others very often. She tends to support others. • Cenisa's parents or teachers are not mentioned. Evidence from the recommendation letter: • Cenisa is independent and tends to seek her own counsel. • Her adviser reported not being approached with a problem Cenisa could not handle herself. Evidence from the application: • No evidence is presented. Summary of the scoring: • Cenisa does not show a strong support person, although she seems to have at least one teacher available, so she gets a 2.	2
6. Successful Leadership Experience	**Score**
Evidence from the personal statement: • Cenisa has acted as an informal source of information on health careers for other students.	4

Evidence from the recommendation letter:

- She has developed some source material that her teacher uses in class.
- Other students look up to her.

Evidence from the application:

- She lists several health-related jobs and summer activities.

Summary of the scoring:

- Cenisa has shown some initiative in helping others and taking the lead in some areas, so she gets a 4.

7. Demonstrated Community Service	Score

Evidence from the personal statement: 4

- Cenisa has done some work on health issues in the larger community.

Evidence from the recommendation letter:

- Cenisa is always busy with some project that may involve a number of people outside the school.

Evidence from the application:

- Cenisa did some work at a community health center.

Summary of the scoring:

- Cenisa has been active in several areas in the community, so she gets a 4.

8. Knowledge Acquired in or About a Field (Nontraditional Learning)	Score

Evidence from the personal statement: 5

- She has learned a great deal about science and health careers from reading and working in a health center.

Evidence from the recommendation letter:

- Cenisa seems to always be reading something outside the required reading for homework.
- She seems to have picked up a great deal of information about her school subjects on her own.

Evidence from the application:

- Cenisa lists some extensive outside reading that has informed her decision to follow her career in medicine.

(Continues)

(Continued)

Summary of the scoring: • Cenisa has pursued information in a number of ways and gets a 5.	
Total Score	34

APPLICATION 8: ALEX MARIN IS A 21-YEAR-OLD BISEXUAL MALE FROM THE SOUTH

1. Positive Self-Concept	Score
Evidence from the personal statement: • Alex has struggled with who he is, but now he knows he is bisexual. • He doesn't worry about what others think of him. • He has done a lot of reading on sexuality, and he is comfortable with his identity. Evidence from the recommendation letter: • Alex is one of the best students. • He has found the space to be comfortable with his religion. • Alex is best at interpersonal issues and has helped many students with his advice. • Alex has volunteered to work in the counseling center on campus. Evidence from the application: • No evidence is presented. Summary of the scoring: • Evidence of Alex's positive self-concept shows that he takes initiative, has handled religious difficulties, and has taught himself and assisted others, so he gets a 5.	5
2. Realistic Self-Appraisal	Score
Evidence from the personal statement: • Alex has spent time figuring out who he is. • Alex realizes he will not be understood by many on campus. Evidence from the recommendation letter: • He has faced an issue on his identity and is doing well. • Alex will make a good graduate student in psychology. Evidence from the application: • Alex has been involved in campus groups on bisexual issues.	4

Summary of the scoring:
- Alex shows evidence of realistic self-appraisal by expressing his interests in the topic of bisexuality and helping other students. Alex's letter of recommendation says he can handle a difficult situation, so he gets a 4.

3. Understands and Knows How to Navigate the System and Racism	Score
Evidence from the personal statement: • He knows he is at a campus where religion does not allow for bisexuality. • Alex would like to stay enrolled and graduate from his college. • He feels bisexual individuals should have their own identities and groups, not just be part of gay, lesbian, and transgender groups. Evidence from the recommendation letter: • Alex is handling the pressures on him to conform well. • Alex is expected to graduate from this school and move on to graduate school. Evidence from the application: • He is open and honest about his sexual orientation and his interests in working with others on the topic. • His view of bisexuality as a separate identity is sophisticated. Summary of the scoring: • Alex receives a 5. He is in an environment where many oppose his sexual preference but has worked the system enough to survive.	5
4. Prefers Long-Range Goals to Short-Term or Immediate Needs	Score
Evidence from the personal statement: • His short-term goal has been to be honest about his sexuality, while having the longer range goal to go to graduate school to study psychology. • His long-term goal is to work with bisexual clients as a career. Evidence from the recommendation letter: • Alex is expected to succeed in completing his goals. • Setting goals is a strength for Alex. He would like to attend one of several graduate schools he has selected. • He is taking some advanced courses at a local community college.	5

(Continues)

(Continued)

Evidence from the application: • He has shown his interest in psychology through courses and activities. Summary of the scoring: • Alex shows long-term goals tied to shorter term ones and gets a 5.	
5. Availability of Strong Support Person	**Score**
Evidence from the personal statement: • Alex has had to find himself without the help of others. • He has found one counselor connected with his religion off campus who has been of some help. • Alex had trouble finding someone to write a letter of recommendation. Evidence from the recommendation letter: • His parents are not supportive of his coming out as bisexual. • His one sibling is active in his church and does not understand his decision. • One faculty member feels he has potential but hopes he finds his way back to his religion. Evidence from the application: • No evidence is presented. Summary of the scoring: • There is only minimal evidence of having a support person, so Alex gets a 2.	2
6. Successful Leadership Experience	**Score**
Evidence from the personal statement: • He organized a group of bisexual students and others off campus. • Alex has worked as a volunteer in advising students in the campus counseling center. Evidence from the recommendation letter: • Alex is a leader by personal example. Classmates come to him for assistance in pursuing their goals in many areas. • Alex has been a group leader in many class projects. • His classmates look to him for his knowledge and leadership.	5

Evidence from the application:	
• Alex is a project leader in several classes. • He organized a bisexual student group. Summary of the scoring: • Alex shows leadership by being a project leader and teaching others. He is seen by others as a leader in multiple areas, so he receives a 5.	

7. Demonstrated Community Service	**Score**
Evidence from the personal statement: • Alex has volunteered in the community on campus on multiple topics. • He started a group open to on- and off-campus people on bisexuality. Evidence from the recommendation letter: • Alex is involved in his campus and the off-campus community as well. Evidence from the application: • Alex has nearly 100 total hours of community service. Summary of the scoring: • Alex gets a 5, because he has shown his activity on multiple topics, including bisexuality, on and off campus.	5

8. Knowledge Acquired in or About a Field (Nontraditional Learning)	**Score**
Evidence from the personal statement: • Alex has learned a great deal about sexuality and bisexuality on his own. • Alex has developed a perspective about bisexuality that is not a traditional view. Evidence from the recommendation letter: • Although Alex is not always well understood, he appears motivated and creative and should do well in his future. Evidence from the application: • Alex organized a group on bisexuality.	5

(Continues)

(Continued)

• He took courses on campus and at a local community college in psychology. • He has clear long-term goals. Summary of the scoring: • Alex shows an interest in many aspects of bisexuality and related topics and has sought the knowledge and information available from multiple sources. He has shared this knowledge through his work on campus and in the community, so he gets a 5.	
Total Score	36

Noncognitive Items That Can Be Employed in Interview, Short-Answer, Essay, or Application Review Formats

It is best to score how focused and specific the response is. A word limit of 100 words or less is recommended for short-answer items. This could be expanded to 200 words for more advanced students. For essays, 500 words is usually best, but it may vary with the level of the person being evaluated (e.g., less for secondary students, more for graduate students). However, there should be a word limit on the responses. In part, you are testing students' ability to be succinct.

Interviewers should be trained to be succinct in their evaluations as well. Scores can be assigned to each noncognitive variable using the following system.

Noncognitive Variable Scoring System

When scoring each of the noncognitive variables for each applicant, be sure to consider the complete application. The following is a description of a five-point system that can be used to assign scores.

Score	Description
1 Low score	There is evidence that the applicant *does not do well* on the variable. Examples: • Not sure of ability • Plans to leave school before finishing • Avoids seeking help from others • Is a loner

(Continues)

(Continued)

Score	Description
2 Minimal evidence	There is some *slight positive evidence* on the variable. Examples: • Minimal involvement in a community • Low-level leadership shown in a group • Handles small examples of racism • Has medium-range goals
3 Neutral or inconsistent evidence	There is *contradictory or no information* on the demonstration of success on the variable. This is the *default option* if the evidence is unclear. Examples: • Some good examples and some bad examples of external learning • No information provided on goal setting • Ambivalence on the value of a support person
4 Solid evidence	*Clear evidence* of success on the variable is presented. Examples: • Experience with a cultural or racial group • Knowledge of a field that the applicant has not formally studied in school • Has a mentor • Evaluates good and bad experiences
5 Outstanding evidence	There is evidence that is *unusually well done or consistent* over time on the variable. *Ten percent of applicants or less will score this highly.* Examples: • Goals that are interconnected in stages over time • Leadership at many levels and situations over time • Can articulate strengths and weaknesses and what can or has been done on them • Noncognitive variables are well integrated (e.g., long-term goals are tied to leadership, feelings about self, and extramural learning)

Variable 1: Positive Self-Concept

- *I am good at most things.* Do you agree or disagree with this statement, and why?
- *I do not expect to have trouble in school.* Do you agree or disagree with this statement, and why?

- *Women make better students than men.* Do you agree or disagree with this statement, and why?

Variable 2: Realistic Self-Appraisal

- Which course in school do you expect to have the most trouble with, and why?
- Describe something in your field that you would *not* like to do, and why?
- What kinds of people would you work *best* with, and why?

Variable 3: Understands and Knows How to Navigate the System and Racism

- *I have never encountered discrimination against me.* Do you agree or disagree with this statement, and why?
- *There is no important discrimination against groups in the society.* Do you agree or disagree with this statement, and why?
- Describe a situation when you were not treated fairly.

Variable 4: Prefers Long-Range Goals to Short-Term or Immediate Needs

- *I would like to be a supervisor someday.* Do you agree or disagree with this statement, and why?
- If you do *not* get accepted into a graduate school, what alternative career would you pursue?
- Aside from jobs in your field, what other goals do you have in your life?

Variable 5: Availability of Strong Support Person

- *I work best on my own.* Do you agree or disagree with this statement, and why?
- *When I have a problem in my life, I like to seek advice on how to handle it.* Do you agree or disagree with this statement, and why?
- Describe your relationship with someone who has given you advice about a career. Why it was good or bad?

Variable 6: Successful Leadership Experience

- *A new employee's role is to follow the lead of supervisors, even when they may be wrong.* Do you agree or disagree with this statement, and why?
- *It is possible to be a leader and a follower at the same time.* Do you agree or disagree with this statement, and why?
- *I have not been successful when I have tried to lead others.* Do you agree or disagree with this statement, and why?

Variable 7: Demonstrated Community Service

- *I prefer to study on my own rather than in a group.* Do you agree or disagree with this statement, and why?
- *In nursing, it is critical to make your own decisions.* Do you agree or disagree with this statement, and why?
- *An employee is a member of a team.* Do you agree or disagree with this statement, and why?

Variable 8: Knowledge Acquired in or About a Field (Nontraditional Learning)

- Describe something you have learned about your field outside school.
- Describe something you have learned about other fields outside school.
- Describe a crisis in your life and what you learned from it.

Noncognitive Items in Likert (Agree–Disagree) Formats

Items marked with an asterisk are reversed in polarity, and a low score is positive.

Variable 1: Positive Self-Concept

- I am good at most things.
- I am *not* sure what I like and don't like.*
- My feelings about myself change a lot.*
- I usually make a mistake in most things I try to do.*
- I like who I am.
- I *don't* like who I am.*
- I do *not* expect to have trouble doing well in college.*
- When I start something new, I am *not* always sure how it will work out.*
- I have strong opinions.
- Once I make up my mind, I "stick with it."
- I am a good listener.
- I can have a good time anywhere.
- I can have a good time with anyone.
- Life without risks is *not* possible.
- I usually "play it safe."*
- If an opportunity comes up, I would "go for it."

Variable 2: Realistic Self-Appraisal

- There are some things I *do not* do well.
- I surprise myself sometimes about what I *can do*.
- I surprise myself sometimes at what I *can't do*.
- Everyone has strengths and weaknesses.
- I know what I do *best*.

- I know my faults.
- I can do anything I set my mind to do.
- I am better at some things than others.
- I have a plan to work on my limitations.
- I am challenged by something I *do not* do well.
- Unless you try something, you *don't* know if you can do it.
- I *don't* like to discuss things I can't do well.*
- You can learn from your failures.
- If I fail at something, I avoid it the next time.*
- I *don't* do things that will not bring success.*
- I tend to repeat my mistakes.*
- I never repeat a mistake.*
- Failure is a poor teacher.*

Variable 3: Understands and Knows How to Navigate the System and Racism

- I like to take advantage of any opportunity that comes my way.
- I sometimes take on too much.*
- I face many obstacles in achieving my objectives.*
- I can solve just about any problem that gets in my way.
- I know how to get good grades.
- I can usually talk a teacher into giving me a higher grade.
- Sometimes I get help on my homework from friends.
- I work harder on subjects I *don't* like.
- I *don't* understand how to get high grades.*
- Getting high grades is mostly luck.*

Variable 4: Prefers Long-Range Goals to Short-Term or Immediate Needs

- I like to take things as they come.*
- If you plan too far ahead, things might *not* work out.*
- I like to start each day without knowing exactly what will happen.*
- I like to make sure I finish today's goals before I worry about tomorrow's.*
- Overplanning makes for a dull life.*
- I like to make plans even if I change them.*
- You *cannot* plan too much.
- Most of my plans *don't* work out.*

- Planning can be fun.
- I like to plan each day the night before.
- If I *don't* plan, things *don't* work out.
- My friends think I plan too much.
- I have the most fun when I *don't* plan ahead.*
- Planning is *not* a good idea because things always change.*
- People are always getting in the way of my plans.*
- I have a plan for my future.
- I know what I will be doing next year.
- I am always changing my plans.*

Variable 5: Availability of Strong Support Person

- When I have a problem in my life, I like to handle it myself.*
- When I have a problem in my life, I like to seek advice on how to handle it.
- I have someone in my life that I have turned to when I needed advice.
- I have had a teacher who has given me good advice.
- No one in my family can give me good advice on academic issues.*
- No one in my family can give me good advice on personal issues.*
- It is best to keep your problems to yourself.*
- I *don't* have problems I need help with.*
- Usually the advice you get from others is *not* good.*
- I *don't* like to listen to others on handling my issues.*
- Everyone needs help sometimes.
- Most people are too involved with their own issues to give good advice.*
- When I am *not* sure of something, I have someone I check it out with.
- I am good at figuring things out for myself.*
- When things are tough, I know where to go.

Variable 6: Successful Leadership Experience

- I like to take the lead in activities in my family.
- I *don't* like to be responsible for the learning of others in class.*
- It is *not* possible to be a leader and follower in a group at different times.*
- People seek my advice.
- I am good at advising others.
- I usually go along with the group.*

- If it's a good idea, I can usually get others to go along.
- I can usually get others to go along with me.
- Others often turn to me when they can't figure something out.
- If I *can't* figure something out easily, I suggest someone else who may have the answer.*
- People usually *don't* seek my advice.*
- I am a leader.
- Others seem to naturally do what I think is best without my help.*
- I like to keep my opinions on what others should do to myself.*
- Most leaders are born that way.*
- I am good at following orders.*
- I am better at following than leading.*
- Leaders often bully people.*
- I *don't* like to "boss" people.*
- People should do what they want and not listen to others.*
- I like to have others follow up on my ideas.
- I am usually the leader in any group.
- You can learn to be a leader.
- More people should do their work and not bother others.*

Variable 7: Demonstrated Community Service

- I prefer to study in a group.
- I prefer to study on my own.*
- I get my *best* work done on my own.*
- I prefer to be with friends rather than meet new people.*
- Working in a group slows me down.*
- In groups there is usually someone who holds the group back.*
- Groups solve problems better than individuals.
- I usually need to discuss my ideas with a group before they are clear.
- Groups are a waste of time.*
- I "hang out" regularly with a group.
- I like to hear what others have to say about different issues of the day.
- There is usually too much talk in a group to get things done.*
- I like to share my problems with others.
- I keep my problems to myself.*
- I usually get some help from groups I belong to.
- Groups can be fun, but they usually *don't* get much done.*
- I would rather figure things out for myself than seek help from others.*
- I need time to study rather than to spend time in a group.*

- I *don't* like group projects in class.*
- A group presentation for a class can be a hassle.*
- Groups are fine for socializing but not for being productive.*
- I like to help others.
- I can usually get more done working by myself than with others.*
- All people should help one another.
- You *cannot* be friendly to everyone.*
- I want my work to make a difference in the world.
- Working in a group can be frustrating.*
- You can learn a lot by studying with others.
- I am in a group that meets regularly to discuss things.
- I am in a social group that does things together.

Variable 8: Knowledge Acquired in or About a Field (Nontraditional Learning)

- I am good at solving problems.
- Most problems will solve themselves with time.*
- I usually need help in figuring things out.*
- I enjoy puzzling over something.
- Sometimes you can overanalyze something.*
- I *don't* like it when others bring me their problems to solve.*
- I have yet to get answers to some questions I have had in my life.
- Solving some problems leads to other problems.
- People rarely ask my advice on solving a problem.*
- I can get to the heart of any matter quickly.
- I often come up with too many solutions to a problem.
- It is *best* to work on one problem at a time.*
- I am *not* creative.*
- Some of my classes are boring.*
- *Not* all learning is interesting.*
- It is better to have one solution to a problem than to have many.*
- Either you are creative or you are *not*.*
- Creativity can be easily recognized.
- What you learn in life *doesn't* help much in school.*
- I learn *best* from reading.*
- I learn *best* from figuring things out on my own.
- I learn *best* from teachers.*
- I can learn in many ways.
- At times I suddenly see things coming together clearly.
- I have used things I learned outside school to do well in school.

Noncognitive Items in Multiple-Choice Formats

Multiple-Choice Items

Choose the one best option of those offered. Scoring will be a 1 for the option noted in italics, and 0 for any other response.

Variable 1: Positive Self-Concept

You are about to do something you have never done before. Which *best describes* how you feel before you begin?

1. Worried something will probably go wrong
2. Unprepared
3. Not sure of how it will come out
4. *Confident that I can do it*

When you believe something strongly, which *best* describes you?

1. I will probably change my mind in the future.
2. I may change with new information.
3. *I am open to change, but I am unlikely to do so.*
4. I am not sure.

Which of the following jobs would *most appeal* to you? Choose one.

1. One where I could be close to my family
2. One that paid a lot
3. One where I could use what I learned in school
4. *One that was different from what I was used to*
5. One that involved working with people

Variable 2: Realistic Self-Appraisal

You feel one of your teachers has given you a lower grade than you deserve. What would you *most likely* do?

1. Report the teacher to his or her supervisor
2. Say nothing but try to prove the teacher wrong next time
3. *Go talk to the teacher and make your case*
4. Complain to friends but do nothing
5. Leave the teacher a note, complaining

Which option *best* describes you?

1. *I know what I do best.*
2. I am surprised at the way some people think of me.
3. I spend time figuring out what I should do.
4. A test can't tell me what I know.
5. I am like most people.

What do you do best?

1. I am not sure.
2. No one knows until they try something.
3. I stick to what I know.
4. *I do some things well and others less well.*
5. I do most things well.

Variable 3: Understands and Knows How to Navigate the System and Racism

Which of these statements do you *most agree* with?

1. Discrimination is in the eye of the beholder.
2. I have never been discriminated against.
3. *The system is fairer for some people than others.*
4. Racism is not a big problem in society.
5. Anyone can achieve if he or she works hard.

Which of these statements do you *most agree* with?

1. Women who complain about sexism have a problem.
2. I have never been racist in my actions.

3. I don't know why people cry "racism" over simple issues.
4. *Some have a more difficult time because of their race.*
5. People who see racism everywhere should get over it.

Which of these statements do you *most agree* with?

1. Few people are racists.
2. Life is fair for most people.
3. If you do not succeed, it is your own fault.
4. *I have overcome obstacles based on who I am.*
5. I can't help the way people treat me.

Variable 4: Prefers Long-Range Goals to Short-Term or Immediate Needs

Which of these statements do you *most agree* with?

1. Planning is not a good idea because things always change.
2. People are always getting in the way of my plans.
3. I do not have a clear plan for my future.
4. *I know what I will be doing next year.*
5. I like to be flexible in planning.

Which of these statements do you *most agree* with?

1. I like to take things as they come.
2. If you plan too far ahead, things might not work out.
3. I like to start each day without knowing exactly what will happen.
4. I like to make sure I finish today's goals before I worry about tomorrow's.
5. *Overplanning makes for a dull life.*

Which of these statements do you *most agree* with?

1. Planning is not fun.
2. I do not like to plan each day beforehand.
3. *If I do not plan, things don't work out.*
4. My friends plan more than I do.
5. I have the most fun when I do not plan ahead.

Variable 5: Availability of Strong Support Person

Which of these statements do you *most agree* with?

1. It is best to keep your problems to yourself.
2. I don't have problems I need help with.
3. Usually the advice you get from others is not good.
4. I don't like to listen to others on handling my issues.
5. *I have someone I talk to about my problems.*

Which of these statements do you *most agree* with?

1. *Everyone needs help sometimes.*
2. Most people are too involved with their own issues to give good advice.
3. I am not sure where I would go to solve a personal problem.
4. I am good at figuring things out for myself.
5. No one in my family can give me good advice on personal issues.

Which of these statements do you *most agree* with?

1. When I have a problem in my life, I like to handle it myself.
2. *I have someone in my life that I have turned to when I needed advice.*
3. I do not have a teacher who has given me good advice.
4. No one in my family can give me good advice on academic issues.
5. Sometimes it is best to handle your own problems.

Variable 6: Successful Leadership Experience

You have been given a group project in a class. *What would you probably do?*

1. Work on my part alone until it was finished
2. *Get the group together where we each are in charge of part of it*
3. Take charge and decide what each person is to do
4. Get the group together and get someone else to take the lead
5. Not sure

Imagine that your family is dealing with a difficult problem. *What kind of role might you play?*

1. *The leader; you can come up with ideas*
2. An active member; you might be able to add something helpful
3. Someone who does what the leader suggests
4. Someone who tries to stay out of the discussion
5. Not sure

A friend comes to you with a problem concerning a relationship he or she has and wants your advice. *Which best describes your reaction?*

1. Think about it for a long period of time and then offer advice
2. Ask someone else what he or she thinks
3. Immediately offer advice
4. *Think about it briefly and then offer advice without consulting anyone*
5. Not get involved

Imagine the disagreements you regularly get into with someone in your life. *What usually is the end result?*

1. *You persuade him or her to see things your way.*
2. The person persuades you to see things his or her way.
3. You fight, and each person sticks to his or her viewpoint.
4. You never have disagreements.
5. I'm not sure.

Two friends come to you for advice, individually, on how to resolve an issue between them. *What would you do?*

1. Avoid giving advice because you do not want to hurt either one
2. *Try to bring them together to work things out*
3. Choose one friend's logic and try to get the other to agree
4. Decide what to do for them
5. Not sure

Variable 7: Demonstrated Community Service

Which of these options *best describes* your *feeling about work?* Choose one.

1. It should satisfy me
2. *It should help others*
3. It should pay a lot
4. It should pay enough to meet my needs
5. It should teach me something

You are running late for an important meeting and see someone by the side of the road trying unsuccessfully to change a tire. What would be your *most likely* reaction?

1. Feel sorry for the person and hope he or she can change the tire
2. *Stop and help*

3. Assume he or she has called for assistance
4. Feel guilty but do not stop
5. Go on to your meeting; it's not your problem

Which of these options *best* describes your perspective?

1. I work best alone.
2. Working in a group is usually a waste of time.
3. *Problems are best solved in groups.*
4. Individual effort gets the job done.
5. Most people prefer their own way of doing things.

Variable 8: Knowledge Acquired in or About a Field (Nontraditional Learning)

Which option do you *most agree* with?

1. I learn best in a class.
2. I learn best from outside reading.
3. I learn best when I have fun.
4. I learn best from a job.
5. *There are lots of ways to learn.*

Which option do you *most agree* with?

1. *I have learned more outside of school than in school.*
2. I am not creative.
3. I do not enjoy puzzling over something.
4. Most problems take care of themselves over time.
5. It is best to solve one problem at a time.

Which of these statements do you *most agree* with?

1. What you learn in life doesn't help much in school.
2. *I learn best from figuring things out on my own.*
3. Sometimes you can overanalyze something.
4. I am not sure how I learn best.
5. It is better to have one solution to a problem than to have many.

Universal Diverse Orientation (UDO) Scale–Short Form

All items are scaled from 1 (*strongly agree*) to 5 (*strongly disagree*). Items 11 through 15 are reverse coded.

1. I would like to join an organization that emphasizes getting to know people from different countries.
2. I would like to go to dances that feature music from other countries.
3. I often listen to music of other cultures.
4. I am interested in learning about the many cultures that have existed in this world.
5. I attend events where I might get to know people from different racial backgrounds.
6. Persons with disabilities can teach me things I could not learn elsewhere.
7. I can best understand someone after I get to know how he or she is *both* similar to and different from me.
8. Knowing how a person differs from me greatly enhances our friendship.
9. In getting to know someone, I like knowing how he or she *both* differs from me and is similar to me.
10. Knowing about the different experiences of other people helps me understand my own problems better.
11. Getting to know someone of another race is generally an uncomfortable experience for me.
12. I am only at ease with people of my race.
13. It's really hard for me to feel close to a person from another race.
14. It is very important that a friend agrees with me on most issues.
15. I often feel irritated by persons of a different race.

References for UDO Scale

Fuertes, J. N., Miville, M. L., Mohr, J. J., Sedlacek, W. E., & Gretchen, D. (2000). Factor structure and short form of the Miville–Guzman Universality–Diversity Scale. *Measurement and Evaluation in Counseling and Development, 33*(3), 157–169.

Longerbeam, S. L., & Sedlacek, W. E. (2006). Attitudes toward diversity and living-learning outcomes among first- and second-year college students. *National Association of Student Personnel Administrators Journal, 49*(1), 40–55.

Singley, D. B., & Sedlacek, W. E. (2004). Universal-diverse orientation and precollege academic achievement. *Journal of College Student Development, 45*, 84–89.

Singley, D. B., & Sedlacek, W. E. (2009). Differences in universal-diverse orientation by race and gender. *Journal of Counseling and Development, 87*(4), 404–411.

Example Behaviors for Evaluating University Police Officers

The following scale can be used to evaluate campus police officers for promotion (five-point scale: 1 = *very negative*, 5 = *very positive*).

Behavior	Mean	SD
Put on formal reprimand	1.03	0.11
Received a letter of complaint	1.34	0.34
Does not follow orders	1.63	0.55
Has difficulty with one or more racial groups	1.97	0.67
Does not resolve disputes on-site	2.27	0.61
Appearance not regular dress (e.g., uniform, shoes)	2.51	0.49
Does not initiate new ideas	2.79	0.62
Belongs to at least two police organizations	3.04	0.68
Is an officer in a police organization	3.36	0.44
Has gotten advanced police training	3.61	0.53
Has had human relations training	3.90	0.34
Speaks a foreign language	4.18	0.57

Behavior	Mean	SD
Has done community police work	4.45	0.22
Is an adviser to a student cultural organization	4.62	0.21
Has received an unsolicited letter of praise	4.86	0.12

Principles of Interviewing for Noncognitive Variable Diagnosis

These 21 principles of interviewing are based on those presented in Sedlacek (2004b).

1. *Provide conditions conducive to good interviews.* The school atmosphere should reflect an orientation toward the individual, a flexible curriculum and instructional methods, and general use of grades and data in ways that will encourage students to seek personal help.

2. *Assemble and relate to the problem and have all the facts available.* Ideally a cumulative personnel record should be accessible to student service workers.

3. *Meet the interviewee cordially.* The friendly spirit needs to be natural, but not condescending or patronizing, and in harmony with your personality.

4. *Begin the interview with a topic that is secondary but of interest to you and of potential interest to the interviewee.* Before the main issue is approached, build rapport by encouraging a short period during which you and the interviewee can discuss an issue that is of common interest.

5. *Approach the problem as soon as rapport is assumed.* Ask the students for a statement of the problem as they see it.

6. *Uncover the real difficulties.* Listen to the obvious problems but watch for clues pointing to the real problems often existing behind them.

7. *Isolate the central problem by asking interviewees questions that direct their attention to salient issues.* Give the students a chance to put several sets of facts together to reach new conclusions about their problems.

8. *Do not embarrass the interviewee unnecessarily.* To make it easy for the students to disclose essential material, do not pry into matters not related to the problems at hand.

9. *Face the facts professionally.* Do not convey surprise or shock or show emotional tension at disclosures.

10. *Observe closely the student's behavior.* As a natural manifestation of your interest while listening, you may give attention to the student's

mannerisms and facial expressions (e.g., you may notice the student giving poor eye contact).

11. *Avoid putting the student on the defensive.* In case of resistance, resulting particularly from a difference of opinion, yield as much as possible.

12. *Alleviate the shock of disillusionment.* Identifying the student's misinformation, error, or difficulty as similar to that of many other persons often helps to allay chagrin, shock, embarrassment, or new fears.

13. *Establish a reputation for being helpful and fair and for keeping confidences.* Personal information should be kept confidential without exception.

14. *Give advice sparingly, if at all.* If your advice is requested, you may say you would rather not advise, but you can review the relevant circumstances and encourage the students to formulate their own conclusions.

15. *Give information as needed.* Unless you feel they would be better served by being required to search out essential information for themselves, you may feel free to supply facts about educational or vocational opportunities or requirements.

16. *Make certain that all vital considerations relevant to a decision are brought forward.* If you expect interviews to go beyond one interview, you may need to develop a list of the many essential points to be reviewed.

17. *Present alternatives for the interviewee's consideration.* Possible courses of action may be proposed without the implication that you are trying to impose your own views.

18. *Make other services available to interviewees.* Refer to librarians, professors, clinicians, and any other experts who can help the interviewees gain insight into their problems.

19. *The interviewees formulate their conclusions or plans of action.* The interviewees' program of action must grow out of their thinking.

20. *Achieve something definite.* Do not let the interview close until recognizable progress has been made and agreements have been reached on at least the next step.

21. *Make subsequent interviews easy.* Do not attempt to move too fast.

REFERENCES

Aamodt, M. G., & Williams, F. (2005, April). Reliability, validity, and adverse impact of references and letters of recommendation. In M. G. Aamodt (Chair), *References and recommendation letters: Psychometric, ethical, legal, and practical issues.* Symposium conducted at the 20th annual conference of the Society for Industrial-Organizational Psychology, Los Angeles, CA.

ACT. (2014). Estimated relationship between ACT composite score and SAT CR+M+W score. Retrieved from http://www.act.org/aap/concordance/estimate.html

Adelstein, S. M., Sedlacek, W. E., & Martinez, A. C. (1983). Dimensions underlying the characteristics and needs of returning women students. *Journal of the National Association for Women Deans, Administrators, and Counselors, 46*(4), 32–37.

Alder, S. L. (n.d.). Retrieved from https://www.goodreads.com/quotes/1097820-anyone-can-plot-a-course-with-a-map-or-compass

African American Registry. (2015). *Nigger (the word): A brief history.* Retrieved from http://www.aaregistry.org/historic_events/view/nigger-word-brief-history

Allen, W. R. (1992). The color of success: African American college student outcomes at predominantly White and historically Black public colleges and universities. *Harvard Educational Review, 62*(1), 26–44.

Allen, W. R., Bobo, L., & Fleuranges, P. (1984). *Preliminary report: 1982 undergraduate students attending a predominantly White state-supported university.* Ann Arbor, MI: Center for Afro-American and African Studies.

American Association of Collegiate Registrars and Admissions Officers. (2013a, September 3). *7 principles of holistic/broad based admissions.* Retrieved from http://www.aacrao.org/resources/resources-detail-view/7-principles-of-holistic-broad-based-admissions

American Association of Collegiate Registrars and Admissions Officers. (2013b, April 1). *Beyond GPA: Assessing the whole student.* Retrieved from http://www.aacrao.org/resources/resources-detail-view/beyond-gpa--assessing-the-whole-student

American Association of Collegiate Registrars and Admissions Officers. (2014, February 24). *Should standardized testing submissions be optional?* Retrieved from http://www.aacrao.org/resources/resources-detail-view/should-standardized-testing-submissions-be-optional

American Astronomical Society. (2016, January 16). *AAS statement on limiting the use of GRE scores in graduate admissions in the astronomical sciences.* Retrieved from https://aas.org/governance/council-resolutions#GRE

American Dental Education Association. (2012). *Dental school enrollees by race/ethnicity in U.S. dental schools, 2000 to 2011.* Washington, DC: Author.

American Psychological Association. (2002). Eminent psychologists of the 20th century. *Monitor on Psychology, 33*(7), 29.

Anastasi, A. (1984). Aptitude and achievement tests: The curious case of the indestructible strawperson. *Social and Technical Issues in Testing: Implications for Test Construction and Usage,* No. 9, 129–140. Retrieved from http://digitalcommons.unl.edu/burostestingissues/9

Ancis, J. R., Bennett-Choney, S. K., & Sedlacek, W. E. (1996). University student attitudes toward American Indians. *Journal of Multicultural Counseling and Development, 24,* 26–36.

Ancis, J. R., & Phillips, S. D. (1996). Academic gender bias and women's behavioral agency and self-efficacy. *Journal of Counseling and Development, 75,* 131–137.

Ancis, J. R., & Sedlacek, W. E. (1997). Predicting the academic achievement of female students using the SAT and noncognitive variables. *College and University, 72*(3), 1–8.

Ancis, J. R., Sedlacek, W. E., & Mohr, J. J. (2000). Student perceptions of the campus cultural climate by race. *Journal of Counseling and Development, 78*(2), 180–185.

Angoff, W. H. (1971). *The College Board admissions testing program.* New York, NY: College Entrance Examination Board.

Aries, E., Oliver, R. R., Blount, K., Christaldi, K., Feldman, S., & Lee, T. (1998). Race and gender as components of the working self-concept. *Journal of Social Psychology, 138*(3), 277–290. doi:10.1080/00224549809600381

Arnold, K. D., Fleming, S., Castleman, B. L., De Anda, M. A., Lynk Wartman, K., & Price, P. (2008, March). *The summer flood: The gap between college admission and matriculation among low-income students.* Paper presented at American Educational Research Association Annual Meeting, New York.

Arnold, K. D., Soto, E. B., Methven, L., & Brown, P. (2014, November). *Postsecondary outcomes of innovative high schools: The BPL longitudinal study.* Paper presented at Association for the Study of Higher Education Annual Meeting, Washington, DC.

Associated Press. (2015, March 15). *Timeline: List of recent sorority and fraternity racist incidents.* Retrieved from http://college.usatoday.com/2015/03/15/timeline-list-of-recent-sorority-and-fraternity-racist-incidents/

Association of American Medical Colleges. (2012). *Diversity in medical education: Facts and figures 2012.* Washington, DC: Author.

Astin, A. W. (1977). *What matters most in college: Four critical years.* San Francisco, CA: Jossey-Bass.

Astin, A. W. (1993). *What matters in college? Four critical years revisited.* San Francisco, CA: Jossey-Bass.

Awad, G. H. (2007). The role of racial identity, academic self-concept, and self-esteem in the prediction of academic outcomes for African American students. *Journal of Black Psychology, 33*(2), 188–207. doi:10.1177/0095798407299513

Ayivor, I. (n.d.). Retrieved from http://www.goodreads.com/quotes/1155663-tradition-is-the-prison-where-change-is-detained-to-make

Balenger, V. J., Hoffman, M. A., & Sedlacek, W. E. (1992). Racial attitudes among incoming White students: A study of ten-year trends. *Journal of College Student Development, 33*, 245–252.

Balón, D. G. (2005, April 26). Asian Pacific American college students on leadership: Culturally marginalized from the leader role? *NetResults.* Washington, DC: National Association of Student Personnel Administrators.

Bandalos, D. L., & Sedlacek, W. E. (1989). Predicting success of pharmacy students using traditional and nontraditional measures by race. *American Journal of Pharmaceutical Education, 53*, 143–148.

Baron, A., & Constantine, M. G. (1997). A conceptual framework for conducting psychotherapy with Mexican-American college students. In J. G. Garcia & M. C. Zea (Eds.), *Psychological interventions and research with Latino populations* (pp. 108–124). Boston, MA: Allyn and Bacon.

Beck, B. L., Koons, S. R., & Milgrim, D. L. (2000). Correlates and consequences of behavioral procrastination: The effects of academic procrastination, self-consciousness, and self-handicapping [Special issue]. *Journal of Social Behavior and Personality, 15*(5), 3–13.

Belasco, A. S., Rosinger, K. O., & Hearn, J. C. (2014, June 12). The test-optional movement at America's selective liberal arts colleges: A boon for equity or something else? *Educational Evaluation and Policy Analysis.* doi:10.3102/0162373714537350

Bennett, C. I. (2002). Enhancing ethnic diversity at a Big Ten university through project TEAM: A case study in teacher education. *Educational Researcher, 31*, 21–29.

Bennett, C., & Okinaka, A. M. (1990). Factors related to persistence among Asian, Black, Hispanic, and White undergraduates at a predominantly White university: Comparison between first and fourth year cohorts. *Urban Review, 22*, 33–60.

Berger, J., & Milem, J. (2000). Exploring the impact of historically Black colleges in promoting the development of undergraduates' self-concept. *Journal of College Student Development, 41*, 381–393.

Bernstein, E. (2003, September 9). Want to go to Harvard Law? *Wall Street Journal,* p. W1.

Berra, Y. (n.d.). Retrieved from http://www.goodreads.com/quotes/499411-if-you-don-t-know-where-you-re-going-you-ll-end-up

Bertrand, M., & Mullainathan, S. (2004). Are Emily and Greg more employable than Lakisha and Jamal? A field experiment on labor market discrimination. *American Economic Review, 94*(4), 991–1013. doi:10.1257/0002828042002561

Bettinger, E. P., & Baker, R. B. (2013, September 18). The effects of student coaching: An evaluation of a randomized experiment in student advising. *Educational Evaluation and Policy Analysis.* doi:10.3102/0162373713500523

Betz, N. E., & Fitzgerald, L. F. (1987). *The career psychology of women.* San Diego, CA: Academic Press.

Big Picture Learning. (2008, December 11). *Annual principal retreat*. Seattle, WA: Author.

Big Picture Learning. (2012). *High school alumni report*. Berkeley, CA: MPR Associates.

Big Picture Learning. (2014). *The role of noncognitive skills for student success: Building and implementing noncognitive competencies in school design*. San Diego, CA: Author.

Bill & Melinda Gates Foundation. (2015). *College ready education*. Retrieved from http://www.gatesfoundation.org/What-We-Do/US-Program/College-Ready-Education

Bowen, W. G., & Bok, D. (1998). *The shape of the river: Long-term consequences of considering race in college and university admissions*. Princeton, NJ: Princeton University Press.

Boyer, S. P., & Sedlacek, W. E. (1988). Noncognitive predictors of academic success for international students: A longitudinal study. *Journal of College Student Development, 29*, 218–222.

Brenneman, J. E. (2010). *Finding education's sweetness: On the state of Goshen College*. Retrieved from https://www.goshen.edu/news/pressarchive/brenneman-stateof-college.html

Brooks, G. C., Jr., & Sedlacek, W. E. (1972). The racial census of college students. *College and University, 47*, 125–127.

Brush, S. G. (1991). Women in science and engineering. *American Scientist, 79*, 404–419.

Bureck, J. P., Malmstrom, T., & Peppers, E. (2003). Learning environments and learning styles: Non-traditional student enrollment and success in an Internet-based versus a lecture-based computer science course. *Learning Environments Research, 6*(2), 137–155.

Burkhardt, J. C., & Zimmerman-Oster, K. (1999). How does the richest, most widely educated nation prepare leaders for its future? *Proteus, 16*(2), 9–12.

Burrelli, J., Rapoport, A., & Lehming, R. (2008). *Baccalaureate origins of S&E doctorate recipients* (NSF 08–311). Arlington, VA: National Science Foundation.

Butters, J. M., & Winter, P. A. (2002). Professional motivation and career plan differences between African-American and Caucasian dental students: Implications for improving workforce diversity. *Journal of the National Medical Association, 94*, 492–504.

Cabrera, A. F., & Nora, A. (1994). College students' perceptions of prejudice and discrimination and their feelings of alienation: A construct validation approach. *Review of Education, Pedagogy, and Cultural Studies, 16*(3–4), 387–409.

Capodilupo, C. M., Nadal, K. L., Corman, L., Hamit, S., Lyons, O. B., & Weinberg, A. (2010). The manifestation of gender microaggressions. In D. W. Sue (Ed.), *Microaggressions and marginality: Manifestations, dynamics, and impact* (pp. 193–216). Hoboken, NJ: Wiley.

Carney, P. I., & Sedlacek, W. E. (1985). *Attitudes of young adults toward children* (Research Report No. 4-85). College Park, MD: University of Maryland Counseling Center.

Carter, R. T., White, T. J., & Sedlacek, W. E. (1987). White students' attitudes toward Blacks: Implications for recruitment and retention. *Journal of Social and Behavioral Sciences, 33,* 165–175.

Carter, S. L. (1996). *Integrity.* New York, NY: HarperCollins.

Castañeda et al. v. The Regents of the University of California, U.S. District Court for the Northern District of California, Civil Action No. C. 99-0525 (1999).

Castellanos J., Gloria, A. M., Besson, D., & L. O. Clark Harvey. Mentoring matters: Racial ethnic minority undergraduates' cultural fit, mentorship, and college and life satisfaction. (2016). *Journal of College Reading and Learning, 46*(2), 2016.

Ceasar, S. (2014). *For students at L.A.'s BPL charter school, downtown is their classroom.* Retrieved from http://www.latimes.com/local/education/la-me-downtown-charter-20141228-story.html

Centers for Disease Control and Prevention. (2016). *Cervical cancer rates by race and ethnicity.* Retrieved from http://www.cdc.gov/cancer/cervical/statistics/race.htm#_blank

Chandler, D. L. (2014, August 27). *Straight facts on Mike Brown shooting case.* Retrieved from http://newsone.com/3047840/mike-brown-shooting-facts/

Changing Minds. (2016). *Reaction formation definition.* http://changingminds.org/explanations/behaviors/coping/reaction_formation.htm

Chaples, E. A., Sedlacek, W. E., & Brooks, G. C., Jr. (1972). Measuring prejudicial attitudes in a situational context: A report on a Danish experiment. *Scandinavian Political Studies, 7,* 235–247.

Chaples, E. A., Sedlacek, W. E., & Miyares, J. (1978). The attitudes of tertiary students to aborigines and New Australians. *Politics, 13*(1), 167–174.

Chávez, C. (1984, November). *Address to the Commonwealth Club in San Francisco.* Retrieved from http://www.goodreads.com/quotes/47934-once-social-change-begins-it-cannot-be-reversed-you-cannot

Chen, H. L., & Mazow, C. (2002). *Electronic learning portfolios and student affairs.* Washington, DC: National Association of Student Personnel Administrators.

Chin, J. L. (1998). Mental health services and treatment. In L. C. Lee & N. W. Zane (Eds.), *Handbook of Asian American psychology* (pp. 485–504). Thousand Oaks, CA: Sage.

Christensen, K. C., & Sedlacek, W. E. (1974). Differential faculty attitudes toward Blacks, females and students in general. *Journal of the National Association for Women Deans, Administrators, and Counselors, 37,* 78–84.

Chung, B. Y., & Sedlacek, W. E. (1999). Ethnic differences in career, academic, and social self-appraisals among college freshmen. *Journal of College Counseling, 2*(1), 14–24.

Chung, D. K. (1992). Asian cultural commonalities: A comparison with mainstream American culture. In D. K. Chung, K. Murase, & F. Ross-Sheriff (Eds.), *Social work practice with Asian Americans* (pp. 27–44). Newbury Park, CA: Sage.

Clark, C. (2003). Diversity initiatives in higher education: A case study of multicultural organizational development through the lens of religion, spirituality, faith, and secular inclusion. *Multicultural Education, 10,* 48–54.

Clark, R. (2004). Interethnic group and intraethnic group racism: Perceptions and coping in Black university students. *Journal of Black Psychology, 30*(4), 506–526.

Clinton, H. (n.d.). Retrieved from http://www.brainyquote.com/quotes/quotes/h/hillarycli163821.html?src=t_communities

Cokley, K. (2000). An investigation of academic self-concept and its relationship to academic achievement in African American college students. *Journal of Black Psychology, 26*(2), 148–164. doi:10.1177/0095798400026002002

College Board. (2014a). *SAT-ACT concordance tables*. Retrieved from http://research.collegeboard.org/programs/sat/data/concordance

College Board. (2014b). *The redesigned SAT*. Retrieved from https://www.collegeboard.org/delivering-opportunity/sat/redesign

Collins, A. M., & Sedlacek, W. E. (1973). Student demonstrations and riots: Past, present and future? *College Student Journal, 7*, 87–90.

Comeaux, E. (2011). A study of attitudes toward college student-athletes: Implications for faculty-athletics engagement. *Journal of Negro Education, 80*(4), 521–532.

Conley, D. (2005). *College knowledge: What it really takes for students to succeed and what it takes to get them ready*. San Francisco, CA: Jossey-Bass.

Conley, D. T. (2013). What's in a name? *Education Week, 32*(18), 20–21.

Connelly, K., & Heesacker, M. (2012). Why is benevolent sexism appealing? Associations with system justification and life satisfaction. *Psychology of Women Quarterly, 36*(4), 432–443.

Contrera, J. (2015, March 22). *Starbucks will stop writing race together on your cups now*. Retrieved from http://www.washingtonpost.com/blogs/style-blog/wp/2015/03/22/starbucks-will-stop writing-race-together-on-your-cups-now/

Curtin, N., Stewart, A. J., & Ostrove, J. M. (2013). Fostering academic self-concept: Advisor support and sense of belonging among international and domestic graduate students. *American Educational Research Journal, 50*(1), 108–137. doi:10.3102/0002831212446662

Curtis, D. A., Lind, S. L., Plesh, O., & Finzen, F. C. (2007). Correlation of admissions criteria with academic performance in dental students. *Journal of Dental Education, 71*, 1314–1321.

D'Augelli, A. R., & Patterson, C. J. (1995). *Lesbian, gay, and bisexual identities over the lifespan: Psychological perspectives*. New York, NY: Oxford University Press.

D'Costa, A. G., Bashook, P., Elliott, P., Jarecky, R., Leavell, W., Prieto, D., & Sedlacek, W. E. (1974). *Simulated minority admissions exercise workbook*. Washington, DC: Association of American Medical Colleges.

D'Costa, A. G., Bashook, P., Elliott, P., Jarecky, R., Leavell, W., Prieto, D., & Sedlacek, W. E. (1975). *Simulated minority admissions exercise workbook: Analysis and discussion*. Washington, DC: Association of American Medical Colleges.

DeHaemers, J., & Sandlin, M. (2015). Delivering effective admissions operations. In D. Hossler & B. Bontrager (Eds.), *Handbook of strategic enrollment management* (pp. 377–395). San Francisco, CA: Jossey-Bass.

Deniz, M. E., Tras, Z., & Aydogan, D. (2009). An investigation of academic procrastination, locus of control, and emotional intelligence. *Educational Sciences: Theory and Practice, 9*, 623–632.

Dewey, J. (n.d.). Retrieved from http://www.goodreads.com/quotes/664197-we-do-not-learn-from-experience-we-learn-from-reflecting

Diamond, P., & Rothschild, M. (Eds.). (1989). *Uncertainty in economics.* Salt Lake City, UT: Academic Press.

DiCesare, A., Sedlacek, W. E., & Brooks, G. C., Jr. (1972). Nonintellectual correlates of Black student attrition. *Journal of College Student Personnel, 13,* 319–324.

Dirschl, D. R., & Adams, G. L. (2000). Reliability in evaluating letters of recommendation. *Academic Medicine, 75*(10), 1029.

Dooley, K. E. (1999). Towards a holistic model for the diffusion of educational technologies: An integrative review of educational innovation studies. *Educational Technology and Society, 2*(4), 35–45.

Dovidio, J. F., & Gaertner, S. L. (1986). *Prejudice, discrimination and racism.* Orlando, FL: Academic Press.

Duckworth, A. L. (2011). The significance of self-control. *Proceedings of the National Academy of Sciences, 108*(7), 2639–2640.

Duckworth, A. L., Peterson, C., Matthews, M. D., & Kelly, D. R. (2007). Grit: Perseverance and passion for long-term goals. *Journal of Personality and Social Psychology, 92*(6), 1087–1101. doi:10.1037/0022–3514.92.6.1087

Duckworth, A. L., Quinn, P. D., & Seligman, M. E. P. (2009). Positive predictors of teacher effectiveness. *Journal of Positive Psychology, 4*(6), 540–547.

Duffy, R. D., & Sedlacek, W. E. (2007). Presence of and search for a calling: Connections to career development. *Journal of Vocational Behavior, 70,* 590–601.

Duffy, R. D., & Sedlacek, W. E. (2010). The salience of a career calling among college students: Exploring group differences and links to religiousness, life meaning, and life satisfaction. *Career Development Quarterly, 59,* 27–41.

Dugan, J. P. (2006). Explorations using the social change model: Leadership development among college men and women. *Journal of College Student Development, 47,* 217–224.

Edwards, A. L. (1957). *Techniques of attitude scale construction.* New York, NY: Appleton Century Crofts.

Edwards, A. L., & Gonzalez, R. (1993). Simplified successive intervals scaling. *Applied Psychological Measurement, 17,* 21–27.

Ehrenberg, R. (2002). Reaching for the brass ring: The *U.S. News & World Report* rankings and competition. *The Review of Higher Education, 26,* 145–162.

El-Khawas, E. H. (1980). Differences in academic development during college. In *Men and women learning together: A study of college students in the late 70s.* Providence, RI: Office of the Provost, Brown University.

Engstrom, C. M., & Sedlacek, W. E. (1991). A study of prejudice toward university student-athletes. *Journal of Counseling and Development, 70,* 189–193.

Engstrom, C. M., & Sedlacek, W. E. (1997). Attitudes of residence life staff toward lesbian, gay, and bisexual students. *Journal of College Student Development, 38*(6), 565–576.

Engstrom, C. M., Sedlacek, W. E., & McEwen, M. K. (1995). Faculty attitudes toward male revenue and nonrevenue student-athletes. *Journal of College Student Development, 36*, 217–227.

Ezeala, C. C., Ezeala, M. O., & Swami, N. (2012, November 30). Strengthening the admissions process in health care professional education: Focus on a premier Pacific Island medical college. *Journal of Educational Evaluation for Health Professions, 9*(11). doi:10.3352/jeehp.2012.9.11

FairTest. (2007). *The ACT: Biased, inaccurate and misused.* Jamaica Plain, MA: Author. Retrieved from http://www.fairtest.org/act-biased-inaccurate-and-misused

FairTest. (2014). *Colleges and universities that do not use SAT/ACT scores for admitting substantial numbers of students to bachelor degree programs.* Jamaica Plain, MA: Author. Retrieved from http://www.fairtest.org/university/optional

Farmer v. Ramsay et al., U.S. District Court for the District of Maryland, case No. L-98-1585 (1998).

Farrington, C. A., Roderick, M., Allensworth, E., Nagaoka, J., Keyes, T. S., Johnson, D. W., & Beechum, N. O. (2012). *Teaching adolescents to become learners: The role of noncognitive factors in shaping school performance; A critical literature review* (ERIC ED542543). Chicago, IL: Consortium on Chicago School Research.

Farver, A. S., Sedlacek, W. E., & Brooks, G. C., Jr. (1975). Longitudinal predictions of university grades for Blacks and Whites. *Measurement and Evaluation in Guidance, 7*, 243–250.

Faubert, M. (1992). *Cognitive and ego development of successful African-American rural youth: Deliberate psychological education* (Unpublished dissertation). North Carolina State University, Raleigh, NC.

Faubert, M., & Sedlacek, W. E. (2008, December). *Applications of noncognitive variables in alternative schools.* Presentation at the annual Principal Retreat-BPL Learning, Seattle, WA.

Fauria, R. M., & Zellner, L. J. (2014, November). College students speak success. *Journal of Adult Development.* doi:10.1007/s10804–014–9203–0

Findlinson, N., Strong, K., & Blackwelder, T. (2014, March–April). *Brigham Young University's holistic review: More than just grades and test scores.* Paper presented at the American Association of Collegiate Registrars and Admissions Officers annual meeting, Denver, CO.

Fisher and Michalewicz v. University of Texas No. 09-50822, Fifth Circuit Court of Appeals (2009), p. 22.

Fisher v. University of Texas et al. No. 14-981, U.S. Supreme Court (June 23, 2016).

Fitzgerald, L. F., Shullman, S. L., Bailey, N., Richards, M., Swecker, J., Gold, Y., Ormerod, M., & Weitzman, L. (1988). The incidence and dimensions of sexual harassment in academia and the workplace. *Journal of Vocational Behavior, 32*, 152–175.

Fleming, J. (1994). *Blacks in college.* San Francisco, CA: Jossey-Bass.

Forrer, S. E., Sedlacek, W. E., & Agarie, N. (1977). Racial attitudes of Japanese university students. *Research in Higher Education, 6,* 125–137.

Foster, M. E., Sedlacek, W. E., Hardwick, M. W., & Silver, A. E. (1977). Student affairs staff attitudes toward commuters. *Journal of College Student Personnel, 18,* 291–297.

Fowler, J. W. (1981). *Stages of faith: The psychology of human development and the quest for meaning.* San Francisco, CA: Harper San Francisco.

Fox, J. W. (1995). *Attitudes of heterosexual African American resident assistants toward lesbians and gay students at historically Black universities* (Unpublished master's thesis). University of Maryland, College Park, MD.

Frankenburg, R. (1993). *The social construction of Whiteness: White women, race matters.* Minneapolis, MN: University of Minnesota Press.

Fredericksen, N. O. (1954). The evaluation of personal and social qualities. In F. H Bowles et al., *College admissions* (pp. 93–105). New York, NY: New York College Entrance Examination Board.

Fries-Britt, S., & Turner, B. (2002). Uneven stories: Successful Black collegians at a Black and a White campus. *Review of Higher Education, 25,* 315–330.

Fuertes, J. N., Miville, M. L., Mohr, J. J., Sedlacek, W. E., & Gretchen, D. (2000). Factor structure and short form of the Miville–Guzman Universality–Diversity Scale. *Measurement and Evaluation in Counseling and Development, 33*(3), 157–169.

Fuertes, J. N., & Sedlacek, W. E. (1993). Barriers to the leadership development of Hispanics in higher education. *National Association of Student Personnel Administrators Journal, 30,* 277–283.

Fuertes, J. N., & Sedlacek, W. E. (1994). Predicting the academic success of Hispanic college students using SAT scores. *College Student Journal, 28,* 350–352.

Fuertes, J. N., & Sedlacek, W. E. (1995). Using noncognitive variables to predict the grades and retention of Hispanic students. *College Student Affairs Journal, 14*(2), 30–36.

Fuertes, J. N., Sedlacek, W. E., & Liu, W. M. (1994). Using the SAT and noncognitive variables to predict the grades and retention of Asian-American university students. *Measurement and Evaluation in Counseling and Development, 27,* 74–84.

Fuertes, J. N., Sedlacek, W. E., Roger, P. R., & Mohr, J. J. (2000). Correlates of universal-diverse orientation among first-year university students. *Journal of the First-Year Experience and Students in Transition, 12*(1), 45–59.

Fuertes, J., Sedlacek, W. E., & Westbrook, F. D. (1993). A needs assessment of Hispanic students at a predominantly White university. In G. M. Gonzalez, I. Alvarado, & A. S. Segrera (Eds.), *Challenges of cultural and racial diversity to counseling* (Mexico City Conference Proceedings Vol. 2, pp. 44–47). Alexandria, VA: American Counseling Association.

Garcia, M., Hudgins, C. A., McTighe Musil, C., Nettles, M. T., Sedlacek, W. E., & Smith, D. G. (2001). *Assessing campus diversity initiatives: A guide for campus practitioners.* Washington, DC: Association of American Colleges and Universities.

Garrod, A., & Larimore, C. (Eds.). (1997). *First person, first peoples: Native American college graduates tell their stories.* Ithaca, NY: Cornell University Press.

Geneen, H. S. (n.d.). Retrieved from http://www.brainyquote.com/quotes/quotes/h/haroldsge109095.html

George, B. L., & Tingson-Gatuz, C. (2014, February). *High impact practices: Creating a culture of completion.* Paper presented at Retention Conference, Oakland University, MI.

Gerson, S. S., & Sedlacek, W. E. (1992). Student attitudes toward "JAPS": The new anti-Semitism. *College Student Affairs Journal, 11*(3), 44–53.

Gibbon, E. (n.d.). Retrieved from https://www.brainyquote.com/quotes/quotes/e/edwardgibb119400.html

Gilman, L. J. (1983). *Assisting evangelicals in presenting a positive witness to Mormons* (Unpublished doctoral dissertation No. 94941). Golden Gate Baptist Theological Seminary, Mill Valley, CA.

Goldberg, L. R. (1990). An alternative "description of personality": The Big-Five factor structure. *Journal of Personality and Social Psychology, 99,* 1216–1229.

Gratz and Hamacher v. Bollinger et al., U.S. Court of Appeals for the Sixth Circuit, No. 02-516 (2002).

Greene, B. (2011). *The hidden reality: Parallel universes and the hidden laws of the cosmos.* New York, NY: Vintage Books.

Gribben, A. (2011). *Mark Twain's adventures of Tom Sawyer and Huckleberry Finn: The New South edition.* Montgomery, AL. New South.

Grutter v. Bollinger et al., U.S. Court of Appeals for the Sixth Circuit, No. 02-241 (2002).

Guinier, L. (2015). *The tyranny of the meritocracy: Democratizing higher education in America.* Boston, MA: Beacon Press.

Gutierrez, R., & Irving, S. E. (2012). *Latino(a) and Black students and mathematics.* Washington, DC: Jobs for the Future. Retrieved from http://www.jff.org/sites/default/files/publications/materials/Students%20and%20Mathematics_0.pdf

Harber, K. D., Gorman, J. L., Gengaro, F. P., Butisingh, S., Tsang, W., & Ouellette, R. (2012). Students' race and teachers' social support affect the positive feedback bias in public schools. *Journal of Educational Psychology, 104*(4), 1149–1161. doi:10.1037/a0028110

Hargrove, B., & Sedlacek, W. E. (1997). Counseling interests among entering Black university students over a ten-year period. *Journal of the Freshman Year Experience and Students in Transition, 9*(2), 83–98.

Harper, S. R. (2012). *Black male student success in higher education: A report from the national Black male college achievement study.* Philadelphia, PA: University of Pennsylvania Center for the Study of Race and Equity in Education.

Harper, S. R. (2016). *Black male student-athletes and racial inequities in NCAA Division I revenue-generating college sports: 2016 edition.* Philadelphia, PA: University of Pennsylvania Center for the Study of Race and Equity in Education.

Harrington, H. J. (n.d.). Retrieved from http://www.goodreads.com/quotes/632992-measurement-is-the-first-step-that-leads-to-control-and

Hawking, S. (n.d.). Retrieved from http://www.brainyquote.com/quotes/quotes/s/stephenhaw135875.html

Hedgpeth, D. (2015, March). *U of Md. student will not return to school after racist, sexist e-mail.* Retrieved from https://www.washingtonpost.com/local/education/u-of-md-student-will-not-return-to-school-after-racist-sexist-e-mail/2015/03/26/af63f532-d3ab-11e4-ab77-9646eea6a4c7_story.html

Helm, E. G., Prieto, D. O., & Sedlacek, W. E. (1997). Simulated minority admissions exercise at Louisiana State University School of Medicine: An evaluation. *Journal of the National Medical Association, 89*(9), 601–605.

Helm, E., Sedlacek, W. E., & Prieto, D. (1998a). Career advising issues for African American entering students. *Journal of the First-Year Experience and Students in Transition, 10*(2), 77–87.

Helm, E. G., Sedlacek, W. E., & Prieto, D. O. (1998b). The relationship between attitudes toward diversity and overall satisfaction of university students by race. *Journal of College Counseling, 1*(2), 111–120.

Helms, J. E. (1992). Why is there no study of cultural equivalence in standardized cognitive ability testing? *American Psychologist, 47,* 1083–1101.

Helms, J. E. (1995). An update of Helm's White and people of color racial identity models. In J. G. Ponterotto, J. M. Casas, L. A. Suzuki, & C. M. Alexander (Eds.), *Handbook of multicultural counseling* (pp. 181–198). Thousand Oaks, CA: Sage.

Helms, J. E. (2009). Defense of tests prevents objective consideration of validity and fairness. *American Psychologist, 64,* 283–284.

Henley, A., Miklaucic, S., Sandeford-Lyons, S., Jones-Cameron, S., & Medlock, G. (2016, June). *Casting the mold: Outlining the strengths-based perspective.* Charlotte, NC: Center for the Study of Metacognitive Variables, Johnson C. Smith University.

Herman, M. H., & Sedlacek, W. E. (1973). Sexist attitudes among male university students. *Journal of College Student Personnel, 14,* 544–548.

Hicks, D. (2003). *Religion and the workplace: Pluralism, spirituality, and leadership.* Cambridge, UK: Cambridge University Press.

Hill, M. D., & Sedlacek, W. E. (1994). *Using historical research methods in higher education* (Research Report No. 8–94). College Park, MD: University of Maryland Counseling Center.

Hill, W. (1995). *The academic retention and graduation status of African American students: Factors in a public university* (Unpublished doctoral dissertation). North Carolina State University, Raleigh, NC.

Hirt, J., Hoffman, M. A., & Sedlacek, W. E. (1983). Attitudes toward changing sex roles of male varsity athletes vs. non-athletes: Developmental perspectives. *Journal of College Student Personnel, 24,* 33–38.

Hiss, W. C., & Franks, V. W. (2014). *Defining promise: Optional standardized testing policies in American college and university admissions.* National Association of College Admission Counselors. Retrieved from http://www.nacacnet.org/research/research-data/nacac-research/Documents/DefiningPromise.pdf

Hoey, J. J. (1997). *Developing a retention risk indicator at North Carolina State University.* Raleigh, NC: North Carolina State University.

Hope, E. C., Chavous, T. M., Jagers, R. J., & Sellers, R. M. (2013). Connecting self-esteem and achievement: Diversity in academic identification and disidentification patterns among Black college students. *American Educational Research Journal, 50*(5), 1122–1151. doi:10.3102/0002831213500333

Hope, E. C., Hoggard, L. S., & Thomas, A. (2016). Emerging into adulthood in the face of racial discrimination: Physiological, psychological, and sociopolitical consequences for African American youth. *Translational Issues in Psychological Science, 1*(4), 342–351.

Hopple, G. W. (1976). Protest attitudes and social class: Working class authoritarianism revisited. *Sociology and Social Research, 60,* 229–246.

Hubbard, D. W. (2014). *How to measure anything: Finding the value of "intangibles" in business.* Hoboken, NJ: John Wiley.

Hune, S., & Chan, K. S. (1997). Special focus: Asian Pacific American demographic and educational trends. In D. J. Carter & R. Wilson (Eds.), *Fifteenth annual status report on minorities in higher education* (pp. 39–67). Washington, DC: American Council on Education.

Hurtado, S. (1992). The campus racial climate: Contexts of conflict. *Journal of Higher Education, 63,* 539–569.

Jansen, T., & Carton, J. S. (1999). The effect of locus of control and task difficulty on procrastination. *Journal of Genetic Psychology, 160*(4), 436–442.

Jaschik, S. (2016, June). An unlikely campaign to move beyond GRE scores. *Inside Higher Education.* Retrieved from https://www.insidehighered.com/news/2016/06/06/ets-plans-encourage-graduate-departments-de-emphasize-gre

Jencks, C., & Crouse, J. (1982). Should we relabel the SAT—Or replace it? In W. B. Schrader (Ed.), *Measurement, guidance, and program improvement: Proceedings of the 1981 ETS Invitational Conference.* San Francisco, CA: Jossey-Bass.

Johnson C. Smith University. (2012). *Metropolitan college report to the board of trustees.* Charlotte, NC: Author.

Jones, S. R. (1997). Voices of identity and difference: A qualitative exploration of the multiple dimensions of identity development in women college students. *Journal of College Student Development, 38,* 376–385.

Ju, S., Zhang, D., & Katsiyannis, A. (2013). The causal relationship between academic self-concept and academic achievement for students with disabilities: An analysis of SEELS data. *Journal of Disability Policy Studies, 24*(1), 4–14. doi:10.1177/1044207311427727

Kalsbeek, D. H. (2013). Reframing retention strategy: A focus on promise [Special issue]. *New Directions for Higher Education, 2013*(116), 49–57. doi:10.1002/he.20045

Kalsbeek, D. H., Sandlin, M., & Sedlacek, W. E. (2013). Employing noncognitive variables to improve admissions, and increase student diversity and retention. *Strategic Enrollment Management Quarterly, 1,* 132–150. doi:10.1002/sem3.20016

Kaplan, R. M., & Saccuzzo, D. P. (2009). *Psychological testing: Principles, applications, and issues.* Belmont, CA: Wadsworth.

Kelley, T. L. (1927). *Interpretation of educational measurements.* Yonkers, NY: World Book.

Khalil, H., & Ebner, M. (2013). How satisfied are you with your MOOC? A research study on interaction in huge online courses. In J. Herrington et al. (Eds.), *Proceedings of world conference on educational multimedia, hypermedia and telecommunications* (pp. 830–839). Chesapeake, VA: AACE.

Kimball, R. L., & Sedlacek, W. E. (1971). Differences between participants and nonparticipants in campus demonstrations. *College Student Journal, 5,* 72–74.

King, M. L., Jr. (n.d.). Retrieved from http://www.brainyquote.com/quotes/quotes/m/martinluth121065.html

Knapp, L. G., Kelly, J. E., Whitmore, R. W., Wu, S., & Gallego, L. M. (2002). *Enrollment in postsecondary institutions, fall 2000 and financial statistics, fiscal year 2000* (No. 2002212.) Washington, DC: National Center for Education Statistics.

Knight, G. D., & Sedlacek, W. E. (1981). *Religious orientation and the concept of God held by university students* (Research Report No. 7–81). College Park, MD: University of Maryland Counseling Center.

Knight, G. D., Seefeldt, C., & Sedlacek, W. E. (1984). *Measuring the attitudes of adults toward children* (Research Report No. 4–84). College Park, MD: University of Maryland Counseling Center.

Kodama, C. M., McEwen, M. K., Liang, C. T. H., & Lee, S. (2002). An Asian American perspective on psychosocial development theory. In M. K. McEwen, C. M. Kodama, A. N. Alvarez, S. Lee, & C. T. H. Liang (Eds.), *Working with Asian American college students* (pp. 45–60). San Francisco, CA: Jossey-Bass.

Komives, S. R., Lucas, N., & McMahon, T. R. (1998). *Exploring leadership: For college students who want to make a difference.* San Francisco, CA: Jossey-Bass.

Komives, S. R., Owen, J. E., Mainella, F. C., & Osteen, L. (2006). A leadership identity development model: Applications from a grounded theory. *Journal of College Student Development, 47*(4), 401–418.

Koretz, D. (1993). New report of the Vermont project documents challenges. *National Council on Measurement in Education Quarterly Newsletter, 1*(4), 1–2.

Kosoko-Lasaki, O., Sonnino, R. E., & Voytko, M. L. (2006). Mentoring for women and underrepresented minority faculty and students: Experience at two institutions of higher education. *Journal of the National Medical Association, 98*(9), 1449–1459.

Kuh, G. D. (1993). In their own words: What students learn outside the classroom. *American Educational Research Journal, 30,* 277–304.

Kuh, G. D., Kinzie, J., Schuh, J. H., & Whitt, E. J. (2011). Fostering student success in hard times. *Change: The Magazine of Higher Learning, 43*(4), 13–19.

Lahr, H., Pheatt, L., Dougherty, K., Jones, S., Natow, R., & Reddy, V. (2014, November). *Unintended impacts of performance funding on community colleges and universities in three states* (Working Paper No. 78). New York NY: Community College Research Center, Columbia University.

LaMahieu, P. G., Gitomer, D. H., & Eresch, J. T. (1995). Portfolios in large-scale assessment: Difficult but not impossible. *Educational Measurement: Issues and Practice, 14,* 11–28.

LaSure, G. E. (1993, August). *Ethnic differences and the effects of racism on college adjustment.* Paper presented at the annual meeting of the American Psychological Association, Toronto, Canada.

Lathram, B. (2015, February). *8 noncognitive competencies for college and career readiness.* Retrieved from http://gettingsmart.com/2015/02/8-non-cognitive-competencies-college-career-readiness/

Lea, H. D., Sedlacek, W. E., & Stewart, S. S. (1980). Faculty attitudes toward resident and commuting students. *Southern College Personnel Association Journal, 2,* 23–32.

Lechuga, V. M., Clerc, L. N., & Howell, A. K. (2009). Power, privilege, and learning: Facilitating encountered situations to promote social justice. *Journal of College Student Development, 50,* 229–244.

Lee, C. C. (1984). An investigation of psychosocial variables related to academic success for rural Black adolescents. *Journal of Negro Education, 53,* 424–434.

Lee, C. C. (1985). Successful rural Black adolescents: A psychosocial profile. *Adolescence, 20,* 129–142.

Lemann, N. (2000). *The big test: The secret history of the American meritocracy.* New York, NY: Farrar, Straus & Giroux.

Leong, F. L. T. (1986). Counseling and psychotherapy with Asian-Americans: Review of the literature. *Journal of Counseling Psychology, 33,* 196–206.

Leong, F. T. L., & Schneller, G. (1997). White Americans' attitudes toward Asian Americans in social situations: An empirical examination of potential stereotypes, bias, and prejudice. *Journal of Multicultural Counseling and Development, 25,* 68–78.

Liang, C. T. H., & Sedlacek, W. E. (2003a). Attitudes of White student services practitioners toward Asian Americans. *National Association of Student Personnel Administrators Journal, 40*(3), 30–42. Retrieved from http://publications.naspa.org/naspajournal/vol40/iss3/art2

Liang, C. T. H., & Sedlacek, W. E. (2003b). Utilizing factor analysis to understand the needs of Asian American students. *Journal of College Student Development, 44*(2), 260–266.

Linnell, D. (2001). *College students' attitudes toward two disability populations: Crime victims and police officers* (Unpublished doctoral dissertation). University of Maryland, College Park, MD.

Liu, W. M., & Sedlacek, W. E. (1999). Differences in leadership and co-curricular perception among male and female Asian Pacific American college students. *Journal of the Freshman Year Experience, 11,* 93–114.

Loh, W. D. (2015, March). *Words matter.* Retrieved from http://www.president.umd.edu/statements/campus_message031715.cfm

Longerbeam, S. L., & Sedlacek, W. E. (2006). Attitudes toward diversity and living-learning outcomes among first- and second-year college students. *National Association of Student Personnel Administrators Journal, 49*(1), 40–55.

Longerbeam, S. L., Sedlacek, W. E., & Alatorre, H. M. (2004). In their own voices: Latino student retention. *National Association of Student Personnel Administra-*

tors Journal, *41*(3), 538–550. Retrieved from http://publications.naspa.org/ naspajournal/vol41/iss3/art9

Longerbeam, S. L., Sedlacek, W. E., Balón, D. G., & Alimo, C. (2005). The multicultural myth: A study of multicultural program organizations at three public research universities. *Journal of College Student Development*, *46*(3), 88–97.

Loo, C. M., & Rolison, G. (1986). Alienation of ethnic minority students at a predominantly White university. *Journal of Higher Education*, *57*, 58–77.

Lopez, F. G., Lent, R. W., Brown, S. D., & Gore, P. A. (1997). Role of sociocognitive expectation in high school students' mathematics-related interest and performance. *Journal of Counseling Psychology*, *44*(1), 44–52.

Lopez, N., Self, K., & Karnitz, J. (2009). Developing a tool for systematic inclusion of non-academic factors in dental school admissions: Towards building diversity in the dental workforce. *Journal of Dental Education*, *73*, 1347–1352.

Majors, M. S., & Sedlacek, W. E. (2001). Using factor analysis to organize student services. *Journal of College Student Development*, *42*(3), 272–278.

Maki, M. T., & Kitano, H. H. L. (2002). Counseling Asian Americans. In P. B. Pedersen, J. G. Draguns, W. J. Lonner, & J. E. Trimble (Eds.), *Counseling across cultures* (5th ed., pp. 109–131). Thousand Oaks, CA: Sage.

Mallinckrodt, B., & Sedlacek, W. E. (2009). Student retention and the use of campus facilities by race. *National Association of Student Personnel Administrators Journal*, *46*(4), 566–572.

Manese, J. E., & Sedlacek, W. E. (1985). Changes in religious behavior and attitudes of college students: 1973–1983. *Counseling and Values*, *30*, 74–77.

Mann, C. C. (2005). *1491: New revelations of the Americas before Columbus*. New York, NY: Knopf.

Marquardt, P. D. (2009). *The effect of accountability-based testing on college bound students: A case study of the Virginia Standards of Learning*. Retrieved from http://ssm.com/absrtact=1405440

Marsh, H. W., Byrne, B. M., & Shavelson, R. J. (1988). A multifaceted academic self-concept: Its hierarchical structure and its relation to academic achievement. *Journal of Educational Psychology*, *80*(3), 366–380. Retrieved from http://dx.doi .org/10.1037/0022–0663.80.3.366

Marshall, D. M. A. (1983). *Attitudes of able-bodied students in integrated and non-integrated residence halls toward blind and wheelchair-bound students* (Unpublished master's thesis). University of Maryland, College Park, MD.

Martin, J. E. (2013, February). *Building the and/plus assessment package*. Retrieved from https://admission.org/blogs/think-tank-blog/item/251-building-the-and-plus-assessment-package

McClellend, K., & Auster, C. J. (1990). Public platitudes and hidden tensions: Racial climates at predominantly White liberal arts colleges. *Journal of Higher Education*, *61*, 607–642.

McGee, E. O. (2009). *A model of mathematical resilience: Black college students negotiating success in mathematics and engineering*. Paper presented at the pre-session of the annual meeting of the National Council of Teachers of Mathematics, Washington, DC.

McNairy, F. G. (1996). The challenge for higher education: Retaining students of color. In I. H. Johnson & A. J. Ottens (Eds.), *Leveling the playing field: Promoting academic success for students of color* (pp. 3–14). San Francisco, CA: Jossey-Bass.

McQuilkin, J. I., Freitag, C. B., & Harris, J. L. (1990). Attitudes of college students toward handicapped persons. *Journal of College Student Development, 31,* 17–22.

McTighe Musil, C., Garcia, M., Hudgins, C. A., Nettles, M. T., Sedlacek, W. E., & Smith, D. G. (1999). *To form a more perfect union: Campus diversity initiatives.* Washington, DC: Association of American Colleges and Universities.

Meyer, I. H. (2003). Prejudice, social stress, and mental health in lesbian, gay, and bisexual populations: Conceptual issues and research evidence. *Psychological Bulletin, 129*(5), 674–697. doi:10.1037/0033-2909.129.5.674

Milem, J. F., & Berger, J. B. (1997). A modified model of college student persistence: Exploring the relationship between Astin's theory of involvement and Tinto's theory of student departure. *Journal of College Student Development, 38,* 387–400.

Miller, C., & Stassun, K. (2014, June). A test that fails. *Nature, 510,* 303–304. doi:10.1038/nj7504-303a

Miller, M., & Lu, M. (2003). Serving non-traditional students in e-learning environments: Building successful communities in the virtual campus. *Educational Media International, 40*(1–2), 163–169.

Min, P. G., & Kim, J. H. (2002). *Religions in Asian America: Building faith communities.* New York, NY: Altamira Press.

Minatoya, L. Y., & Sedlacek, W. E. (1983). The Situational Attitude Scale toward women (SASW): A means to measure environmental sexism. *Journal of the National Association for Women Deans, Administrators, and Counselors, 47*(1), 26–30.

Mitchell, A. A., Sergent, M. T., & Sedlacek, W. E. (1997). Mapping the university learning environment. *National Association of Student Personnel Administrators Journal, 35,* 20–28.

Miville, M. L., Carlozzi, A. F., Gushue, G. V., Schara, S. L., & Ueda, M. (2006). Mental health counselor qualities for a diverse clientele: Linking empathy, universal-diverse orientation, and emotional intelligence. *Journal of Mental Health Counseling, 28*(2), 151–165.

Miville, M. L., Molla, B., & Sedlacek, W. E. (1992). Attitudes of tolerance for diversity among university freshmen. *Journal of the Freshman Year Experience, 4*(1), 95–110.

Miville, M. L., & Sedlacek, W. E. (1994). Attitudes of freshmen toward Arab-Americans: A university campus dilemma. *Journal of the Freshman Year Experience, 6*(2), 77–88.

Moffitt, T. E., Arseneault, L., Belsky, D., Dickson, N., Hancox, R. J., Harrington, H., . . . Caspi, A. (2011). A gradient of childhood self-control predicts health, wealth, and public safety. *Proceedings of the National Academy of Sciences of the United States of America, 108*(7), 2693–2698.

Mohr, J. J., Israel, T., & Sedlacek, W. E. (2001). Counselors' attitudes regarding bisexuality as predictors of counselors' clinical responses: An analogue study of a female bisexual client. *Journal of Counseling Psychology, 48*, 212–222.

Mohr, J. J., & Sedlacek, W. E. (2000). Perceived barriers to friendship with lesbians and gay men among university students. *Journal of College Student Development, 41*(1), 70–79.

Montgomery College: Closing the Achievement Gap Task Force. (2013, December). *Final report and recommendations.* Rockville, MD: Author.

Moore, S. K. (1995). *Indicators of academic success and the student characteristics of international students at Santa Monica College* (Unpublished doctoral dissertation). Pepperdine University, Malibu, CA.

Moyer, J. (2015, March). *University of Oklahoma fraternity closed after racist chant.* Retrieved from http://www.washingtonpost.com/news/morning-mix/wp/2015/03/09/university-of-oklahoma-fraternity-suspended-after-racist-chant/

Muchinsky, P. M. (1987). *Psychology applied to work: An introduction to industrial and organizational psychology.* Chicago, IL: Dorsey Press.

Musk, E. (2014, June). *All our patent are belong to you.* Retrieved from http://www.teslamotors.com/blog/all-our-patent-are-belong-you

Nadal, K. L. (2010). Gender microaggressions: Implications for mental health. In M. A. Paludi (Ed.), *Feminism and women's rights worldwide: Mental health and physical health* (Vol. 2, pp. 155–175). Santa Barbara, CA: Praeger.

National Center for Education Statistics, U.S. Department of Education. (2013). *Digest of Education Statistics, 2012* (NCES 2014–015). Washington, DC: Author.

Native Americans unite to speak out against racially offensive mascot name. (n.d.). Retrieved from http://www.changethemascot.org/wp-content/uploads/2014/09/Native-Nations-Unite-to-Speak-Out-Against-Racially-Offensive-Mascot-Name.pdf

Neville, H. A., Heppner, P., & Wang, L. (1997). Relations among racial identity attitudes, perceived stressors, and coping styles in African American college students. *Journal of Counseling and Development, 75*, 303–311.

New, J. (2015, April). *Punishment, post-Oklahoma.* Retrieved from https://www.insidehighered.com/news/2015/04/01/some-college-leaders-are-responding-quickly-racist-and-sexist-incidents

Nilson-Whitten, M. K., Morder, B., & Kapakla, G. M. (2007). *Relationship between locus of control, optimism, and academic performance.* Proceedings of the annual conference of the New Jersey Counseling Association, Eatontown NJ.

Nisbet, J., Ruble, V. E., & Schurr, K. T. (1982). Predictors of academic success with high-risk college students. *Journal of College Student Personnel, 23*, 227–235.

Noonan, B. M., Sedlacek, W. E., & Veerasamy, S. (2005). Employing noncognitive variables in admitting and advising community college students. *Community College Journal of Research and Practice, 29*, 463–469.

Obama, B. (2015, June). *Podcast interview.* Retrieved from http://potus.wtfpod.com/

O'Callaghan, K. W., & Bryant, C. (1990). Noncognitive variables: A key to Black-American academic success at a military academy. *Journal of College Student Development, 31*, 121–126.

O'Neal, N. (2010, July). *"Anchor baby" phrase has controversial history.* ABCNews.com. Retrieved from http://abcnews.go.com/Politics/anchor-baby-phrase-controversial-history/story?id=11066543

Osgood, C. E., Suci, G. J., & Tannenbaum, P. H. (1957). *The measurement of meaning.* Urbana, IL: University of Illinois Press.

Ossana, S. M., Helms, J. E., & Leonard, M. M. (1992). Do "womanist" identity attitudes influence college women's self-esteem and perceptions of environmental bias? *Journal of Counseling and Development, 70*, 402–408.

Owens, T., & Beaty, R. (2016). *Faces of Change 2.* Fayetville, GA: Foundation for Educational Success.

Paniagua, F. A. (1994). *Assessing and treating culturally diverse clients: A practical guide.* Thousand Oaks, CA: Sage.

Park, H., McLean, A., Roberts, G., & Tse, A. (2012). *The events leading to the shooting of Trayvon Martin. New York Times.* Retrieved from http://www.nytimes.com/interactive/2012/04/02/us/the-events-leading-to-the-shooting-of-trayvon-martin.html?_r=0

Pascarella, E. T., & Terenzini, P. T. (1991). *How college affects students: Findings and insights from twenty years of research.* San Francisco, CA: Jossey-Bass.

Patai, R. (1973). *The Arab mind.* New York, NY: Charles Scribner's Sons.

Patterson, A. M., Jr., Sedlacek, W. E., & Perry, F. W. (1984). Perceptions of Blacks and Hispanics in two campus environments. *Journal of College Student Personnel, 25*, 513–518.

Patterson, A., Sedlacek, W. E., & Scales, W. R. (1988). The other minority: Disabled student backgrounds and attitudes toward their university and its services. *Journal of Postsecondary Education and Disability, 6*, 86–94.

Peabody, S. A., & Sedlacek, W. E. (1982). Attitudes of younger university students toward older students. *Journal of College Student Personnel, 23*, 140–143.

Perrin, N. (1998, October). How students at Dartmouth came to deserve better grades. *Chronicle of Higher Education*, p. A68.

Perrone, K. M., Sedlacek, W. E., & Alexander, C. M. (2001). Gender and ethnic differences in career goal attainment. *Career Development Quarterly, 50*, 168–178.

Pfeifer, C. M., Jr., & Sedlacek, W. E. (1971). The validity of academic predictors for Black and White students at a predominantly White university. *Journal of Educational Measurement, 8*, 253–261.

Pfeifer, C. M., Jr., & Sedlacek, W. E. (1974). Predicting Black student grades with nonintellectual measures. *Journal of Negro Education, 43*, 67–76.

Phillips Exeter Academy. (2013). The Sedlacek eight in play. In Secondary School Admission Test Board (Ed.), *Think tank on the future of assessment* (p. 19). Princeton, NJ: Secondary School Admission Test Board.

Posselt, J. R. (2016). *Inside graduate admissions: Merit, diversity and faculty gatekeeping.* Cambridge, MA: Harvard University Press.

Powell, K. (2013, December). Higher education on the lookout for true grit. *Nature, 504*, 471–473. doi:10.1038/nj7480–471a

Prieto, D. O., Bashook, P. G., D'Costa, A. G., Elliott, P. R., Jarecky, R. K., Kahrahrah, B., . . . Sedlacek, W. E. (1978). *Simulated minority admissions exercise workbook* (Rev. ed.). Washington, DC: Association of American Medical Colleges.

Prieto, D. O., Quinones, E., Elliott, P., Goldner, A., & Sedlacek, W. E. (1986). *Simulated minority admissions exercise* (3rd ed.). Washington, DC: Association of American Medical Colleges.

Quintana, S. M., Vogel, M. C., & Ybarra, V. C. (1991). Meta-analysis of Latino students' adjustment in higher education. *Hispanic Journal of Behavioral Science, 13*, 155–168.

Racism. (n.d.). *Race.* Retrieved from http://dictionary.reference.com/browse/race

Ranasinghe, P., Ellawela, A., & Gunatilake, S. B. (2012). Non-cognitive characteristics predicting academic success among medical students in Sri Lanka. *BMC Medical Education, 12*, 66. doi:10.1186/1472–6920–12–66

Ranney, R. R., Wilson, M. B., & Bennett, R. B. (2005). Evaluation of applicants to predoctoral dental education programs: Review of the literature. *Journal of Dental Education, 69*, 95–106.

Reeve, C. L., & Hakel, M. D. (2001, June). *Criterion issues and practical considerations concerning noncognitive assessment in graduate admissions.* Paper presented at the symposium on Noncognitive Assessments for Graduate Admissions, Graduate Record Examinations Board, Toronto, Canada.

Rich, A. (n.d.). Retrieved from http://www.goodreads.com/quotes/44367-that-s-why-i-want-to-speak-to-you-now-to

Rickard, J. (2015). University of Puget Sound gives applicants an alternative to standardized test scores. Retrieved from pugetsound.edu/admission/apply/optional-application-questions

Riddle-Crilly, M. (2009). *What are the identifiable causes of low self-esteem among lesbian, gay, bisexual, or transgender individuals?* (Unpublished B.A. thesis). Chapman University College, Orange, CA.

Roberts, K. J. (1998, November). *Thurstone's method of equal-appearing intervals in measuring attitudes: An old method that is not forgotten.* Paper presented at the Mid-South Educational Research Association annual meeting, New Orleans, LA.

Rogers, E. M. (2003). *Diffusion of innovations* (5th ed.). New York, NY: Free Press.

Rojstaczer, S., & Healy, C. (2010, March). Grading in American colleges and universities. *Teachers College Record.* ID No. 15928. Retrieved from http://www.tcrecord.org

Rojstaczer, S., & Healy, C. (2012). Where A is ordinary: The evolution of American college and university grading, 1940–2009. *Teachers College Record, 114*(7). ID No. 16473. Retrieved from http://www.tcrecord.org

Roorda, M. (2016, March). *ACT statement on ACT-SAT concordance.* Retrieved from http://www.act.org/content/act/en/about-act/perspectivesandhappenings.html

Roper, L., & Sedlacek, W. E. (1988). Student affairs professionals in academic roles: A course on racism. *National Association of Student Personnel Administrators Journal, 26*(1), 27–32.

Rotter, J. B. (1966). Generalized expectancies for internal versus external control of reinforcement. *Psychological Monographs, 80*(1), 1–28. doi:10.1037/h0092976

Rucker, J. M., Neblett, E. W., & Anyiwo, N. (2014). Racial identity, perpetrator race, racial composition of primary community, and mood responses to discrimination. *Journal of Black Psychology, 40*(6), 539–562.

Sackett, P. R., Borneman, M. J., & Connelly, B. S. (2008). High stakes testing in higher education and employment: Appraising the evidence for validity and fairness. *American Psychologist, 63*(4), 215–227. doi:10.1037/0003-066X.63.4.215

Sahin, I. (2006). Detailed review of Rogers' diffusion of innovations theory and educational technology-related studies based on Rogers' theory. *The Turkish Online Journal of Educational Technology, 5*(2), Article 3.

Sánchez, E. L. (2014, April). *4 messed up sexist things that happen to women of color: Gender and racial inequalities combined with sexism ravage both our physical and mental health.* Retrieved from http://www.alternet.org/gender/4-messed-sexist-things-happen-women-color

Sandler, B. R. (1987). The classroom climate: Still a chilly one for women. In C. Lasser (Ed.), *Educating men and women together: Coeducation in a changing world* (pp. 113–123). Urbana, IL: University of Illinois Press.

Sandlin, M. L. (2008). The "Insight Résumé": Oregon State University's approach to holistic assessment. In B. Lauren (Ed.), *The college admissions officer's guide* (pp. 99–108). Washington, DC: American Association of Collegiate Registrars and Admissions Officers.

Sandlin, M. L., & Sedlacek, W. E. (2013). *Employing noncognitive variables to improve admissions and increase student retention.* AACRAO Consulting Solutions Article No. 0113. Retrieved from http://williamsedlacek.info/files/ACS%20Noncognitive-Jan-2013.pdf

Santos, S. J., & Reigadas, E. (2002). Latinos in higher education: An evaluation of a university faculty mentoring program. *Journal of Hispanic Higher Education, 1*, 40–50.

Sawyer, R. (2008). *Benefits of additional coursework and improved course performance in preparing students for college* (ACT Research Report 2008-1). Iowa City, IA: ACT.

Schlosser, L. Z., & Sedlacek, W. E. (2001a). Hate on campus: A model for evaluating, understanding, and handling critical incidents. *About Campus, 6*(1), 25–27.

Schlosser, L. Z., & Sedlacek, W. E. (2001b). The relationship between undergraduate students' perceived past academic success and perceived academic self-concept. *Journal of the First-Year Experience and Students in Transition, 13*(2), 93–105.

Schlosser, L. Z., & Sedlacek, W. E. (2003). Christian privilege and respect for religious diversity: Religious holidays on campus. *About Campus, 7*(6), 31–32.

Schmidt, D. K., & Sedlacek, W. E. (1971). An analysis of the attitudes and behavior associated with student demonstrations on the Vietnam War. *College Student Journal, 5*, 44–50.

Schmitt, N., Billington, A., Keeney, J., Reeder, M., Pleskac, T. J., Sinha, R., & Zorzie, M. (2011). *Development and validation of measures of noncognitive college student potential* (Research Report 2011-1). Princeton, NJ: College Board.

Schroeder, K. (2014, December). *Here is the controversial cake that landed one sorority in hot water [Photo]*. Retrieved from http://www.opposingviews.com/i/society/sorority-sister-posts-photo-arguably-racist-birthday-cake

Schuette v. Coalition to Defend Affirmative Action, No. 12-682. US Supreme Court (April 22, 2014).

Schultheis, L. (2014, February). *Should standardized testing submissions be optional? The role of holistic admissions.* Retrieved from http://www.aacrao.org/resources/resources-detail-view/should-standardized-testing-submissions-be-optional

Schwalb, S. J., & Sedlacek, W. E. (1990). Have college student attitudes toward older people changed? *Journal of College Student Development, 31,* 127–132.

Secondary School Admission Test Board. (2013). *Think tank on the future of assessment.* Princeton, NJ: Author.

Secondary School Admission Test Board. (2014, October). *Measuring what matters in admission and beyond.* Retrieved from http://www.admission.org/news/detail.aspx?pageaction=ViewSinglePublicandLinkID=1999andModuleID=28andandNEWSPID=1

Sedlacek, W. E. (1972). Unique predictors of Black student success. *The Advisor (Association of American Medical Colleges), 8,* 2–4.

Sedlacek, W. E. (1974). Issues in predicting Black student success in higher education. *Journal of Negro Education, 43*(4), 512–516.

Sedlacek, W. E. (1976). Recent developments in test bias research. *Compass Points (Maryland Personnel and Guidance Association), 21*(4), 3–4.

Sedlacek, W. E. (1977a). Should higher education students be admitted differentially by race and sex? The evidence. *Journal of the National Association of College Admissions Counselors, 22*(1), 22–24.

Sedlacek, W. E. (1977b). Test bias and the elimination of racism. *Journal of College Student Personnel, 18,* 16–20.

Sedlacek, W. E. (1983). Teaching minority students. In J. H. Cones III, J. Noonan, & D. Janha (Eds.), *Teaching minority students: New directions for teaching and learning* (pp. 39–50). San Francisco, CA: Jossey-Bass.

Sedlacek, W. E. (1987). Blacks in White colleges and universities: Twenty years of research. *Journal of College Student Personnel, 28,* 484–495.

Sedlacek, W. E. (1988). Evaluating student support services. In *Evaluating campus programs and services* (pp. 49–57). San Francisco, CA: Jossey-Bass.

Sedlacek, W. E. (1989, Fall). Noncognitive indicators of student success. *Journal of College Admissions,* No. 125, 2–10.

Sedlacek, W. E. (1991). Using noncognitive variables in advising nontraditional students. *National Academic Advising Association Journal, 11*(1), 75–82.

Sedlacek, W. E. (1993). Employing noncognitive variables in admissions and retention in higher education. In *Achieving diversity: Issues in the recruitment and retention of underrepresented racial/ethnic students in higher educa-*

tion (pp. 33–39). Alexandria, VA: National Association of College Admission Counselors.

Sedlacek, W. E. (1994a). Advising nontraditional students: The big bang or another universe? *National Academic Advising Association Journal, 14*(2), 103–104.

Sedlacek, W. E. (1994b). Issues in advancing diversity through assessment. *Journal of Counseling and Development, 72,* 549–553.

Sedlacek, W. E. (1995a). *Improving racial and ethnic diversity and campus climate at four-year independent Midwest colleges* (An evaluation report of the Lilly Endowment Grant Program). Indianapolis, IN: Lilly Endowment.

Sedlacek, W. E. (1995b). Using research to reduce racism at a university. *Journal of Humanistic Counseling and Development, 33,* 131–140.

Sedlacek, W. E. (1996). An empirical method of determining nontraditional group status. *Measurement and Evaluation in Counseling and Development, 28,* 200–210.

Sedlacek, W. E. (1997). An alternative to standardized tests in higher education. *Higher Education Extension Service.* Retrieved from www.review.org

Sedlacek, W. E. (1998a). Admissions in higher education: Measuring cognitive and noncognitive variables. In D. J. Wilds & R. Wilson (Eds.), *Minorities in higher education 1997–98: Sixteenth annual status report* (pp. 47–71). Washington, DC: American Council on Education.

Sedlacek, W. E. (1998b). Multiple choices for standardized tests. *Priorities, 10,* 1–16.

Sedlacek, W. E. (2000). A campus climate survey: Where to begin. *Diversity Digest, 4*(3), 24–25.

Sedlacek, W. E. (2003a). Alternative admissions and scholarship selection measures in higher education. *Measurement and Evaluation in Counseling and Development, 35*(4), 263–272.

Sedlacek, W. E. (2003b). *Using noncognitive variables in first-year student programs. First Year Assessments Listserv.* Retrieved from http://www.brevard.edu/fyc/listserv/remarks/sedlacek.htm

Sedlacek, W. E. (2004a). A multicultural research program. In F. W. Hale (Ed.), *What makes racial diversity work in higher education?* (pp. 256–271). Sterling, VA: Stylus.

Sedlacek, W. E. (2004b). *Beyond the big test: Noncognitive assessment in higher education.* San Francisco, CA: Jossey-Bass.

Sedlacek, W. E. (2004c). Why we should use noncognitive variables with graduate and professional students. *The Advisor: The Journal of the National Association of Advisors for the Health Professions, 24*(2), 32–39.

Sedlacek, W. E. (2007). Conducting research that makes a difference. In C. C. Lee & G. R. Walz (Eds.), *Counseling for social justice* (pp. 223–237). Alexandria, VA. American Counseling Association.

Sedlacek, W. E. (2008). Using noncognitive variables in K–12 and higher education. In *University of Michigan summit on college outreach and academic success: Summary report from meetings at the School of Education, August 11–12, 2008* (pp. 35–42). Ann Arbor, Michigan.

Sedlacek, W. E. (2010). Noncognitive measures for higher education admissions. In P. L. Peterson, E. Baker, & B. McGaw (Eds.), *International encyclopedia of education* (3rd ed., pp. 845–849). Amsterdam, the Netherlands. Elsevier.

Sedlacek, W. E. (2011). Using noncognitive variables in assessing readiness for higher education. *Readings on Equal Education, 25,* 187–205.

Sedlacek, W. E. (2013). *Closing the success gap for young men of color.* Mendham, NJ: Ten2One.

Sedlacek, W. E. (2014a, February). *Free higher education for all! [Insidetrack Blog].* Retrieved from www.insidetrack.com/wp-content/uploads/2014/10/williamsedlacek_oped.pdf?ba0439

Sedlacek, W. E. (2014b, August). *Noncognitive assessment and its role in recruiting, admissions and post-matriculation programs [WEBinar Sponsored by Innovative Educators].* Retrieved from file:///C:/Documents%20and%20Settings/William/My%20Documents/Downloads/williamsedlacek_oped.pdf

Sedlacek, W. E. (2014c, January). *The proper use of GRE scores and non-cognitive measures for enhancing diversity and excellence in astronomy and physics graduate programs.* Discussant at the 223rd meeting of the American Astronomical Society, Washington, DC.

Sedlacek, W. E. (in press). Measures worth considering in diversity research and programming. *Readings on Equal Education.*

Sedlacek, W. E., & Adams-Gaston, J. (1992). Predicting the academic success of student-athletes using SAT and noncognitive variables. *Journal of Counseling and Development, 70,* 724–727.

Sedlacek, W. E., Benjamin, E., Schlosser, L. Z., & Sheu, H. B. (2007). Mentoring in academia: Considerations for diverse populations. In T. D. Allen & L. T. Eby (Eds.), *The Blackwell handbook of mentoring: A multiple perspectives approach* (pp. 259–280). Malden, MA: Blackwell.

Sedlacek, W. E., & Brooks, G. C., Jr. (1970). Black freshmen in large colleges: A survey. *Personnel and Guidance Journal, 49,* 307–312.

Sedlacek, W. E., & Brooks, G. C., Jr. (1972). Race of experimenter in racial attitude measurement. *Psychological Reports, 30,* 771–774.

Sedlacek, W. E., & Brooks, G. C., Jr. (1973). Racism and research: Using data to initiate change. *Personnel and Guidance Journal, 52,* 184–188.

Sedlacek, W. E., & Brooks, G. C. (1976). *Racism in American education: A model for change.* Chicago, IL: Nelson-Hall.

Sedlacek, W. E., & Brooks, G. C., Jr. (1981). Eliminating racism in educational settings. In O. Barbarin, P. R. Good, O. M. Pharr, & J. A. Siskind (Eds.), *Institutional racism and community competence* (pp. 223–229). Rockville, MD: U.S. Department of Health and Human Services, Public Health Service.

Sedlacek, W. E., Brooks, G. C., Jr., Christensen, K. C., Harway, M. H., & Merritt, M. S. (1976). Racism and sexism: A comparison and contrast. *Journal of the National Association for Women Deans, Administrators, and Counselors, 39,* 120–127.

Sedlacek, W. E., Brooks, G. C., Jr., & Horowitz, J. L. (1972). Black admissions to large universities: Are things changing? *Journal of College Student Personnel, 13,* 305–310.

Sedlacek, W. E., Brooks, G. C., Jr., & Mindus, L. A. (1973a). Black and other minority admissions to large universities: Three-year national trends. *Journal of College Student Personnel, 14,* 16–21.

Sedlacek, W. E., Brooks, G. C., Jr., & Mindus, L. A. (1973b). Racial attitudes of White university students and their parents. *Journal of College Student Personnel, 14,* 517–520.

Sedlacek, W. E., Lewis, J. A., & Brooks, G. C., Jr. (1974). Black and other minority admissions to large universities: A four-year national survey of policies and outcomes. *Research in Higher Education, 2,* 221–230.

Sedlacek, W. E., Merritt, M. S., & Brooks, G. C., Jr. (1975). A national comparison of universities successful and unsuccessful in enrolling Blacks over a five-year period. *Journal of College Student Personnel, 16,* 57–63.

Sedlacek, W. E., & Pelham, J. C. (1976). Minority admissions to large universities: A national survey. *Journal of Non-White Concerns in Personnel and Guidance, 4,* 53–63.

Sedlacek, W. E., & Prieto, D. O. (1982). An evaluation of the Simulated Minority Admissions Exercise (SMAE). *Journal of Medical Education, 57,* 119–120.

Sedlacek, W. E., & Prieto, D. O. (1990). Predicting minority students' success in medical school. *Academic Medicine, 3*(65), 161–166.

Sedlacek, W. E., & Sheu, H. B. (2004a). Academic success of Gates Millennium Scholars. *Readings on Equal Education, 20,* 181–197.

Sedlacek, W. E., & Sheu, H. B. (2004b). Correlates of leadership activities of Gates Millennium Scholars. *Readings on Equal Education, 20,* 249–264.

Sedlacek, W. E., & Sheu, H. B. (2005). Early academic behaviors of Washington State Achievers. *Readings on Equal Education, 21,* 207–222.

Sedlacek, W. E., & Sheu, H. B. (2008). The academic progress of undergraduate and graduate Gates Millennium Scholars and non-scholars by race and gender. *Readings on Equal Education, 23,* 143–177.

Sedlacek, W. E., & Sheu, H. (2013). Selecting and supporting Asian American and Pacific Islander students in higher education. In S. D. Museus, D. C. Maramba, & R. T. Teranishi (Eds.), *The minority within the minority: Asian Americans in higher education* (pp. 327–339). Sterling, VA: Stylus.

Sedlacek, W. E., Troy, W. G., & Chapman, T. H. (1976). An evaluation of three methods of racism-sexism training. *Personnel and Guidance Journal, 55,* 196–198.

Sedlacek, W. E., & Webster, D. W. (1978). Admission and retention of minority students in large universities. *Journal of College Student Personnel, 19,* 242–248.

Seifert, T. (2007). Understanding Christian Privilege: Managing the tensions of spiritual plurality. *About Campus, 12*(2), 10–17.

Sergent, M. T., & Sedlacek, W. E. (1989). Perceptual mapping: A methodology in the assessment of environmental perceptions. *Journal of College Student Development, 30,* 319–322.

Sergent, M. T., Woods, P. A., & Sedlacek, W. E. (1992). University student attitudes toward Arabs: Intervention implications. *Journal of Multicultural Counseling and Development, 20*, 123–131.

Shaw, E. J., & Milewski, G. B. (2004). *Consistency and reliability in the individualized review of college applicants* (Research Notes RN-20). Princeton, NJ: College Board, Office of Research and Development.

Sheets, R. L., Jr., & Mohr, J. J. (2009). Perceived social support from friends and family and psychosocial functioning in bisexual young adult college students. *Journal of Counseling Psychology, 56*(1), 152–163.

Sherry, L. (1997). The Boulder Valley Internet project: Lessons learned. *THE Technological Horizons in Education Journal, 25*(2), 68–73.

Sheu, H. B., & Sedlacek, W. E. (2004). An exploratory study of help-seeking attitudes and coping strategies among college students by race and gender. *Measurement and Evaluation in Counseling and Development, 37*(3), 130–143.

Sheu, H. B., & Sedlacek, W. (2009). Cross-cultural issues in counseling research. In D. Burnhill, A. L. Butler, C. P. Hipolito-Delgado, M. Humphrey, C. C. Lee, O. Muñoz, & H. Shin (Eds.), *Elements of culture in counseling: Theory and practice* (pp. 226–241). Boston, MA: Allyn & Bacon.

Sheu, H. B., Sedlacek, W. E., & Singley, D. B. (2003). *Effects of universal-diverse orientation and adjustment on life satisfaction* (Research Report No. 10–03). College Park, MD: University of Maryland Counseling Center.

Singley, D. B., & Sedlacek, W. E. (2004). Universal-diverse orientation and precollege academic achievement. *Journal of College Student Development, 45*, 84–89.

Singley, D. B., & Sedlacek, W. E. (2009). Differences in universal-diverse orientation by race and gender. *Journal of Counseling and Development, 87*(4), 404–411.

Smith, K., & Tillema, H. (2003). Clarifying different types of portfolios. *Assessment and Evaluation in Higher Education, 28*(6), 625–648.

Spitzer, J. T. (2014). *An examination of the role of gender in understanding faculty perceptions of student-athletes at NCAA Division I institutions* (Unpublished doctoral dissertation). University of Tennessee, Knoxville, TN.

Stericker, A. B., & Johnson, J. E. (1977). Sex role identification and self-esteem in college students: Do men and women differ? *Sex Roles, 3*, 19–26.

Sternberg, R. J. (1985). *Beyond IQ.* London, UK: Cambridge University Press.

Sternberg, R. J. (1986). What would better intelligence tests look like? In *Measures in the college admissions process* (pp. 146–150). New York, NY: College Entrance Examination Board.

Sternberg, R. J. (1996). *Successful intelligence.* New York, NY: Plume.

Sternberg, R. J. (2010). Momentum for non-cognitive reviews. *Inside Higher Education.* Retrieved from https://www.insidehighered.com/news/2010/09/13/ppi

Sternberg, R. J., & the Rainbow Project collaborators. (2006). The Rainbow Project: Enhancing the SAT through assessments of analytical, practical, and creative skills. *Intelligence, 34*, 321–350.

Sternberg, R. J., & Williams, W. M. (1997). Does the Graduate Record Examinations predict meaningful success in the graduate training of psychology? A case study. *American Psychologist, 52,* 630–641.

Stinson, D. W. (2008). Negotiating sociocultural discourses: The counter-storytelling of academically (and mathematically) successful African American male students. *American Educational Research Journal, 45*(4), 975–1010.

Stinson, D. W. (2013). Negotiating the "White male math myth": African American male students and success in school mathematics. *Journal for Research in Mathematics Education, 44,* 69–99.

St. John, E. P. (2013). *Research, actionable knowledge, and social change: Reclaiming social responsibility through research partnerships.* Sterling, VA: Stylus.

Stovall, C. D. (1989). *Development of a measure of White counselor racial attitude toward Black male client characteristics: The Counselor Situational Attitude Scale (CSAS)* (Unpublished doctoral dissertation). University of Maryland, College Park, MD.

Stovall, C. D., & Sedlacek, W. E. (1983). Attitudes of male and female university students toward students with different physical disabilities. *Journal of College Student Personnel, 24,* 325–330.

Stuart, W. D. (2000). *Influence of sources of communication, user characteristics and innovation characteristics on adoption of a communication technology* (Doctoral dissertation). University of Kansas, Lawrence, KS. Retrieved from ProQuest Digital Dissertations. (UMI No. AAT 9998115)

Sue, D. W., & Sue, D. (2015). *Counseling the culturally diverse: Theory and practice* (7th ed.). New York, NY: Wiley.

Swanson, E. (2015, August). *Things to know about race and Americans' views of policing.* Retrieved from http://www.usnews.com/news/politics/articles/2015/08/05/ap-norc-poll-things-to-know-on-views-of-race-and-police

Swim, J. K., Mallett, R., & Stangor, C. (2004). Understanding subtle sexism: Detection and use of sexist language. *Sex Roles, 51*(3–4), 117–128.

Takaki, R. (1993). *A different mirror: A history of multicultural America.* New York, NY: Back Bay Books.

Texas Tech University Student Counseling Center. (2015). *LGBTQ Pamphlet.* Retrieved from http://www.depts.ttu.edu/scc/virtual_library/lgbtq.php

That's Not Twain. (2011, January 6). *New York Times,* p. A26.

Thomas, K. M., Willis, L. A., & Davis, J. (2007). Mentoring minority graduate students: Issues and strategies for institutions, faculty, and students. *Equal Opportunities International, 26*(3), 178–192. doi:10.1108/02610150710735471

Thomas, L. L., Kuncel, N. R., & Credé, M. (2007). Noncognitive variables in college admissions: The case of the noncognitive questionnaire. *Educational and Psychological Measurement, 67*(4), 635–657.

Thurstone, L. L. (1959). *The measurement of values.* Chicago, IL: University of Chicago Press.

Thurstone, L. L., & Chave, E. J. (1929). *The measurement of attitude.* Chicago, IL: University of Chicago Press.

Ting, S. R. (1997). Estimating academic success in the first year of college for specially admitted White students: A model combining cognitive and psychosocial predictors. *Journal of College Student Development, 38,* 401–409.

Ting, S. R. (2009). Impact of non-cognitive factors on first-year academic performance and retention of NCAA Division I student athletes. *Journal of Humanistic Counseling, Education and Development, 48,* 215–228.

Ting, S. R., & Gales, G. (2014). *Enhancing academic success: Exploring the role of noncognitive skills in student outcomes at North Carolina State University* (Unpublished report). North Carolina State University, Raleigh, NC.

Ting, S. R., & Robinson, T. L. (1998). First-year academic success: A prediction combining cognitive and psychosocial variables for White and African American students. *Journal of College Student Development, 39,* 599–610.

Ting, S. R., & Sedlacek, W. E. (2000). *Validity of the Noncognitive Questionnaire–Revised 2 in predicting the academic success of university freshmen* (Research Report No. 1-00). College Park, MD: University of Maryland Counseling Center. (Also presented at the annual meeting of the American College Personnel Association, Washington, DC, March 2000.)

Ting, S. R., Sedlacek, W. E., Bryant, A., Jr., & Ward, D. (2004, April). *Developing alternative admissions criteria.* Paper presented at American College Personnel Association Convention, Philadelphia, PA.

Tinto, V. (1993). *Leaving college: Rethinking the causes and cures of student attrition* (2nd ed.). Chicago, IL: University of Chicago Press.

Toldson, I. A. (2014). Will the new SAT boost college prospects for Black students? *The Root.* Retrieved from http://www.theroot.com/articles/culture/2014/03/sat_scores_for_Black_students_don_t_predict_success.2.html

Tomlin, L. (n.d.). Retrieved from http://www.brainyquote.com/quotes/quotes/l/lilytomlin379145.html

Tracey, T. J., Leong, F. T. L., & Glidden, C. (1986). Help-seeking and problem perception among Asian Americans. *Journal of Counseling Psychology, 33,* 331–336.

Tracey, T. J., & Sedlacek, W. E. (1981). Conducting student retention research. *National Association of Student Personnel Administrators Field Report, 5*(2), 5–6.

Tracey, T. J., & Sedlacek, W. E. (1984a). Noncognitive variables in predicting academic success by race. *Measurement and Evaluation in Guidance, 16,* 171–178.

Tracey, T. J., & Sedlacek, W. E. (1984b). Using ridge regression with non-cognitive variables by race in admissions. *College and University, 59,* 345–350.

Tracey, T. J., & Sedlacek, W. E. (1985). The relationship of noncognitive variables to academic success: A longitudinal comparison by race. *Journal of College Student Personnel, 26,* 405–410.

Tracey, T. J., & Sedlacek, W. E. (1987). Prediction of college graduation using noncognitive variables by race. *Measurement and Evaluation in Counseling and Development, 19,* 177–184.

Tracey, T. J., & Sedlacek, W. E. (1988). A comparison of White and Black student academic success using noncognitive variables: A LISREL analysis. *Research in Higher Education, 27,* 333–348.

Tracey, T. J., & Sedlacek, W. E. (1989). Factor structure of the Noncognitive Questionnaire–Revised across samples of Black and White college students. *Educational and Psychological Measurement, 49,* 637–648.

Tracey, T. J., Sedlacek, W. E., & Miars, R. D. (1983). Applying ridge regression to admissions data by race and sex. *College and University, 58,* 313–318.

Trent, W., & St. John, E. P. (Eds.). (2008). Resources, assets, and strengths among successful diverse students: Understanding the contributions of the Gates Millennium Scholars Program. In *Readings on equal education* (Vol. 23). New York, NY: AMS Press.

Trimble, J. E. (1988). Stereotypical images, American Indians and prejudice. In P. A. Katz & D. A. Taylor (Eds.), *Eliminating racism: Profiles in controversy* (pp. 181–202). New York, NY: Plenum.

Trippi, J., & Cheatham, H. E. (1989). Effects of special counseling programs for Black freshmen on a predominantly White campus. *Journal of College Student Development, 30,* 35–40.

Trochim, W. K. (2002). *Thurstone scaling.* Retrieved from http://trochim.omni .cornell.edu/kb/scalthur.htm

Twain, M. (1885). *Adventures of Huckleberry Finn.* New York, NY: Charles L. Webster.

Tzu, L. (n.d.). Retrieved from http://www.goodreads.com/quotes/4304-at-the-center-of-your-being-you-have-the-answer

U of California v. Bakke (1978, 438 U.S. 265, 98 S.Ct. 2733, 57 L.Ed. 2d 750).

Uba, L. (1994). *Asian Americans: Personality patterns, identity, and mental health.* New York, NY: Guilford.

U.S. Department of Justice. (2015, March). *Department of Justice report regarding the criminal investigation into the shooting death of Michael Brown by Ferguson Missouri police officer Darren Wilson.* Retrieved from http://www.justice.gov/sites/ default/files/opa/press-releases/attachments/2015/03/04/doj_report_on_shoot-ing_of_michael_brown.pdf

Wagner, J. The 3/5 compromise is a model to which we should aspire. Also, the liberal arts are like slaves and should be treated as such. *Emory Magazine.* 2013. Retrieved from http://www.emory.edu/EMORY_MAGAZINE/issues/2013/winter/register/ president.html

Walton, G. (2015, January). *Presentation at Redefining Student Success: The Role of Non-Cognitive Skill Development.* Chapel Hill, NC.

Wang, Y. Y., Sedlacek, W. E., & Westbrook, F. D. (1992). Asian-Americans and student organizations: Attitudes and participation. *Journal of College Student Development, 33,* 214–221.

Warren, J. M., & Hale, R. W. (2016). Fostering non-cognitive development of underrepresented students through rational emotive behavior therapy: Recommendations for school counselor practice. *The Professional Counselor, 6*(1), 89–106.

Washington, B. T. (n.d.). Retrieved from http://www.brainyquote.com/quotes/quotes/b/bookertwa107996.html

Washington, J. E. (1993). *An investigation of attitudes of heterosexual identified resident assistants toward students based on the sexual orientation of the student* (Unpublished doctoral dissertation). University of Maryland, College Park, MD.

Washor, E., Arnold, K., & Mojkowski, C. (2008). *Taking the long view on student success.* Providence, RI: BPL.

Wawrzynski, M. R., & Sedlacek, W. E. (2003). Race and gender differences in the transfer student experience. *Journal of College Student Development, 44*(4), 489–501.

Webb, C. T., Sedlacek, W. E., Cohen, D., Shields, P., Gracely, E., Hawkins, M., & Nieman, L. (1997). The impact of nonacademic variables on performance at two medical schools. *Journal of the National Medical Association, 89*(3), 173–180.

Webster, D. W., & Sedlacek, W. E. (1982). The differential impact of a university student union on campus subgroups. *National Association of Student Personnel Administrators Journal, 19*(2), 48–51.

Wedemeyer, C. A. (1981). *Learning at the back door: Reflections on non-traditional learning in the lifespan.* Madison, WI: University of Wisconsin Press.

Weick, K. E. (1984). Small wins: Redefining the scale of social problems. *American Psychologist, 39*, 40–49.

Weiner, J., & Stutzman, R. (2015, February). George Zimmerman will not face federal charges in Trayvon Martin shooting. Retrieved from http://www.orlandosentinel.com/news/trayvon-martin-george-zimmerman/os-george-zimmerman-trayvon-martin-no-charges-20150224-story.html

Westbrook, F. D., & Sedlacek, W. E. (1988). Workshop on using noncognitive variables with minority students in higher education. *Journal for Specialists in Group Work, 13*, 82–89.

Westbrook, F. D., & Sedlacek, W. E. (1991). Forty years of using labels to communicate about nontraditional students: Does it help or hurt? *Journal of Counseling and Development, 70*, 20–28.

White, C. J., & Shelley, C. (1996). Telling stories: Students and administrators talk about retention. In I. H. Johnson & A. J. Ottens (Eds.), *Leveling the playing field: Promoting academic success for students of color* (pp. 15–34). San Francisco, CA: Jossey-Bass.

White, T. J., & Sedlacek, W. E. (1986). Noncognitive predictors of grades and retention for specially admitted students. *Journal of College Admissions, 3*, 20–23.

Wilbur, S. A., & Bonous-Hammarth, M. (1998). Testing a new approach to admissions: The Irvine experience. In G. Orfield & E. Miller (Eds.), *Chilling admissions: The affirmative action crisis and the search for alternatives.* Cambridge, MA: Harvard Education Publishing Group.

Wilkshire, D. M. (1989). *Differential attitudes of student affairs professionals toward commuter and resident students* (Unpublished master's thesis). University of Maryland, College Park, MD.

Willingham, W. W. (1985). *Success in college: The role of personal qualities and academic ability.* New York, NY: College Entrance Examination Board.

Willingham, W. W., Lewis, C., Morgan, R., & Ramist, L. (1990). *Predicting college grades: An analysis of institutional trends over two decades.* Princeton, NJ: Educational Testing Service.

Wilson, E. S. (1955). Sorting by personal factors. In *College admissions 2.* New York, NY: College Entrance Examination Board.

Wilson, M. B., Sedlacek, W. E., & Lowery, B. L. (2014). An approach to using noncognitive variables in dental school admissions. *Journal of Dental Education, 78,* 567–574.

Winkle, C. A. (2014). *University partnerships with the corporate sector: Faculty experiences with for-profit matriculation pathway programs.* Boston, MA: Brill.

Woodruff, D. J., & Ziomek, R. L. (2004). *High school grade inflation from 1991 to 2003* (ACT Research Report 2004-04). Iowa City, IA: ACT.

Wouters, S., Germeijs, V., Colpin, H., & Verschueren, K. (2011). Academic self-concept in high school: Predictors and effects on adjustment in higher education. *Scandinavian Journal of Psychology, 52*(6), 586–594. doi:10.1111/j.1467-9450.2011.00905.x

Yablon, M. (2001). Test flight: The scam behind SAT bashing. *New Republic, 30,* 24–25.

Yeh, C., & Wang, Y. W. (2000). Asian American coping attitudes, sources, and practices: Implications for indigenous counseling strategies. *Journal of College Student Development, 41*(1), 94–103.

YES Prep Public Schools. (2014, June). *College initiatives redefined: A responsive approach to college counseling and alumni support.* Houston, TX: Author.

Young, E. Y. (2011). The four personae of racism: Educators' (mis)understanding of individual vs. systematic racism. *Urban Education, 46*(6), 1433–1460.

Zimbalist, S. (Producer), & Wyler, W. (Director). (1959). *Ben-Hur* [Motion picture]. United States: Metro-Goldwyn-Mayer.

Also available from Stylus

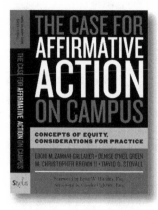

The Case for Affirmative Action on Campus
Concepts of Equity, Considerations for Practice

Eboni M. Zamani-Gallaher, Denise O'Neil Green,
M. Christopher Brown II, and David O. Stovall

"This text provides a comprehensive overview of the state of affirmative action law and the climate for related policies on college campuses. It suggests a persistent need for affirmative action even decades after the civil rights movement, and lays out the arguments in favor of these controversial policies. By delving into deep divides and grappling with tough questions, this volume articulates a compelling case for affirmative action—and will help its readers make this case to the higher education world."—
Diversity & Democracy (AAC&U)

Advancing Black Male Student Success From Preschool Through Ph.D.
Restoring Rigor, Motivating Students, and Saving Faculty Time

Edited by Shaun R. Harper and J. Luke Wood

"Harper and Wood have provided a timely and definitive text that offers rich conceptual, empirical, and practical analysis on Black males and education. This book explains the challenges Black boys and men encounter in pursuit of education and offers meaningful ways to disrupt these troubling trends. It is mandatory reading for scholars, practitioners, and policymakers."—***Tyrone C. Howard***, *Professor and Director, UCLA Black Male Institute*

Closing the Opportunity Gap
Identity-Conscious Strategies for Retention and Student Success

Edited by Vijay Pendakur

Foreword by Shaun R. Harper

"Closing the achievement gap for low-income, first-generation, and students of color in American higher education needs to be a national priority. This book is a roadmap that outlines the dimensions of a systemic approach towards decreasing the attainment gap for our most underrepresented students. The upfront focus on racial identity and the need for systemic change make this a 'must-read' for college presidents, provosts, and senior administrators who seek real equity at their colleges and universities."—*Kevin Kruger*, *President, NASPA—Student Affairs Administrators in Higher Education*

22883 Quicksilver Drive
Sterling, VA 20166-2102

Subscribe to our e-mail alerts: www.Styluspub.com

INTEREST-BASED INTERNSHIPS

WHOLE COMMUNITY INVOLVEMENT: ADVISERS, PEERS, PARENTS, AND MENTORS

PERSONALIZED LEARNING PLANS, PUTTING STUDENTS AT THE CENTER

DIFFUSING INNOVATION ACROSS THE COUNTRY AND THE WORLD

For more than 20 years, Big Picture Learning (BPL) has been reinventing and reimaginging education, creating truly student-centered schools and personalized, real-world learning opportunities for young people and communities across the country and the world.

Big Picture schools exist in over 22 states and eight countries around the world.

84% of BPL students head to college each year

96% of non-college attending BPL alumni work full time, often at places in which they interned

88% of BPL students remain in contact with their advisers two years after graduation

BIG PICTURE LEARNING

STUDENTS AT THE CENTER PRACTICE AT THE EDGE

bigpicture.org | @bigpiclearning

Meet DJ

DJ had an all-too-familiar early high-school experience. He was bored and unconnected and considered dropping out. Yet he yearned to go to college. Then he learned about a local BPL school where you could "learn what you want to learn." He transferred, quickly landed an internship, and discovered a flair for business. While still in high school, DJ lauched a successful soda company and was soon rewarded with multiple college scholarships. He's now attending Howard University where he majors in, what else, Business Management.

Meet more BPL students:
www.bigpicture.org/students